Mathematical Knowledge for Primary Teachers

Third Edition

Also available:

Understanding Primary Mathematics
Christine Hopkins, Sue Pope and Sandy Pepperell
1-84312-012-7

Mathematics in the Primary Schools 2e
A Sense of Progression
Christine Hopkins, Susan Gifford and Sandy Pepperell
1-85346-592-5

Mathematical Knowledge for Primary Teachers

Third Edition

● ● ● **Jennifer Suggate, Andrew Davis
and Maria Goulding**

David Fulton Publishers

This edition reprinted 2006 by Routledge
2 Park Square, Milton Park, Abingdon, Oxon, OX14 4RN
Simultaneously published in the USA and Canada
By Routledge
270 Madison Avenue, New York, NY 10016

First published in Great Britain in 2006 by David Fulton Publishers

10 9 8 7 6 5 4 3 2

British Library Cataloguing in Publication Data
A catalogue record for this book is available from the British Library.

ISBN 1 84312 424 6
EAN 9781843124245

Typeset by Servis Filmsetting Ltd, Manchester
Printed and bound in Great Britain

Contents

Note to third edition

In response to changes in regulations and practice in schools, we have taken this opportunity to:

- completely rewrite the chapter on fractions, decimals and percentages
- rewrite the section on graphs
- expand the comments on mental methods of calculation
- re-examine the relation between mental and written methods of calculation
- include a CD with some programs for the computer which illustrate mathematical concepts in new ways.

We hope the new format and other minor alterations will help make the book more accessible.

Jennifer Suggate, Andrew Davis and Maria Goulding
May 2006

For Alan, Margaret and Pete
In gratitude for their unfailing help and encouragement

Acknowledgements

We are all a product of our own histories and are rarely aware of all the people and experiences which have influenced us. So in a real sense it is impossible to acknowledge all the sources of ideas in this book. We have acknowledged those of which we are conscious and hope others will forgive our lapses of memory. Of those we can name, we must first mention students in the School of Education in Durham over the years. By their enthusiastic questioning they have inspired us to think in new ways about the mathematics we use. This book is written primarily for them.

Although the responsibility for any mistakes rests firmly with us, we are most grateful to those who kindly read drafts and pointed out errors and inconsistencies. First among these is Brian Woodhouse, our colleague at Durham, who has also helped develop our ideas over many years. Alan Suggate, Margaret Davis and Sue Smith have all made invaluable suggestions for clarification and improvement.

Introduction

This book has been written especially for those preparing to be teachers in primary schools who need support in developing their mathematical subject knowledge. The knowledge of mathematics required of those intending to teach either Key Stage 1 or Key Stage 2 children differs significantly from that developed and tested by traditional GCSE courses, or by conventional higher education mathematics courses. Accordingly both the content and style of this book set it apart from mathematics texts used in secondary schools.

There is much about teaching mathematics which this book does not cover. At regular intervals 'Links with the classroom' suggest connections between the material presented at an adult level, and contexts in which young children are learning mathematics. However, these concentrate on how teachers' knowledge is likely to impinge on the way they might explain mathematics to children, or question children about mathematics. You should look elsewhere for a comprehensive treatment of the teaching of the topics covered here. At the same time you may well consult this book on occasion when planning specific lessons. This is because there are classic topics such as fractions which challenge the subject knowledge of many teachers. If the challenge cannot be met the lesson plans will suffer accordingly.

As befits a self-study text, there are many collections of exercises. These are an integral part of the book. Answers to these exercises may be found on the CD. A deliberate attempt has been made to indicate connections and interconnections between many of the concepts. This reflects our view of the nature of mathematics itself, and a little more will be said about this in Chapter 1. It also means that you are encouraged to follow a variety of routes through the material. While we have tried to offer content in a reasonably logical and coherent sequence, we are well aware that there is no one best order in which to attempt to learn the mathematics concerned. The book also contains a comprehensive glossary of terms used. In some cases this simply duplicates material within chapters, but we make no apology for that.

 The Third Edition includes a CD Rom, which contains several pieces of software to support the reader grappling with some of the mental strategies outlined in the book. The software runs on any standard PC. It uses a variety of visual representations in the hope that these will contribute to the proper understanding of the methods concerned.

The flexibility of the software design means that readers can concentrate on those representations that they find most helpful, and also that they can compare and contrast different ways of visualising the relevant operations. The CD Rom also contains a 'self-audit test' designed to help readers assess their own level of mathematical ability, as well as all of the answers to the 'check' questions dotted throughout the text.

Each Part of the book offers an introduction to the several chapters immediately following. The organisation of the Part is explained, and the introduction outlines some general principles which are then developed in detail in the relevant chapters.

In addition to finding your way through this book in various directions we also hope that you will develop and practise your skills in mental arithmetic and in estimating the answers to calculations. For detailed discussion of these matters see especially Part Two. Developing and practising number skills of this kind is much closer to working on athletic skills than you might suppose. You may surprise yourself with just how skilful you become after a period of regular practice.

Just now we used the word 'learn' rather than 'revise', and perhaps some of you will find that inappropriate. You may deem yourselves perfectly competent mathematicians, and feel that you are only turning to this book to revisit one or two things. You may feel like reminding us that you have your GCSE grade C or better, or you would not have been accepted on your course.

If so, we hope to persuade you to think a little differently. This book is emphatically not a GCSE revision text. Precisely what kind of subject knowledge supports effective primary teaching is a complex and still controversial issue. This question will be explored further in Chapter 1. At the moment we can state firmly that the knowledge required certainly does not equate with that needed for GCSE. It is both much more and less. This seemingly paradoxical claim will be discussed in Chapter 1.

Mathematics has a troubled place in the emotions of many highly intelligent learners. Some of our readers may have been mentally scarred by past experiences of failure. This is probably associated with incompetent and insensitive teaching. Is such teaching especially likely in the case of mathematics? It has often been suggested, rather uncharitably, that the subject actually attracts a disproportionate number of teachers lacking perception and insight. This book cannot settle how much truth that suggestion contains. However, part of the problem may lie in the kind of understanding which the mathematics teacher has of his or her subject, and in consequence the type of understanding that teacher attempts to develop in pupils. Such a hypothesis underlies the approach of this book and, as we will see in Chapter 1, is borne out by recent research into what makes an effective teacher of numeracy. A different kind of difficulty which some adults experience when returning to the learning of mathematics is that when younger they were not allowed to fail when tackling the subject. Their teachers made the learning too 'safe'. Yet for a number of perfectly intelligent people some fairly basic mathematics can prove quite tough, at least when first encountered. It may be argued that it is no bad thing for pupils to experience 'supported' failure; to come to appreciate that when you are trying to grasp certain ideas or to solve certain kinds of problems in mathematics a significant level of mental effort may be required. Failure, at least in the first instance, is not the end of the world. Certain kinds of failure, handled correctly, seem almost essential for real learning to take place. While much of this book should prove straightforward to most readers, there are some more challenging sections, especially perhaps in Chapter 2 which deals with proof. 'Proof' is relatively unfamiliar, even to those who were successful in A-level mathematics. You can always study other chapters and return to Chapter 2 if you find it rather heavy-going at first.

We have been thinking about mathematics subject knowledge at Durham for many years, and our current perspective on the form that knowledge should take has not been easily won. Tutors providing professional mathematics courses at Durham had long been unhappy with aspects of students' subject knowledge. At the same time, we lacked detailed knowledge of what they actually knew about mathematics. Hence we were not in the best position to judge whether our courses fitted student needs.

In a well-intentioned but rash venture, we decided to find out what the students knew about some aspects of algebra. We devised a written test. We were well aware of the limitations of written assessment and how taken alone a written test could not probe understanding of mathematics in any kind of depth. The test was planned to be supplemented by follow-up interviews by tutors and Secondary PGCE students. Since we wished to discover what our students knew as such, rather than what they knew after some kind of revision, we did not inform them in advance, but sprung the test upon them. We made it very clear that the test results would in no way count as part of their degree classification, and that we simply wanted to probe their understanding to help us deliver effective maths courses. This did nothing to placate them. They were angry and resentful. Some queried the level of subject knowledge we were investigating. We looked at mathematics roughly up to level 7 of the National Curriculum, and the students felt that they simply did not need that level of knowledge to be able to teach effectively to the top of Key Stage 2. In the light of these vehemently expressed sentiments, one Secondary PGCE student wondered wryly why she was expected to have a degree in mathematics to teach up to A-level in the subject.

As tutors we certainly felt vulnerable, since while we had a vague conviction that the students should be at least a few steps ahead of the pupils, we were unable to defend a requirement for any particular 'level' of subject knowledge. Indeed, it became increasingly clear that the notion of a 'level' of knowledge was pretty unhelpful when trying to think of the subject expertise required by a good primary mathematics teacher. Moreover, it was by no means evident that intending Key Stage 2 teachers needed 'more' mathematical knowledge than Key Stage 1. If anything, the latter needed a deeper grasp than the former. Yet another burden of complaint voiced by our student victims was that they should have been told in advance about the test, since they then could have revised for it and obtained higher scores. It was many years, they said, since they had taken their GCSE mathematics and they had forgotten much. In vain did we protest that the scoring was irrelevant, and that part of what we wished to know was just how much they had forgotten. Their feelings about the subject and about being tested were so strong that they did not believe us. Incidentally it was fascinating to discover the variation in 'forgetting' between students who had taken the same GCSE at the same time and obtained the same grade.

With the benefit of hindsight we can see why we provoked such a hostile reaction, and can understand how we might have handled matters differently, at least in some ways. Fundamentally we had underestimated the emotional baggage adult students of mathematics frequently bring with them to the enterprise.

This book is written several years on from that traumatic episode. Its writers have now gained extensive experience of trying to help students feel better about the subject and to overcome a range of mental 'blocks', especially relating to algebra and fractions. Students have even been detected having some fun in connection with such topics!

An explicit subject knowledge element in the professional mathematics courses for intending primary teachers is now well established at Durham. These components have gradually been extended and refined. It was clear from the start of this development that what was needed differed significantly from mathematics courses found either in Secondary Schools or at Higher Education level. Indeed, we had a PGCE student with a first class degree in mathematics who turned out to lack some of the basic understanding which our subject knowledge course was designed to promote and which we felt was essential for all students teaching at Key Stages 1 and 2.

We have not changed our view that better subject knowledge is required. We continue to test student subject knowledge at various points during their 'training', or as we still quaintly like to style it on occasion, 'education'. However, the 'audit' as it is known is a transparent process which is on the whole understood by the students. They have opportunities to explain their performance in audits, and thus to provide us with richer evidence of what they actually grasp.

We now have a better idea than we used to have of the quality of subject knowledge which supports teachers in explaining mathematics to young children. We have a greater appreciation of what is needed to inform teacher questioning likely to stimulate mathematical understanding and indeed to support all aspects of the interactive whole-class teaching favoured in the 'Numeracy Hour'. Once students begin to develop this kind of knowledge themselves, we are confident that they can readily see the value of it. They are motivated to acquire more, through self-study, peer tutoring, or directly from tutors. We hope that this book will facilitate all these processes.

Note on references

A conscious decision has been made not to sprinkle the text with many detailed academic references. The book is not an academic research text, though of course we hope that the material offered here is properly informed by relevant professional and scientific literature.

Setting the scene

Much of this book looks systematically at specific areas of mathematical content. However, Part One differs in that it discusses some wider issues, some of which have already been raised in the introduction. Both Chapter 1 and Chapter 2 discuss aspects of mathematical knowledge in general, Chapter 1 taking up the theme of understanding, while Chapter 2 deals with problem solving and proof.

The nature and purpose of mathematics: brief remarks

If this were a very different work, a good deal of fascinating but abstruse discussion could be devoted to analysing the nature of mathematics. Despite the 'absolute'-seeming character of the subject, there is no consensus of opinion as to its nature. Bertrand Russell remarks: '. . . mathematics may be defined as the subject in which we never know what we are talking about, nor whether what we are saying is true' (Russell 1917, pp. 59–60). In the light of this, it is perhaps puzzling that he also observes in another essay in the same volume: 'Mathematics, rightly viewed, possesses not only truth, but supreme beauty – a beauty cold and austere, like that of sculpture, without appeal to any part of our weaker nature, without the gorgeous trappings of painting or music, yet sublimely pure, and capable of a stern perfection such as only the greatest art can show' (Russell 1917, p. 49).

Knowledge, including knowledge of mathematics, is seen very differently by some recent writers in what is known as the 'situated cognition' tradition: 'Learners . . . participate in communities of practitioners and . . . the mastery of knowledge and skill requires newcomers to move towards full participation in the sociocultural practices of a community' (Lave and Wenger 1991, p. 29).

In this tradition, learning mathematics might be compared to an apprenticeship, with all the human and fallible trappings that this process seems to imply. The writers of this book also see mathematics as a human construction. We view learning mathematics as a process in which pupils, partly through interaction with those who are in possession of fuller versions, invent for themselves an understanding of the subject. You can read more about this in Davis and Pettitt (1994). It is less clear than some claim that this wholly rules out Russell's perspective as expressed in the 'supreme beauty' quotation, but no more can be said about that here. Readers who are interested might try Ernest (1991) for one verdict on this argument.

Mathematics for many children offers its own intrinsic satisfactions, but it also has essentially practical applications in everyday life. It enables us to communicate thinking and reasoning about number, quantity, shape and space. It embodies a precise language in which technological and scientific claims can be made. Those working in the field of the expressive arts also may make use of mathematics. Design and architecture are two obvious examples.

We are working on the assumption that for the vast majority of Key Stage 1 and 2 children, mathematics which cannot be used or applied in a range of practical circumstances is mathematics which is not understood.

References

Davis, A. and Pettitt, D. (1994) *Developing Understanding in Primary Mathematics*. London: Falmer Press.

Ernest, P. (1991) *The Philosophy of Mathematics Education*. London: Falmer Press.

Lave, J. and Wenger, E. (1991) *Situated Learning*. Cambridge: Cambridge University Press.

Russell, B. (1917) *Mysticism and Logic*. London: Unwin Books.

1

Mathematical understanding

ONE OF THE problems to be overcome by many seeking to teach mathematics to young children is that they have the wrong kind of understanding of their subject. It is not that they know too little, though they may, but rather that their knowledge is not of an appropriate kind. Thirty years ago the psychologist Richard Skemp coined a distinction between two sorts of understanding. He described and contrasted what he called relational understanding and instrumental understanding. His distinction can help us grasp the nature of the knowledge of mathematics we should be seeking as primary teachers (Skemp 1989).

Suppose two people, Anna and Sarah, are each making their way to a wedding in a town which is unfamiliar to them. Both have been supplied by the host with a series of directions. 'Left after the first roundabout on the way into town, under the railway bridge, third right, past the park and second left by the hypermarket. The church is on the right a few hundred yards down that road.' Anna has no map of the town, whereas Sarah has a splendid map and can also read it. If Anna meticulously follows the directions supplied she will make it to the wedding. It only needs one slip, however, for Anna to be miserably lost. Sheer chance may lead her to her goal, but she is more likely to circle the roads in a state of increasing frustration and panic. How blessed is Sarah in comparison. She can follow the directions with confidence, knowing that if she strays she has a remedy. This may make her less likely to go wrong in the first place. If she does make a mistake she can find her way back to the sequence of directions, or even pick out a new way to the church.

Anna's situation models the instrumental understanding which is all that many of us possess in respect of our mathematics. We may know what to do to obtain the right answer. But we only know one way of doing it, and we have little idea why the sequence of moves we make is a sensible one. If we go wrong, we may not be able to recover. We have no other route to the solution. We lack the understanding which might enable us to construct a route for ourselves. We are likely to be in possession of a number of mathematical rules which we implement 'without reason'. Certain examples have become classics and are usually quoted in this connection. To divide fractions, 'turn upside down and multiply'. When dealing with equations, if you 'change the side you change the sign'. To multiply by 10, 'add a zero'. (This one is not even universally correct, of course.)

In contrast, Sarah offers an analogy for those who have relational understanding of their mathematics. She has a map. Armed with a 'cognitive map' of the relevant mathematics, those with relational understanding are able to find a number of ways to solve a given problem. If they forget a particular procedure, or make a mistake in it, they can use and even construct an alternative route.

Some have understood Skemp to be extolling the virtues of relational understanding at the expense of instrumental understanding. In this book about subject knowledge in mathematics we take the view that both kinds of understanding are important. Knowing rules and procedures can be extremely useful and efficient. However, they need to be embedded within a rich relational understanding of the concepts concerned. Without this understanding, as Skemp points out, much strain is placed on the memory, and feelings of frustration and panic are more likely. Moreover, someone with mere instrumental understanding of mathematics cannot 'use and apply' it. They are likely only to be able to implement the procedure in contexts which closely resemble the situations in which they were taught the procedures. For instance, they can do 'long division' with paper and pencil, but are unable to work out how many dollars they will get for their pounds when they take a holiday in the States, even though the calculation required would in fact be a division operation. Their mathematics is rigid and inert. Those whose knowledge is limited in this way will, in a sense with total justification, consider mathematics as a pointless and tedious subject. This is hardly a desirable state of mind for a primary teacher who plays a significant part in shaping not only what young children know about mathematics but also how they feel about the subject.

A teacher in a recent study of effective teachers of primary mathematics remarks: 'I did maths for A-level . . . but actually I hadn't really sorted out how number worked . . . I'd always performed tricks until it was pointed out what the sums actually meant . . . I was sold on the idea they (pupils) really do need to know to be able to *apply* it, they really need to know what they're doing with number. . . . We have lots of using and applying . . . and I think that has got to be done alongside teaching new concepts' (Askew *et al.* 1997, p. 45).

We have noted the negative feelings which are often associated with mathematics. Sometimes positive feelings can also prove unhelpful. It is easy to be over-confident if your understanding is merely instrumental or procedural, if you happen to have found the acquisition of this kind of knowledge quite easy, and if you are unaware that you lack an associated relational understanding. We referred in the introduction to a past student with a first class degree in mathematics. His knowledge of mathematics turned out to be quite rule-bound and unreflective. He lacked much in the way of 'cognitive maps' of his subject. Presumably he had a good memory, and had been able to learn the procedures required for passing quite difficult examinations without much problem. Yet his understanding in the richer or relational sense wa: limited. His confidence which stemmed from his rather thin procedural knowledge actually prevented him from learning what he needed to become an effective teacher of primary mathematics. It may sound odd to say this, but a desirable state of mind for the aspiring primary mathematics teacher is informed uncertainty, at least for some of the time while learning to teach.

Let us return to the nature of mathematics itself, in order to appreciate the full importance of relational understanding. Knowing isolated mathematical facts or concepts makes little sense, since these individual items have no meaning or identity without their interconnections with a whole range of other mathematical facts or concepts. A very young child might 'know' that $7 + 3 = 10$ because an adult had informed her of this fact. Yet if that child has no appreciation of the number system, of the place 7 has within it, of the nature of the addition operation, the relationship between addition and other operations, and so on, 'knowing' may amount merely to a capacity to come up with the right answer of '10' when asked a specific question (see also Davis and Pettitt 1994, Chapter 2).

Maths is not the only subject or topic in which there are networks of interconnected ideas such that individual concepts make little sense considered on their own. Science offers comparable examples. In Newtonian mechanics, force, mass and acceleration are interdefined. A full account of what force actually amounts to cannot be given without appeal to mass and acceleration (and indeed to a number of other ideas).

The notion of interconnectivity is applicable to many contexts. Suppose my queen has a 'strong position' on the chess board. This property cannot be identified in isolation. To uncover its meaning it must be understood in relation to the rest of my pieces, and how they in turn relate to my opponent's pieces. Or again, suppose we are trying to learn about the function of the liver. The nature of that function can only be identified if we make reference to the blood and its function, the heart, breathing and the processing of food, together with much else.

Knowing about a key idea in mathematics, such as fractions, involves knowing how fractions relate to whole numbers, where they belong on a number line, how they link to ideas of ratio and proportion, the connection between fractions and the division operation, the links between a range of modes of representing fractions, and a host of other points. Evidently knowledge of this kind will be a matter of degree. However, without a reasonably comprehensive grasp of the cognitive map in which fractions are situated, a teacher will be hard put to it to frame the variety of explanations and analogies needed to explain this very difficult idea to Key Stage 1 and Key Stage 2 children.

Consider another example: to understand the notion of division, appeal must be made to multiplication. This in turn may be unpacked in a number of ways, one of which is the idea of repeated addition. Addition itself is not thoroughly understood until its relationship to subtraction is covered. Division of course is also connected to the idea of repeated subtraction. We can take this further. There are several different models of addition itself. Representations, characteristic diagrams and pictures, and associated terminology are tied to the various models. Since they are all models of addition, it is essential that their close interconnections are understood by teachers, and ultimately by their pupils.

It appears to be perfectly possible to gain correct answers in conventional GCSE exams, A-level and even in Higher Education tests without fully grasping the relevant networks of connections. This is why the notion of 'levels' of mathematical knowledge required for effective teaching proves so elusive and in the long run misleading. Primary teachers need to know their maths 'differently' just as much as they need to know 'more' mathematics.

Although these points can be justified by commonsense reflection on the nature of mathematics and of what it is to know and understand, it is interesting that recent empirical research supports the claims we make above. We have already made reference to Askew *et al.* (1997). The Teacher Training Agency commissioned researchers at King's College, London, to investigate what distinguished effective teachers of numeracy from their less splendid colleagues. The researchers reached a number of conclusions, a key one of which was expressed thus: 'Highly effective teachers of numeracy themselves had knowledge and awareness of conceptual connections between the areas they taught of the primary curriculum. In this study, being highly effective was not associated with having an A-level or degree in mathematics' (Askew *et al.* 1997).

Try to imagine that the question of 'infinity' comes up when you are teaching an able class of Y2s. What 'knowledge' do you need to answer questions, to offer explanations or to provoke the children into further investigations? Some of you will appreciate that the concept of infinity has been subjected to extremely abstruse investigations by mathematicians. Yet it would be of little use to the teacher confronting these troublesomely curious infants to know of the mathematician Cantor, and his investigation into (or construction of) numbers representing different kinds of infinity, represented by numbers called transfinite cardinals. Indeed, some readers may already be shuddering slightly after reading the last sentence. Instead, what seems to be required is a good basic grasp of the number system, of the different kinds of numbers and the ways of representing these. A child might ask whether infinity is a number. Because the child is unlikely to have a definitive notion in her head of what is, and what is not a number, the question may not be clear. The question could mean this: is infinity a number like other numbers which can be put on a number line, such as the natural numbers beginning 1, 2, 3 . . . ? Put in this way, the answer is evidently no. For any number represented on a number line it is always possible to put one after it. There is no greatest number. The child might be asking the related question whether infinity is the biggest possible number. The thought that 'the biggest possible number' is an incoherent term needs thinking through carefully with the children.

As so often in mathematics, you need some kind of model or analogy which works for young children. When I was a child I was always given a tin of toffees in my Christmas stocking. The tins had beautiful pictures on their lids. The picture always included a person with a tin of toffee, the lid of which was the same beautiful picture, including a picture of a person with a tin of toffee. I used to wonder whether if I had a good magnifying glass I would be able to detect very tiny pictures, and assumed that they went on for ever. This image conveys a good image of infinity, without of course being particularly 'technical' mathematically. It may illuminate the concept of infinity for some pupils. Others may be unmoved. Ideally I have other models, analogies or pictures which I can also try.

Discussion of such issues in informal fashion is perfectly possible with some seven year olds, and can involve sophisticated mathematical thinking without any appeal to Georg Cantor and his baroque landscape of transfinite cardinals. The teacher needs, among other things, a rich understanding of the kinds of abstract items which numbers can be, a grasp of their interrelationships and of key modes of representing and applying them.

Teachers who can flexibly and confidently move in many directions within these complex networks or maps are in a good position to help children to learn to do the same. The teachers are initiating the children into a set of conventions, concepts and rules which constitute mathematics. These rules have been developed since the time of Ancient Egypt, or earlier. Each generation must re-learn them, and continue to develop them. This view of mathematics is known by some as social constructivism. You can read more about it in Ernest (1991), and in Davis and Pettitt (1994).

We may note other connections treated in this book without going into the same kind of detail as we did in the above examples. Probability is connected to ratio and fractions, functions are connected to graphs, the measurement of area is connected to multiplication, pattern is connected to algebra and arguably to virtually everything in mathematics. We could go on.

Try to move around in this book as though you could click on a phrase and move to the relevant section of another chapter. We will issue explicit indications of connections wherever possible.

A popular sentiment, to which we also subscribe, is that 'knowing' plenty of mathematics does not in itself make you a good teacher. Indeed many of us have suffered under teachers who may well have been good mathematicians but were of little use to us. Now we may begin to wonder whether their relational understanding was limited in some ways. Were they really as 'good' at the subject as they thought, and as their qualifications suggested? Having dared to raise this question, we still need to concede that there is much more to teaching mathematics than subject knowledge, however rich. This book only addresses one modest part of what is needed by high quality teachers of primary mathematics.

Summary

- Two kinds of understanding of mathematics are possible, relational and instrumental.
- Instrumental understanding is knowing a particular method or rule for gaining an answer.
- Relational understanding is having a cognitive map of relevant sections of the interconnected network of concepts which constitutes mathematics.
- Many students may begin learning to be primary teachers with only an instrumental understanding. They know rules without reasons.
- Instrumental understanding without relational understanding burdens the memory and may induce negative feelings or even panic.
- Effective teachers of primary mathematics need connected or relational understanding.
- Relational understanding helps to enable the effective teacher to frame explanations in a variety of language, to suggest a range of representations and models, and to inform appropriate questioning in the classroom.

References

Askew, M. *et al.* (1997) *Effective Teachers of Numeracy*. London: King's College.

Davis, A. and Pettitt, D. (1994) *Developing Understanding in Primary Mathematics*. London: Falmer Press.

Ernest, P. (1991) *The Philosophy of Mathematics Education*. London: Falmer Press.

Skemp, R. (1989) *Mathematics in the Primary School*. London: Routledge.

Problem solving and proof

Introduction

Mathematics which stresses results over proof is often called applied mathematics, mathematics which stresses proof tends to be called pure mathematics (or just mathematics).

(Hersh 1997, p. 6)

NOT EVERYONE AGREES that mathematics splits easily in this way, but it is a useful distinction, provided that we remember that there is an important place for both activities. Moreover, the search for a result, something that works, may stimulate us to look at the principles behind our method and to verify some of our reasoning. Having proved something we may then find that the result has a useful application. The growth of mathematics through history has often relied upon a symbiotic relationship between pure and applied mathematics. At the heart of both pure and applied mathematics, however, are problems:

> But anyone who has done mathematics knows what comes first – a problem. Mathematics is a vast network of interconnected problems and solutions . . . (Hersh, 1997)

Many of the problems which pupils encounter at school are little more than practice exercises, and we have included some of these in the book. They have a place in the learning of mathematics but they are just the tip of an iceberg. For a start they can usually be solved quite quickly, provided the learner can recognise the technique needed, and the problem usually has just the right amount of information, no more and no less. These are quite unlike some of the famous problems of mathematics, some of which have remained unsolved for hundreds of years.

Most of you will know the statement of the theorem of Pythagoras:

$$a^2 + b^2 = c^2$$

where a, b and c are the lengths of the sides of a right-angled triangle with c as the hypotenuse. You may also know some whole number values which satisfy the relationship, e.g:

$$3, 4, 5 \qquad 5, 12, 13 \qquad 7, 24, 25$$

Pierre Fermat, a seventeenth-century French lawyer who did mathematics in his spare time, claimed to have a proof that this does not work for powers higher than two, i.e. there are no whole numbers for which

$$a^3 + b^3 = c^3 \quad \text{or} \quad a^4 + b^4 = c^4 \quad \text{or} \quad a^5 + b^5 = c^5 \quad \text{or} \quad a^6 + b^6 = c^6$$

or in fact any power you care to choose. In Fermat's last theorem, as this statement is known, the problem was in fact to provide a proof that something could *not* happen, unlike the Pythagoras relationship in which all right-angled triangles have the required property. Unfortunately Fermat did not write this proof down. He simply scribbled a note in the margin of one of his notebooks to say he had one, and only in the last few years has it yielded to the British mathematician, Andrew Wiles. Throughout the centuries there have been numerous attempts, and some claims which proved to be false, including one by Wiles himself. In the end, it was a combination of persistence, hard work, knowledge, intuition, imagination, the connecting of seemingly disparate branches of mathematics and even competition (someone else looked as if he was near to the solution as well) which contributed to success. There are other problems in mathematics for which there are no known solutions as yet, and some very old problems which have only recently been cracked.

In some of these, like Fermat's last theorem, the problem is to provide a proof. But what is a proof? There are numerous definitions, but the one we like best is from Hersh:

A proof is a conclusive argument which convinces fellow mathematicians . . .

Even this is not straightforward. There is another famous mathematical curiosity, which applies to maps in which countries share common borders and are coloured so that neighbouring countries are coloured differently. In 1852, Francis Guthrie, a recent graduate from University College, London, noticed that the maximum number of colours needed seemed to be four. This result, often called the Four Colour map problem, has only been 'proved' relatively recently by using a computer to check all the different possibilities. Human beings would not live long enough to do the checking themselves so the capacity of the computer to work at high speeds has obviously provided the mathematicians with another potential tool. But this proof is contentious and some mathematicians do not accept it. Who says mathematicians are boring? They are as argumentative and human as any other group in the community. Who says mathematics is dry? It is as full of interest and debate as any subject in the curriculum, but you have to be prepared to seek out this side of its nature.

You may say that this is all very well for the community of professional mathematicians and that they inhabit a different world from that of the primary school teacher. But it is important to realise that such teachers form a community themselves, part of the community of mathematics educators, who have a defining role in what and how we teach mathematics to school pupils. Despite an imposed curriculum, this will not remain static and will always be the subject of debate and consultation. By sharing experiences with other students and teachers, attending courses, keeping up to date with reading, joining a professional association[1] and responding to consultations, the primary school teacher has an opportunity to contribute to the development of the mathematics curriculum. He or she will have an important role in the way children develop their ability to solve appropriate problems and develop ideas of reasoning and proof through a variety of appropriate activities. Their solutions may not be concise or heavily dependent on symbolism, but the seeds of such mathematical thinking can be sown at a very early stage.

The point here is that tackling extended problems for which there are no obvious lines of attack is not just the province of the professional mathematician. Very young children can tackle non-standard problems, provided they are accessible. Some of these are directly related to conventional aspects of the curriculum and others are free-standing. Teachers can take exactly the same problems and extend them or deal with them in greater depth, and in so doing increase their own understanding and appreciation of the richness of mathematical activity. Along the way they may also experience frustration and joy, and learn to use their imagination and intuition as well as standard rules and procedures.

The rest of this chapter illustrates aspects of problem solving and proof through illustrative examples. There will be both practical situations where a solution which works is what is needed as well as abstract situations where we are interested in finding solutions which work, but also knowing why they work, when they work and if they follow logically from our assumptions.

Using mathematics in 'real life' situations

One of the common justifications for the place of mathematics in the curriculum is that it is useful for practical situations in everyday life. This is certainly true but can perhaps be overstated, because the mathematics many of us use in our everyday lives often bears little resemblance to the mathematics we meet at school. For one thing, the methods we use are frequently different since there is often a great deal of approximation and estimation used in the out of school situations. For another, we often have to make more decisions, e.g. deciding which measurements we need, selecting the appropriate instruments, finding and interpreting information, working within constraints of time and money. Above all we have to decide how we are going to tackle the problem.

This was brought home to me a few years ago when I wanted to re-cover a lampshade. Even though I have a school mathematics background, my first method for creating a paper pattern was actually quite rough and ready. It involved tracing out the paper pattern directly onto a piece of newspaper as I turned the lampshade

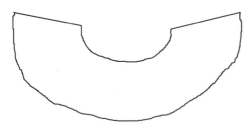

around. (You may wish to try this yourself.) First I had to draw a straight line the length of the seam onto the paper. I placed the seam on top of this, and started to turn the lampshade around, tracing out the path of the larger circular rim first and then that of the smaller rim, until the seam was once more in contact with the paper. I marked the end points of each arc and joined them together with straight line.

As you can see the tracing was slightly wobbly but the pattern was actually quite a good fit, with a little bit of adjustment here and there.

I then decided that I would try another method so I set about taking some measurements.

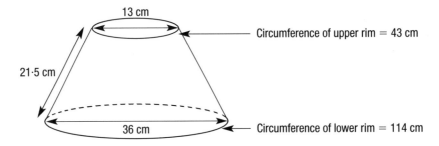

This was where my first problems arose. How do you measure the diameter of a circle when the centre is not marked? I had to gauge where the diameters were by trying to find the longest distance across each of the circles, and these circles were difficult to locate exactly because of the thickness of the material. At least the circumferences of the edges were tangible but I was measuring them with a tape measure and it was difficult to keep to the edge.

I decided to round the slant height to 22 cm. I also felt that my diameter measurements were probably more accurate than the two circumference measurements so I used the diameter measurements to calculate the two circumferences using the formula $C = \pi d$.

Circumference of small circle = $3 \cdot 14 \times 13$

$= 40 \cdot 82$

$= 41$ cm to the nearest cm

Similarly the circumference of the larger circle was 113 cm.

Next I made a diagram of the shape I wanted to cut out, which was clearly part of two concentric circles.

If I could find out the length x and the angle θ I could draw the required arcs using a blackboard compass or a pencil attached to a piece of string.

The calculation of x and θ is a straightforward piece of GCSE mathematics, but I have used this problem with graduate mathematicians and it has never failed to amaze me how long it has taken them to do this bit of the mathematics. It involves numerical ideas of similarity and ratio within the context of 2-D and 3-D shape. So beware – the next bit may be difficult to understand. Go over it a few times, working it through yourself as you read, but if there are still steps you do not understand, you may wish to return to this after you have covered other sections in the book.

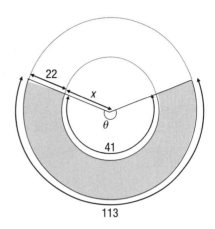

To calculate x, we use the fact that the sector A and the larger sector of which it is part are similar and so the lengths are in proportion.

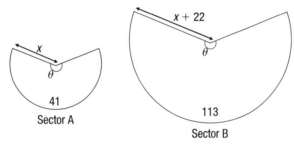

Sector A Sector B

Sector A and Sector B are similar, that is the same shape but different sizes. Therefore the ratios of corresponding lengths are equal.

$\dfrac{\text{radius}}{\text{arc length}}$ of sector A $= \dfrac{\text{radius}}{\text{arc length}}$ of sector B   i.e. $\dfrac{x}{41} = \dfrac{x+22}{113}$

Multiplying both sides by 41×113 gives $113x = 41(x + 22)$

$113x = 41x + 902$

Subtract $41x$ from both sides $72x = 902$

Divide both sides by 72 $x = \dfrac{902}{72}$

$x = 12{\cdot}5$ cm

To find θ we use the fact that the smaller sector A is a fraction $\frac{\theta}{360}$ of the circle, and so the arc length is the same fraction of the whole circumference.

The whole circumference $= \pi \times 25 = 79$ cm

so $\dfrac{\theta}{360} = \dfrac{41}{79}$ $\theta = \dfrac{41 \times 360}{79}$ $\theta = 187°$

Using these values I could draw the pattern on newspaper. I only needed to draw half the shape since I knew I could cut out the material on a fold.

In fact this method gave a pattern which was not quite as good as the rough and ready method, probably because the lampshade itself was slightly distorted. But in case this destroys your confidence in school mathematics there is a further twist to the tale. Some time later, I was visiting an engineering workshop and found an apprentice cutting out a metal flue to join two pipes of different diameters.

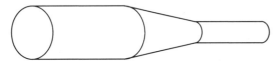

He was having to work very accurately, using a template based on a technical drawing design, and he did not have an existing flue to draw around. The pattern was not instantly recognisable but on close inspection it clearly had its origins in the second method described earlier. It is clearly important to have a range of strategies that we can use depending on the situation and the materials with which we are working. In the primary school we have very little idea of how our pupils will eventually use mathematics in their lives after school, whether in common everyday or specialised vocational and professional situations, and we need to prepare them for a variety of possibilities.

Using intuition

The second example again comes from my personal experience and illustrates the stages in a pure mathematical activity before a problem is formulated completely. I was at an ATM (Association of Teachers of Mathematics) conference, keeping myself up to date, and sitting with a secondary mathematics teacher and two primary teachers from a school which had spent its entire year's staff development budget on sending all the teachers to the conference. We were asked to investigate the number of right angles in polygons.

We immediately attacked this by starting with a triangle and then moving on to a quadrilateral. These first two were easy – a triangle can have at most one right angle and a quadrilateral has at most four.

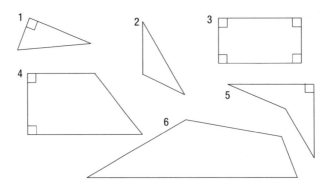

Check 2.1

Why can there be only one right angle in a triangle? Why not two? Can you get a quadrilateral with three but not four right angles?

We started to focus our investigation at this point. Almost imperceptibly we slipped into looking for the maximum number of right angles in a given polygon. This now became our problem, so we needed to do some clarification. We decided that we would not allow shapes like this:

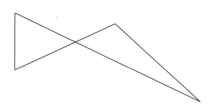

because it could either be thought of as a quadrilateral with crossing sides or a hexagon. We also decided that the activity would be rather limited unless we allowed angles greater than 180° as in the fourth polygon (of the seven shown in the diagram below).

We started to draw, and as we drew we recorded our results in a table. At first our drawings were quite random and then we started to work more systematically, by cutting corners, making 'inserts' and creating 'bulges'.

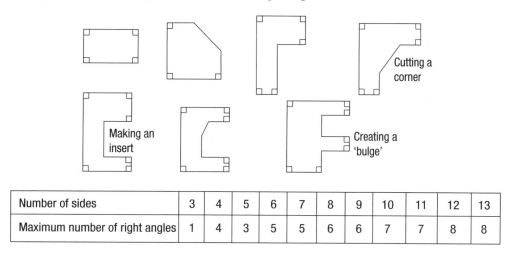

Cutting a corner

Making an insert

Creating a 'bulge'

Number of sides	3	4	5	6	7	8	9	10	11	12	13
Maximum number of right angles	1	4	3	5	5	6	6	7	7	8	8

We were comfortably in our swing now and except for the first few numbers we felt it was settling into a nice pattern. One of our group had earlier made the prediction that a nine sided shape could have seven right angles. Actually, it was more than this since she said she *wanted* the nine sided shape to have seven right angles. The rest of us ignored her.

Another group in the room claimed to have found a general rule which described the number sequence, and it was at this point that the leader of the session decided to intervene by showing us this shape:

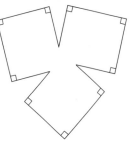

Here was a 12 sided polygon with nine right angles. Now we had to go back to our table. This threw us into confusion but gave inspiration to the woman who wanted to find seven right angles in a nine sided shape. It did not take her long to come up with this:

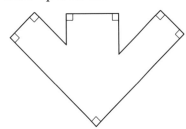

Her intuition had been right all along. I will leave this story at this point, partly because the investigation is still ongoing – we think a pattern is emerging but there are several points at which it seems to break down. Perhaps there are several patterns. The ultimate goal is to find a general formula which we could use to predict the maximum number of right angles in any polygon. We do not know if there is one and we do not know if we can find one and the session leader, David Fielker, is not saying!

Problem posing in the classroom

You may have found the last section rather unusual and perhaps frustrating, because it is very rare to hear accounts of mathematics in progress. This is a shame because professional mathematicians spend most of their time being stuck, playing around with their problems, waiting for inspiration and hoping someone will nudge them in the right direction with a chance remark. Too much of this can be dispiriting, but teachers and pupils alike should learn how to cope with being stuck. More than this, they should recognise that only by getting stuck do they have an opportunity to learn. If you only tackle problems which are easy to solve, you are never going to learn anything new. At the very least it is a good preparation for life!

Probably the most important thing is to have problems which are just outside your reach, but manageable with a little help from peers and teachers. Many problems come to us ready made, but Marion Walter has made a speciality out of helping teachers and pupils to *pose* problems.

Here are some of the problems which developed out of using a dustbin as a starting point.

How many dustbins are needed to collect the week's school litter?

How high is it?

How many ways can you fit the lid on this bin?

What do you think would fit in this bin . . . an elephant, a bird . . . ?'

This ubiquitous addition problem

$$
\begin{array}{r}
342 \\
+ \ 534 \\
\hline
876
\end{array}
$$

led to:

> Make up other addition problems of two 3 digit numbers whose sum is 876.
>
> Make up other 3 digit addition problems whose answers consist of three consecutive digits.
>
> Rearrange the digits of each 3-digit number in 342 + 534 to get the largest possible total.
>
> Find all the different totals you can get by rearranging the digits . . .

The fractions calculation $\frac{2}{3} + \frac{1}{5}$ stimulated

> When in real life would you ever have to add these two fractions?
>
> Is the answer less or more than 1?
>
> By how much does $\frac{2}{3}$ differ from 1?
>
> By how much does $\frac{1}{5}$ differ from 1?
>
> What must be added to $\frac{2}{3} + \frac{1}{5}$ to obtain a total of 1?

Marion Walter was deliberately using ideas which related to conventional topics in the mathematics curriculum, so pupils tackling them would be given valuable opportunities to practise skills but also to think more widely and deeply about those conventional topics. I particularly like her account of the regular hexagon starting point and her initial question: 'What does one want students to know about a regular hexagon anyway?'

My own problems derived from this would include

> One way of splitting the regular hexagon into triangles is shown:
>
> Can you find another way of splitting it into triangles,
> using only vertices of the hexagon as vertices of the triangles?
> What are the angles of the triangles?

> Join each vertex of the hexagon to every other vertex.
> How many lines have you drawn?
> Find the lengths of the lines
> Find all the angles in the shape

Ways of approaching problems

There has been a great deal of debate about how to improve pupils' problem solving skills, with some writers advocating a routine for solving problems. Others find this too mechanical, and suggest that we cannot teach thinking skills in a vacuum since each problem has its own context and content.

John Mason with Leone Burton and Kaye Stacey (1988) suggest that there are two intertwining factors:

1 the processes of the mathematical enquiry – specialising, generalising, conjecturing, convincing

2 the emotional state – getting started, getting involved, getting stuck, mulling, keeping going, being sceptical, contemplating

in any process of mathematical thinking. As far as the mathematical enquiry is concerned, the questions 'What do I know?' 'What do I want?' 'What can I introduce?' may help the learner during the 'Entry phase'. In the 'Attack phase' the processes of conjecturing, collecting data, discovering patterns, then justifying and convincing may all be involved. During this process the learner should be constantly reviewing progress, and towards the end reflecting on the whole process. This reflection period may in turn suggest new avenues of enquiry or ways in which the original activity can be extended.

At several points along this journey the emotional state of the learner may take over – either through paralysis when stuck or through hot-headedness when in full cry. Mason, Burton and Stacey point out the importance of recognising these emotional states and harnessing the positive side of seemingly negative feelings. For instance, they suggest that being stuck is an honourable state and that instead of immediately responding with a cry for help, trying to do something about being stuck is the first step to a resolution.

The writers give a framework within which to work, rather than a set of rules of how to proceed, and they give an invaluable piece of advice for improving mathematical thinking. This is to practise, i.e. to get into the habit of doing mathematical problems, but always accompanied by reflection. They argue that practice can 'wash over you leaving no permanent marks', but that looking back over your work, marking critical moments and drawing out their significance will help you to approach new problems from a stronger base.

Much will depend on whether you are working individually, with a group or using a combination of the two. All three modes have their own advantages and disadvantages, as you may find when working through this book. Working on your own means you will be going at your own pace, but you will be denied the opportunity of other people's ideas and knowledge. Working in a group can be excellent for pooling ideas, talking through problems, and using each other as sounding boards but if there are dominant characters who will not listen to others the experience can be isolating. Hopefully, you will also have access to tutors who can monitor the way the group is working, curb unhelpful members and encourage less confident ones. They may be sufficiently detached to make you stand back and review the mathematics you are doing, acting as a mirror to your thinking. They may also give hints and in some cases just tell you things which may be useful.

Finally, if the teacher is in the habit of doing problems herself, and reflecting on the experience, she may be better able to help pupils solve problems themselves. In this book, there are a variety of problems. It is important to try all of them – the starters, the routine exercises and the challenges – because each type will give you different experiences. Some will help you refresh your memory, others will provoke discussion and debate and some will require deep thinking. Together they should provide a rich experience of mathematical activity which will refresh and extend your present understanding.

Using reasoning

Finding the elephant

There is a very enjoyable game which appears on the SMILE[2] collection of mathematical software in which an elephant is hidden at one of the crossroads in a square grid representing the streets of New York. The player types in a set of coordinates and is given the direct distance of the coordinates from the elephant. The object of the game is to find the elephant as quickly as possible.

After a few guesses a successful player may be looking at a screen like the one below. The first guess was 5 units way, the second was closer at 2·24 units, the third was closer still and the fourth was slightly further away. However, the whole number solution led to success on the fifth attempt.

The player has probably been trying to improve her guesses in the light of the feedback information, rather than working randomly. For instance, after her first guess she may have realised that she could be 5 units away along either a horizontal or vertical line, or along the hypotenuse of a 3, 4, 5, right-angled triangle. This is not always the case, however. It is fascinating to watch pupils playing this game and look to see if they appear to be think through their strategy or playing in an unthinking way.

Even for the intelligent player above, however, a more rigorous use of reasoning could have

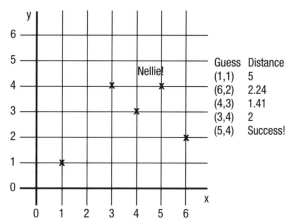

Guess	Distance
(1,1)	5
(6,2)	2.24
(4,3)	1.41
(3,4)	2
(5,4)	Success!

given the answer after much fewer guesses. Since the first guess was five units away from the hidden elephant, we can draw an arc of a circle radius 5 units centred at (1,1) – the position of the first guess. This arc contains all the possible points where the elephant could be since all the points on the arc are 5 units away from the first guess. Then we can draw a second arc, radius 2·24, centred on (6,2). This includes all the points which are 2·24 units away from the second guess. Where the two arcs

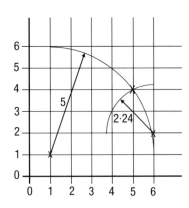

meet, at (5,4), is the point which is 5 units away from (1,1) and also 2·24 away from (6,2). This is the only point where the arcs meet on the grid so Nellie must be hiding there.

Using the grid actually makes life easier in this problem since the elephant can only hide at a crossroads. But in fact, even without a grid, the maximum number of guesses you would need in order to win would be three. After the first guess there are an infinite number of possible positions around the circumference of the circle.

After the second guess the two circles drawn will intersect at two points – narrowing down the possibilities to just two points which are both the required distance away.

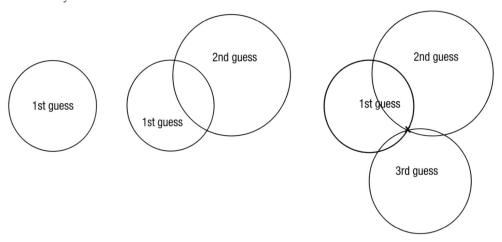

After the third guess, the only possible place which is the required distance from each of the three guesses is the point, X, at which all the circles intersect. Of course when playing the game at the computer screen without compasses handy a certain amount of estimating where the circles lie may be necessary!

Playing the elephant game intelligently would be an example of using mathematical reasoning; if you regularly find the elephant after four or five attempts you are clearly demonstrating a trial and improvement strategy, based on reason. If you had developed the reasoning used above which shows that that the maximum number of guesses needed is three, then you are actually providing a logical mathematical proof. Interestingly, and counter to many people's expectations, this proof relies upon a written argument and an illustrative diagram, and there is not an algebraic symbol in sight. It has, however, moved away from the context of the original game and does look more abstract.

Check 2.2

1 Where is Nellie?

Guess	Distance
(4,2)	2·8
(1,3)	1·4
(0,4)	2

2 Play the elephant game yourself on paper with a partner.
Hint: The person being the computer can either measure the distances or calculate distances using Pythagoras' theorem and a handy calculator.

Using patterns

Number grids

These can be a rich source of number patterns and have some interesting relationships embedded in the structure.

Consider this 100 grid:

1	2	3	4	5	6	7	8	9	10
11	12	13	14	15	16	17	18	19	20
21	22	23	24	25	26	27	28	29	30
31	32	33	34	35	36	37	38	39	40
41	42	43	44	45	46	47	48	49	50
51	52	53	54	55	56	57	58	59	60
61	62	63	64	65	66	67	68	69	70
71	72	73	74	75	76	77	78	79	80
81	82	83	84	85	86	87	88	89	90
91	92	93	94	95	96	97	98	99	100

You will see patterns in the units and tens digits as you move across rows and down columns and along diagonal lines. Within the grid, there are also patterns and relationships which are not so immediately obvious.

If you take any 2 × 2 section of the grid such as:

24	25
34	35

The sum of the top row of numbers = 49
The sum of the bottom row of numbers = 69

If you try any other 2 × 2 section the actual values of the sum will differ from these but we will always have a difference of 20. While it is possible to check every single possibility in this grid it would be tedious and it is very straightforward to formalise what seems intuitively obvious.

The first number in the section will vary across the grid, and so we can represent this by the letter 'x'. The value in the cell to the right of x will be 1 more, and the value in the cell below it will be 10 more, because of the structure of the grid. We can therefore fill in the value in each cell in terms of x.

x	$x + 1$
$x + 10$	$x + 1 + 10$

or

x	$x + 1$
$x + 10$	$x + 11$

Sum of numbers in top row $= x + x + 1$
$$= 2x + 1$$

Sum of numbers in second row $= x + 10 + x + 11$
$$= 2x + 21$$

It is obvious that whatever the value of x, these sums will differ by 20 but we can formalise this algebraically:

Difference $= (2x + 21) - (2x + 1)$
$$= 2x + 21 - 2x - 1$$
$$= 20$$

Similar relationships can be found for differences between sums in rows or in diagonals, and on different sized grids. You will also find relationships if you alter the size and shape of the section. Try to justify these algebraically.

Arithmagons

In an article by Diane Stoncel for *Mathematics Teaching* there is a write up of a Year 3 child's work on arithmagons. These are figures where the sum of the two numbers in the circles at either end of each side is placed in the corresponding square.

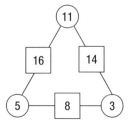

Jonathan found that if consecutive numbers are placed in the circles, then the sum of the numbers in the squares is twice the sum of the numbers in the circles. His invented symbolism for this is a lovely example of mathematical compression. With 1,2,3 in the circles which gave 3,4,5, in the squares he wrote

$$+ \bigcirc = 6$$
$$= 18$$
$$+ \square = 12$$

Can you follow what he was doing here? What do you think he would write for other sets of consecutive numbers placed in the circles? You may wish to investigate this yourself further.

We can easily prove that the relationship between the sum of the numbers in the circles and the squares holds for any starting numbers, not necessarily consecutive. We can choose any values for the numbers in the circles, so we can represent them by a, b and c.

Then the values in the squares will be $a + b$, $b + c$, and $a + c$.
Sum of the numbers in circles $= a + b + c$
Sum of the numbers in squares $= a + b + b + c + a + c$
$= a + b + c + a + b + c$

This is obviously twice the sum of the numbers in the circles. We could also write this sum as $2a + 2b + 2c = 2(a + b + c)$. Both expressions indicate that the sum of the numbers in the squares is twice the sum of the numbers in the circles whatever the original values placed in the circles. It holds **in general**.

Check 2.3

1 Misleading patterns

Consider the relationship between the number of points on the circumference of a circle (n) and the number of regions (R) formed by joining each pair of points with straight lines:

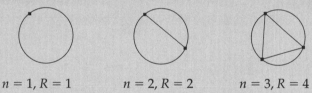

$n = 1, R = 1$ $n = 2, R = 2$ $n = 3, R = 4$

As you continue this sequence, make sure that no more than two lines cross at any point in the interior of the circle. See if you can see a pattern developing and start predicting and testing your predictions. What happens?

Always, sometimes or never true

In the question above (1 in 2.3) you may have found that the relationship you thought was emerging, turned out to be wrong when you tried more cases. This can happen with other mathematical conjectures

It must have a bigger area, because the perimeter is bigger

This statement from an 11-year-old pupil in a mixed ability class in a secondary school was a perfect example for the teacher to respond with 'Is that always true?'

The pupil had several examples for which the conjecture did work:

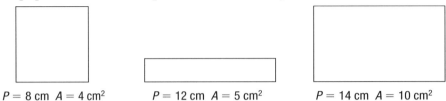

$P = 8$ cm $A = 4$ cm^2 $P = 12$ cm $A = 5$ cm^2 $P = 14$ cm $A = 10$ cm^2

but when he tried a few more examples he soon found a contradiction.

$P = 12$ cm $A = 9$ cm^2 $P = 16$ cm $A = 7$ cm^2

Here the perimeter of the second shape is larger than that of the first, but the area is smaller.

 Check 2.4

Discuss these statements and try a few examples. Decide whether you think they are always, sometimes or never true.

1 The sum of four even numbers is divisible by four.
2 A parallelogram has a line of symmetry.
3 Half a circle is a semi-circle.
4 Solid shapes have at least six faces.
5 A triangle must have at least one acute angle.
6 All four sided shapes tessellate.

Euclidean geometry

It is astonishing to realise that a work on geometry, compiled by a Greek mathematician between 300 and 275 BC, survived in translation as a standard school text until well into the twentieth century. In 'The Elements', Euclid, the first head of the mathematics department at the University of Alexandria, drew together a rigidly deductive system based on precisely defined axioms which were considered to be self-evident 'truths'. From these, new relationships were deduced.

For example, amongst definitions in Book 1 (Fauvel and Grey 1993, pp. 100–102) we have:

A point is that which has no part.
A line is a breadthless length.
A figure is that which is contained by any boundary or boundaries.

Amongst the postulates we have:

> That, if a straight line falling on two straight lines makes the interior angles on the same side less than two right angles, the two straight lines, if produced indefinitely, meet on that side on which are the angles less than the two right angles.
>
>   You may need to sketch this to clarify what it means.

Amongst the common notions we have;

> Things which are equal to the same thing are also equal to one another.

Within its terms of reference, Euclidean geometry is an elegantly rigorous system applying to the properties of two- and three-dimensional shapes constructed using only compasses and an ungraduated ruler. Different geometries, with alternative axiomatic foundations, have since been invented by mathematicians, and the recent teaching of geometry has adopted more intuitive and less rigorously logical approaches in the last thirty years, but no chapter on reasoning and proof would be complete without some reference to Euclid.

One key idea, which certainly sticks in my memory from studying Euclidean geometry at school, is that of congruence. If you could prove that two shapes, usually triangles, were congruent then a whole host of further relationships could be deduced.

Congruent shapes are identical in shape and size but not necessarily position.

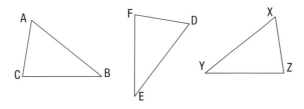

We can slide $\triangle$ABC and turn it so that it fits exactly on top of $\triangle$DEF. We can also reflect it so that it fits exactly on top of $\triangle$XYZ. These triangles are all congruent since their corresponding sides and angles are equal. i.e.

$$AB = DE = XY \quad \angle A = \angle D = \angle X$$
$$AC = DF = XZ \quad \angle B = \angle E = \angle Y$$
$$BC = EF = YZ \quad \angle C = \angle F = \angle Z$$

but [cross shape] is not congruent to [smaller cross shape]

because although the shapes are the same, they are different sizes.

Also etched on my memory from school geometry are the minimum conditions needed to prove that two triangles are congruent. It is not necessary to know that each corresponding side and each corresponding angle are equal. For instance, if you know that each side of a triangle is equal in length to each side of another triangle, then they will necessarily be congruent. The shorthand for this is S.S.S. and is easy to justify by constructing a triangle knowing only the lengths of the three sides AB, AC and BC.

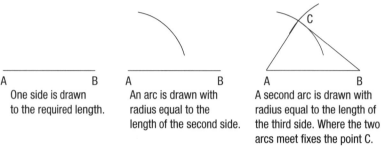

A   B   A   B   A   B

One side is drawn to the required length.   An arc is drawn with radius equal to the length of the second side.   A second arc is drawn with radius equal to the length of the third side. Where the two arcs meet fixes the point C.

Since we are including reflections as congruent, there is one and only one triangle with these particular length sides and so all copies will be congruent to each other. It follows that the corresponding angles are then equal, which may be useful in making further deductions.

Another situation can arise when two sides and the included angle of one triangle are equal to the corresponding sides and angle of another triangle (S.A.S.). Again, these three conditions imply that the two triangles are congruent. This is easy to see from a construction, where the lengths of sides AB, AC and the angle, A, included between them are specified.

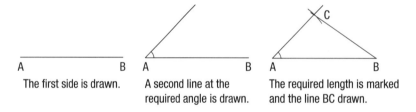

A   B   A   B   A   B

The first side is drawn.   A second line at the required angle is drawn.   The required length is marked and the line BC drawn.

The triangle can now be completed. It is easy to see that there is only one possible triangle with these three measurements, and that any copies will be congruent to each other. It now follows that for all these copies, the third side will be equal, as will the other two corresponding angles.

(Both these results will be used in Chapter 17, in order to make further deductions about shapes.)

Check 2.5

   1 Construct a triangle with sides 6 cm, 3 cm and 4 cm. Measure the angles. Is it possible to construct a triangle with sides 6 cm, 3 cm and 4 cm but with different angles from the first?

   2 Construct a triangle with two sides of 7 cm and 5 cm and the angle between them of 120°. Measure the third side and the other two angles. Is it possible to draw a different triangle with the first three measurements?

3 Construct a triangle with angles 10°, 55°, and 115°. Measure its sides. Is it possible to construct a triangle with the same angles but with different length sides?

4 Construct a triangle ABC so that AB = 7 cm, AC = 5 cm and ∠B = 15°. How many different triangles can be drawn with these measurements?

Proving from basic principles

Odds and evens

Recently, a group of students training to be primary teachers pooled all they knew about odd and even numbers.

A Even Numbers	B Odd numbers
(i) end in 2, 4, 6, 8 . . .	(i) cannot halve them to get a whole number
(ii) are divisible by two	(ii) cannot be divided by two exactly
(iii) when you add, subtract or multiply two even numbers you get an even number	(iii) end in 1, 3, 7, 9 . . .

A(i), and B(iii) are descriptive statements.

A(ii), B(i) and B(ii) are concerned with the properties of odd and even numbers, and A(iii) gives us some general statements about the result of operating on even numbers, which we could try to prove.

In this section, we will look at how to prove some of the statements in A(iii), using the basic properties of odd and even numbers, and a process of **deductive reasoning**. For our purposes, deductive reasoning uses basic general principles to derive other general statements. Further, if the basic principles are true, then the conclusions are also generally (i.e. always) true.

Let us see how the student group approached this. After discussing their list of statements, they were given large sets of counters or Multilink and asked to decide if they had an odd or even number **without counting them all**. There were several strategies:

1 Some students took counters one by one, put them into two separate sets, A and B, by first putting one counter in A and then putting one in B, and continued until all the counters were used up. If the last counter was placed in B, they knew they had an even number; if in A, they knew they had an odd number, e.g. an even number of counters would end up looking like this:

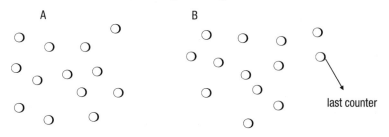

2 Some students took 2 counters at a time, and put one in each of the two sets. If they were left with one spare counter they knew they had an odd number. Otherwise they knew they had an even number.

3 Some students simply grouped their counters in pairs. An odd number would end up looking like this:

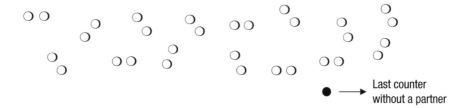

Last counter
without a partner

4 Not surprisingly, students with Multilink tended to link them together either in 'trains' put side by side or in columns joined together:

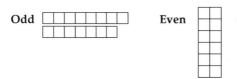

5 More rarely Multilink were joined in pairs

6 One group were able to join their Multilink into little 'wands' of five and announced that they had an even number.

✎ Check 2.6

Which are correct? Which methods would you be inclined to use?

In fact, the last method is incorrect, because it would work for numbers like 10 or 20 but not for 15 or 25. The other methods are all correct and embody the properties of odd and even numbers, albeit in slightly different ways. Each of these correct methods involves a way of deciding if a natural number (see Chapter 3) is exactly divisible by 2 (a fuller exploration of division is made in Chapter 5).

Methods 1 and 4 are examples of the principle that

A number is even if it can be split into two equal whole number parts. If not it is odd.

Methods 3 and 5 illustrate the principle that

> A number is even if it is made up of a whole number of twos. If not it is odd.

Interestingly, method 2 uses both these principles. Each principle has a different visual representation and either is sufficient to prove some new relationship similar to those mentioned earlier.

(a) A visual proof that the sum of two odd numbers is even

We could list lots of pairs of odd numbers, each with an even sum, but that would be inductive reasoning, since we could not be sure that it would work for all odd numbers and we would never be able to test all the possibilities. We need to show that this will work for *any* two starting numbers.

Using the principles stated earlier, we assume that an odd number can either be represented by a train of paired cubes with an extra cube on one layer, or by counters arranged in twos with an extra counter:

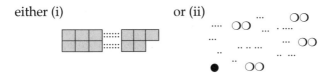

The dots are very important here. They show that there are an unspecified number of blocks, or counters which have not been drawn in, but each arranged like the visible blocks or counters. The number of visible counters or blocks has no significance; they are simply drawn in to show how the Multilink and counters have been arranged. This form of representation means that our reasoning will apply to any two odd starting numbers.

When we find the sum we have :

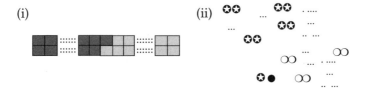

In (i) we have a longer train with two blocks one above the other at each point. The total number of cubes must be even because we could split this into two equal lines. Similarly in (ii) the two odd counters have paired up and we now have a larger number of pairs, so we must have an even number of counters.

(b) A symbolic proof that the sum of two odd numbers is even

Here we are going to use letters to represent the numbers, but we need a way of showing that our two starting numbers can be different.

So I will represent the first odd number as O_1 and the second as O_2.

Then $\quad O_1 = 2 \times t_1 + 1 \quad$ or $\quad O_1 = p_1 \times 2 + 1$

$\qquad\quad O_2 = 2 \times t_2 + 1 \qquad\qquad O_2 = p_2 \times 2 + 1$

Try to relate this to the earlier visual images with t as the length of the paired section of the train and p as the number of pairs of counters.

So $\quad O_1 + O_2 = 2 \times t_1 + 1 + 2 \times t_2 + 1 \qquad O_1 + O_2 = p_1 \times 2 + 1 + p_2 \times 2 + 1$

$\qquad\qquad\qquad = 2 \times t_1 + 2 \times t_2 + 2 \qquad\qquad\qquad\quad = p_1 \times 2 + p_2 \times 2 + 2$

$\qquad\qquad\qquad = 2 \times (t_1 + t_2 + 1) \qquad\qquad\qquad\qquad = (p_1 + p_2 + 1) \times 2$

This represents a train of length $t_1 + t_2 + 1$ $\qquad$ This represents $p_1 + p_2 + 1$ pairs

Both these forms represent an even number because they are each a multiple of 2, i.e. 2 multiplied by the length of the final train, or the number of pairs multiplied by 2.

(c) Proof by exhaustion

Jane, one of the group of students previously mentioned, proved the result for the sum of two odd numbers in an unusual way. She reasoned that any odd number has to have a units digit of 1, 3, 5, 7, or 9 because any other digits represent multiples of ten and hence are even, e.g. 973 = 97 tens (can be split into two exactly) + 3 (cannot be split into two exactly). So the 'oddness' of any number shows up in its units. Similarly an even number has to have units digits of 0, 2, 4, 6, or 8. She then proceeded to work out all the possible units digits produced in the sum:

$1 + 1 \to 2$	$3 + 1 \to 4$	$5 + 1 \to 6$	$7 + 1 \to 8$	$9 + 1 \to 0$
$1 + 3 \to 4$	$3 + 3 \to 6$	$5 + 3 \to 8$	$7 + 3 \to 0$	$9 + 3 \to 2$
$1 + 5 \to 6$	$3 + 5 \to 8$	$5 + 5 \to 0$	$7 + 5 \to 2$	$9 + 5 \to 4$
$1 + 7 \to 8$	$3 + 7 \to 0$	$5 + 7 \to 2$	$7 + 7 \to 4$	$9 + 7 \to 6$
$1 + 9 \to 0$	$3 + 9 \to 2$	$5 + 9 \to 4$	$7 + 9 \to 6$	$9 + 9 \to 8$

These are all even units digits so any pair of odd numbers will give an even sum. This was a way of proving the result by collecting all the different possibilities and proving that the result is true for each case. It can only be done when we have a finite number of cases but it is a perfectly sensible method and is called proof by exhaustion. It has echoes of the computer proof of the Four Colour map problem mentioned at the beginning of the chapter.

Check 2.7

Prove these statements using either a visual or symbolic proof.

1 The sum of an odd and an even number is odd.
2 The sum of three odd numbers is odd.
3 The difference between two odd numbers is even.

Try making up some more of your own.

If you are exhausted by now and wonder where the idea of proof connects with the primary classroom, you will be interested in this example from a Year 2 class (NCC, 1992).

A Year 2 class had been learning about odd and even numbers. A few days later, Paul and Rachel were painting. Their teacher approached:

Paul: If you add two odd numbers together, you get an even number.

Teacher: That's interesting. Are you sure it's always true?

Paul: 3 and 5 make 8; 5 and 7 make 12.

Rachel (after a pause): It's because the odd one from one number goes with the odd one from the other number.

Paul offers a conjecture, and gives specific examples to support it. Rachel seems to get to the underlying structure and gives a logical proof. It is a wonderful example of young children thinking about mathematical generalities and being stimulated by the teacher's question to justify their reasoning.

Summary

- Problem solving is at the heart of mathematics.
- Problems can be 'real life' or abstract.
- Proving something is more than just giving many examples.
- Proofs can use words, pictures or symbols.
- Proofs need to be convincing.
- You can disprove something by finding a counter-example.
- Inductive reasoning is a method of drawing general conclusions from a limited set of observations.
- Deductive reasoning uses logic to draw general conclusions from initial statements or assumptions.

Links with the classroom

Do a Marion Walter, by posing your own problems, based on these starting points:

a $2 + 8 = 10$

b $1.4 \times 5 = 7$

c $0.3 + 0.3 + 0.4 = 1$

d $69 - 27 = 42$

e A triangle

f The class register

g The desks in the classroom

h The class library

Challenges!

1 Solve a selection of the problems from the problem posing section.
2 The bigger the diagonal of a rectangle the bigger the area. True or False?
3 Prove that the sum of four consecutive numbers is even.
4 Prove that the product of three consecutive numbers is divisible by three.

5 Prove that the product of two even numbers is even.

6 Prove that product of two odd numbers is odd.

References

Fauvel, J. and Gray, J. (1993) *The History of Mathematics*. Basingstoke: Macmillan in association with the Open University Press.

Hersh, R. (1997) *What is Mathematics Really*. London: Jonathan Cape.

Mason, J. with Burton, L. and Stacey, K. (1988) *Thinking Mathematically*. Workingham, England: Addison-Wesley.

National Curriculum Council (1992) *Using and Applying Mathematics – Book A*. York: NCC.

Stoncel, D. (1994) 'How far can you go?', *Mathematics Teaching*, **147**, 36–7.

Walter, M. (1989) 'Curriculum topics through problem posing', *Mathematics Teaching*, **128**, 23–5.

Notes

1 The Association of Teachers of Mathematics (ATM) or the Mathematical Association (MA).

2 SMILE software available from the SMILE Centre, 108a Lancaster Road, London W11 1QS.

2

Number and algebra

Introduction

It is generally accepted that primary schools should help their pupils to become both numerate and literate. But it is necessary to discuss what 'numerate' means. Rather than giving a definition, it may be more useful to mention some features that are involved. Lacey (1998) offers this list:

- An at-homeness with number; knowing how numbers relate to each other.
- Visualising number lines or squares or other patterns; being able to 'see' in your head.
- Using mathematical language to communicate ideas orally, and then in writing, using words, diagrams and graphs.
- Mentally calculating, and developing written methods for more complex calculations.

And he goes on: 'Being numerate implies being able to use a toolkit of mathematical knowledge, skills and understanding to solve problems.' This is a wide definition, but a knowledge of and a feeling for our number system is at the heart of it.

Importance of number

These days it seems particularly important to know about numbers for, as David Wells (1986) writes, 'Children in our society are floating in numbers. Whole numbers, fractions, decimals, approximations, estimations, record-breaking large numbers, minusculely small numbers'. Learning to handle numbers in school is taken to include counting, reading and writing numbers, and understanding the four basic operations of addition, subtraction, multiplication and division. To many people this means the ability to do pages of written calculations accurately. However, in these days when electronic calculating aids are so common, other skills may be just as important. Children should develop a 'sense of number'. There is no generally accepted definition of this but Sowder (1992) suggests that 'number sense refers to a well-organised conceptual network that enables one to relate number and operation properties and to solve number problems in flexible and creative ways'. This clearly includes counting, reading and writing and doing calculations but it involves much more than that. Children should be able to use numbers to solve practical problems, to estimate the approximate size of an answer, and to communicate their findings. The stress on relationships between numbers and operations and the inclusion of 'flexible and creative' indicates the breadth of this goal. Sowder also suggests that estimation is an important part of this. This includes mental computation, estimating the results of computation (getting some idea of the size of the result of a calculation), estimating measures (e.g. estimating the length of an object) and estimating numerosity (e.g. the size of a football crowd). These aspects of number sense have only recently been incorporated into the curriculum.

Whatever else is included in primary mathematics, the core of the subject must be the study of our number systems, the basic operations on them and their use in practical situations. To be confident and creative, children must have a sound grasp of concepts and their relationships. These topics are explored in the following chapters. The different types of number systems and operations on them together with the conventions of representation are considered first in Chapter 3. This may be an unfamiliar approach to arithmetic, but it lays sound foundations. The four basic operations are considered in Chapters 4 and 5 together with comments on different methods of carrying out the calculations, both written and mental. There is considerable emphasis these days on helping children develop efficient mental methods. There is no single way to do this, but Lacey says 'There is a single number structure which is perfectly regular and accommodates all numbers' and 'teaching images of the number structure so that it is known and understood by pupils will empower them and enable them to work with numbers in their heads'.

Some of the difficulties which may occur when new types of numbers, such as fractions, decimals and integers, are introduced, are considered in Chapters 6 and 7. In some ways, learning about numbers is like learning a new language. There are special ideas, words, and symbols which must be learnt and a characteristic way of thinking has to be experienced. This takes time and effort.

Nature and place of algebra

If the place of number has been accepted as part of the primary curriculum for a long time, the introduction of algebra is fairly recent. The manipulation of symbols, which is so commonly called algebra in secondary schools, is not suitable for most primary school children. Chapter 8 looks at the beginnings of algebra in the study of patterns and relationships. The development of some understanding of its language, its conventions and the power of its generalisations is appropriate for many primary pupils. Chapter 9 introduces early ideas of functions and graphs which can be interesting and stimulating for primary pupils.

References

Lacey, P. (1998) *Building Numeracy*. Stafford: Robert Powell Publications.

Sowder, J. (1992) 'Estimation and number sense', in Grouws, D. A. (ed.) *Handbook of Research on Mathematics Teaching and Learning*, 371–89. New York: Macmillan Publishing Company.

Wells, D. (1986) *The Penguin Dictionary of Curious and Interesting Numbers*. Harmondsworth: Penguin Books.

3

Properties of numbers and operations

Introduction

The number system we use today has developed over many centuries, including elements from many cultures and so is quite complex. When children first meet numbers they probably think of them as labels, for example the number 6 bus. As they learn to count (see Chapter 5) they discover that numbers are used in other ways, particularly to answer the question 'How many?' But as adults we meet many different types of number used in many different ways. However, they are related to each other in a complex but regular system. In this chapter we shall first look at the most common types of number, then examine some aspects of the structures within which we use them.

Types of number

The main types of number we shall consider are natural number, integers, rational numbers and real numbers. There are many others, but they lie outside the scope of this book.

Natural numbers

The first numbers that children meet are those used in counting 1, 2, 3, 4, . . . which are called the natural numbers. 1 is the first natural number (0 is not usually included in the natural numbers), but there is no largest natural number, as we can go on counting as long as we like (theoretically forever). The numbers are strictly ordered, that is we can always say whether a natural number is bigger or smaller than another different natural number. In fact they can be put in one and only one order on a line.

The difference between two consecutive natural numbers is always the same, namely 1. So the difference between 2 and 3 is 1 and the difference between 46 and 47 is also 1. Much of primary arithmetic deals with these numbers alone, so children become familiar with the way they behave. If we think of the operations on the natural numbers then if two numbers are added, the result is always another natural number. If two natural numbers are multiplied, again the result is always a natural number. The natural number system is said to be closed with respect to addition and multiplication. This means no new number need ever be introduced to solve any addition or multiplication problem given in natural numbers.

However, if we take two natural numbers and subtract them, the result may be a natural number, but not all subtraction problems can be answered within the natural number system. For example, $5 - 2 = 3$ but, if we restrict ourselves to the natural numbers, we have to say $2 - 5$ is impossible. If the problem is to be solved a new kind of number is needed. So the natural number system is not closed under subtraction.

Integers

The need to extend the number system also occurs in practical situations. For example, if the temperature is below freezing, we do not say it is impossible to measure. We record how many degrees below 0°C it is. So the number line is extended to the left of 0.

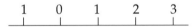

We now need some way of distinguishing those numbers that are more than 0 from those that are less than 0. The ones to the right of 0 (greater than 0) are called positive, and those on the left (less than 0) are called negative. Thus we write:

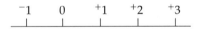

By convention the positive ($+$) and negative ($-$) signs are written above the line immediately before the number to which they refer. So $^+3$ is read as 'positive three' and $^-4$ as 'negative four'. These new numbers are called integers or directed numbers. Now it is always possible to carry out subtraction for $^+5 - {}^+2 = {}^+3$ and $^+2 - {}^+5 = {}^-3$, so the integers are closed under addition, subtraction and multiplication. The operation of subtraction can be modelled by steps along the integer number line. If we start at $^{+}2$ and go 5 steps to the left, we will finish at $^{-}3$.

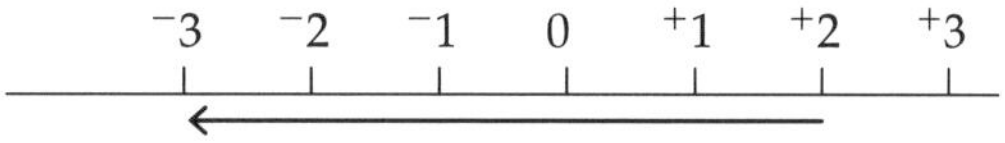

The integers are still equally spaced, like the natural numbers, but there is no first number. They stretch out infinitely in either direction.

However, there is still a problem with some division calculations. In some cases two natural numbers can be divided and the result is a natural number, e.g. $24 \div 3 = 8$. But what happens when we try to divide 10 by 3? If we use a calculator we may get 3·333333, which is neither a natural number nor an integer. We need another type of number.

Rational numbers

Again practical situations also require another sort of number. It is quite possible to divide a single pizza equally between four people.

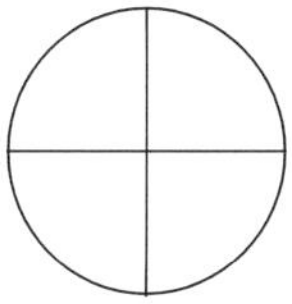

What can we call the parts?

Each part is called a quarter and can be written as $\frac{1}{4}$. These fractions (or rational numbers) are different from the natural numbers and integers in several ways. It is important to be aware of some of the sources of possible confusion here. Although two digits are used, it is the relation between the two which represents a single number. In the pizza model, the separate digits can be related to actual quantities. The denominator (number underneath) shows that there are four equal parts; the numerator (number on the top) indicates the number of parts we are considering, in this case just one. So the fraction is dependent on both numbers. By thinking of this model carefully, children should be able to appreciate that if a pizza is divided into more pieces, then each piece will be smaller, so $\frac{1}{5}$ is less than $\frac{1}{4}$.

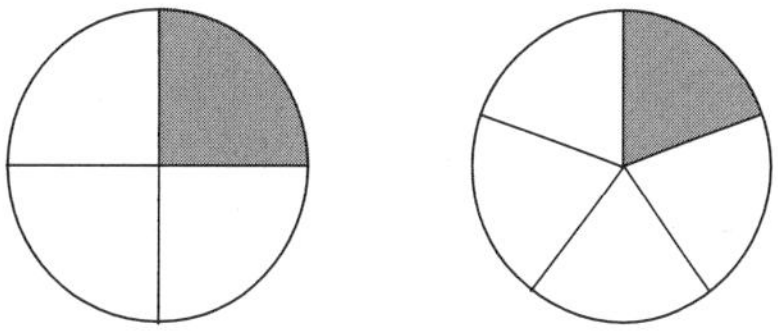

But fractions or rational numbers can apply to many situations. For example, Alex has 12 marbles and $\frac{1}{4}$ of them are red. This does not mean that $\frac{1}{4}$ of each marble is red. Rather it means that all the marbles (the whole lot – represented by the numerator) are divided into 4 (the denominator) equal groups of 3; and each of the marbles in one of these groups (i.e. 3 marbles) is red.

With natural numbers and integers, there is a unique (one and only one) way of writing each one; but with fractions there are many ways of writing the same amount. So $\frac{2}{8}$ is equivalent to $\frac{1}{4}$, $\frac{4}{16}$, or $\frac{25}{100}$.

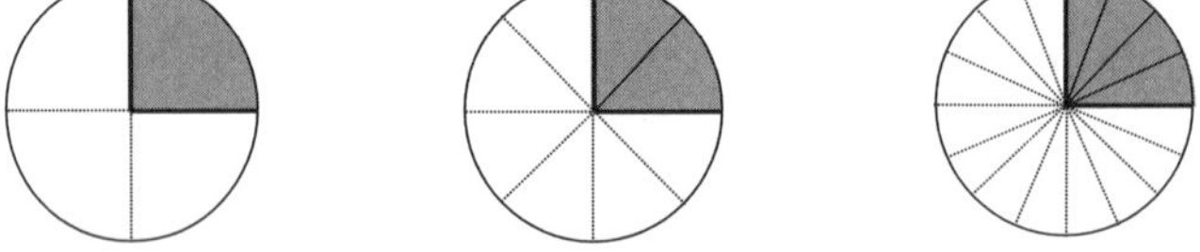

The idea of the same quantity being written in more than one way is confusing to many children. They will write ⅜ = ⁶⁄₁₆ and still say that ⁶⁄₁₆ is the bigger fraction. To avoid this possible source of confusion much discussion and practice is necessary in the classroom.

We can also represent fractions in our decimal place value system. This was first used in the late sixteenth century. A dot (or comma in some European countries) is placed immediately to the right of the units column. Then the numbers immediately to the right of the decimal point represent ¹⁄₁₀ (tenths), those in the next column are hundredths (¹⁄₁₀₀) and so on. This means that ¼ is equivalent to ²⁵⁄₁₀₀ and can be written as 0·25. It is possible to place fractions on the number line at appropriate points between the integers.

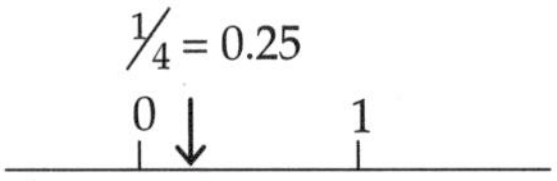

$$¼ = 0.25$$

$$\underset{0 \quad\qquad\qquad 1}{\rule{3cm}{0.4pt}}$$

All fractions can be expressed as decimals, but some of them, like ⅓, are never ending or infinite repeating decimals. This means the numbers after the decimal point repeat continuously. So ⅓ = 0·33333 with the 3 repeated indefinitely. This is usually written as 0·333ċ which means that the number with the dot above it is repeated. With fractions such as ⅐ several digits are repeated. Dots are placed above the first and last of the digits to be repeated so ⅐ = 0·1̇42857̇. Fractions are either finite or infinite repeating decimals.

By introducing these new types of numbers, we now have a system which is closed for the four basic operations of $+, -, \times, \div$. But there are disadvantages. We can no longer say which number is the 'next one'. Suppose we want the 'next' fraction to ¼ (the one which is just a little greater). We might suggest ⅓. But it is possible to calculate a fraction which is greater than ¼ and less than ⅓ by finding their average. (¼ + ⅓) ÷ 2 = ⁷⁄₂₄. If we say this is next to ¼ we can find another which is the average of ¼ and ⁷⁄₂₄. This will be greater than ¼ and less than ⁷⁄₂₄. This is always true whatever fraction we choose.

Irrational numbers

There are other types of number which we use and which cannot be written as rational numbers. For example, the circumference of a circle can be calculated from the formula $C = \pi d$ or $C = 2\pi r$, where C = circumference, d = diameter and r = radius of the circle. But the number π (pi) is an infinite non-recurring decimal which starts 3·14 . . . It cannot be written exactly as one whole number divided by another, although it is quite close to $^{22}/_{7}$ (Greek) or $^{256}/_{81}$ (Egyptian) or $^{355}/_{113}$ (Chinese). The length of the diagonal of a square of side 1 cm is $\sqrt{2}$ cm, which is also an infinite non-recurring decimal starting with 1·414 . . . The numbers which cannot be written as fractions (rationals) are called irrational numbers. They include the square roots of all natural numbers which are not perfect squares, e.g. $\sqrt{3}$, $\sqrt{5}$, $\sqrt{10}$. They can also be placed on the number line:

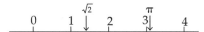

The real number system

Together the rational and irrational numbers make the real number system.

If we recognise different types of number, then we must ask how they are related. There are several ways of thinking about this. All the numbers we have discussed can be represented on a number line. Some points on the line can be named only with one type of number, but others can be represented in several systems. For example, the natural number 2 is equivalent to the integer $^{+}2$, to the fraction $^{2}/_{1}$ or $^{4}/_{2}$ and to the decimal 2·0. In fact we tend to move from one type of number to another according to the problem we are considering. For example, we may start with a problem in the natural number system such as three pizzas divided between four people, and then move to the rational number system (fractions) to solve it. Each person can have $^{3}/_{4}$ of a pizza.

Usually the equivalences (or crossing points) between number systems are fairly clear. Major problems arise when intuitions about and ways of handling numbers in one system are transferred to another system. So, for example, within the natural number system multiplication makes a number bigger (unless the number is 1). Children often continue to feel this must be true, even when they are dealing with fractions. In fact the situation is far from simple. If both numbers are greater than 1, then it is still true; but if one or both are less than 1 (and greater than zero) the result is less than the bigger number. If we also consider negative rationals the situation becomes quite complicated. Look at these examples:

natural numbers	rational numbers		integers	negative rationals	
3 × 4	3 × $^{2}/_{5}$	3 × 0·4	$^{-}3$ × $^{-}4$	3 × $^{-2}/_{5}$	3 × $^{-}0·4$
= 12	= $1^{1}/_{5}$	= 1·2	= $^{+}12$	= $^{-}1^{1}/_{5}$	= $^{-}1·2$

In primary school, children should be introduced to the fraction form of rational numbers by discussing various models, so that they understand the notation. The decimal form of rational numbers appears much simpler; but children are inclined to carry over intuitions from their experience with natural numbers. Considerable practice and discussion are necessary to help them adjust their understanding both of the numbers and the effects of operations on them.

Operations

Although numbers alone can be used to answer questions such as 'how many?' or 'how much?' their real power in problem solving involves understanding how they may be combined (or 'operated on'). In primary school, children are introduced not only to numbers but also to ways in which they may be combined or acted upon. The four basic actions or operations are addition, subtraction, multiplication and division. The operations, such as 'add', act on two or more numbers (or elements). So if 3 is added to 5 the result is 8. This means that the 3 and 5 are put together and the result is a single number, namely 8. This is the most common way to think about numbers and methods of combining them. However, there is another way of viewing 3 + 5. The first number (3 in this case) is acted upon or changed by an operator, in this case 'add 5'. The operator not only defines the type of action (addition) it also specifies its magnitude (5). This alternative view can be useful when we come to fractions and percentages in Chapter 7. Sometimes fractions appear to behave like numbers, e.g. if Bill ate ½ of one pizza and ⅓ of another, how much did he eat altogether? In this case the ½ and ⅓ are both numbers and the appropriate operation is addition. At other times they appear more like operators, e.g. What is ½ of £40? Here the number of pounds (40) is the number and the ½ looks more like an operator. However we think of it, one of the problems in primary school is the identification of an appropriate operation to solve a given problem. This will be considered further in Chapter 4 (addition and subtraction) and Chapter 5 (multiplication and division). Although we take these operations for granted, the 'concepts' themselves are quite complicated as they each have several facets.

Notation

There are powerful and concise ways of writing down mathematical ideas. These have developed over long periods and are largely a matter of convention, but they must be learned and understood correctly. It is a bit like learning a game. Unless you understand the rules and abide by them, you cannot play. In fact the common symbols of + and − were first used in the fifteenth century by merchants in German warehouses. The = sign appears to have been first used in the mid-sixteenth century by Robert Record in a book of practical mathematics. He writes 'and to avoide the tediouse repetition of these wordes "is equalle to" I will sette as I doe often in woorke books, a paire of paralleles . . . thus: ═══ because noe 2 thynges can be moare equalie'.

Although the situations giving rise to addition and subtraction calculations may vary, the way they are represented in mathematical notation is standard. 'Four add five' or 'four and five' is written as 4 + 5. 'Seven take away three' or 'the difference between seven and three' is written as 7 − 3. However, multiplication and division can be shown in more than one way. The usual symbol for multiplication is ×, so 3 × 6 can be read as 'three multiplied by six' or 'three times six' or 'three sets of six'.

When letters are used to represent numbers, as in algebraic expressions, the $\times$ can be confused with x, so the convention has developed that $3a$ means 3 multiplied by a. But it is not unreasonable for children to interpret $3a$ following the place value system and think of it as 3 tens and a units. In primary school it is probably better to avoid the abbreviated notation and leave in the $\times$, so writing $3 \times$ length (or whatever word is appropriate) or $3 \times a$, to avoid this source of misunderstanding. 'Twelve divided by three' or 'twelve shared between three' can be written as $12 \div 3$ or $\frac{12}{3}$ or $^{12}\!/_3$. At first sight it is not obvious that these all mean the same, so it is important to discuss the meaning of the notation with children over time and give some guidance about which representation is appropriate in given contexts.

The use of brackets enables complicated expressions to be written quickly and clearly; but again the conventions must be understood and followed. An expression like $8(4 - 2)$ means, first take two away from four, then multiply the result by eight. The number in front of the bracket is to be multiplied by the result of the calculation within the bracket. Again in primary school it may be better to include the $\times$ sign to make the meaning quite clear, so it would be shown as $8 \times (4 - 2)$. In an expression like $(5 - 3)6$ the bracket is written first but this makes no difference to the order of calculation. The bracket is calculated first, so $5 - 3 = 2$ and the result is multiplied by 6, that is $2 \times 6 = 12$.

In complicated fractions such as $\frac{3 + 5}{2}$ the dividing line acts as a bracket, so that the first operation is $3 + 5$ and the result is divided by 2. So $\frac{3 + 5}{2} = \frac{8}{2} = 4$. This could also be written as $(3 + 5) \div 2$. If there are more than one bracket, all values within brackets are worked out before the operations between brackets.

For example
$$
\begin{array}{ll}
(4 + 2) \times (6 - 3) & \text{or} \quad (6 + 3) \div (5 - 2) \\
= 6 \times 3 & \quad\quad = 9 \div 3 \\
= 18 & \quad\quad = 3
\end{array}
$$

Check 3.1

Calculate the values of the following:

Put in brackets so that each expression can have more than one value:

1 $6 \times (8 - 5)$

2 $(10 + 2) \div 4$

3 $(8 + 4) \times (6 - 2)$

4 $(10 + 5) \div (7 - 4)$

5 $3 + 2 \times 4$

6 $5 \times 2 - 6 \div 2$

7 $8 - 5 \times 3 + 10 \div 4$

8 $10 - 4 \div 3$

9 Toni, Lee, Andy and Kirsty have used their calculators to work out this 'sum' $\frac{25 + 36 \cdot 9}{7 \times 44}$. They have each given their answers to 3 decimal places.

Toni gets 256·943   Lee gets 0·201   Andy gets 389·086   Kirsty gets 4·410.

Without using a calculator, work out who could not possibly be correct. Find the correct answer. What have the others done wrong?

Relations between operations

It is important to be aware of the relationships between the four operations. For instance, mathematicians say that addition and subtraction are each the inverse of the other. This means that if a certain number is selected and a second number added to it, and subsequently subtracted from the result, the original number will be unchanged. The same is true if any number is subtracted from, then added to the original number.

For example: $5 + 3 = 8$ and $8 - 3 = 5$ so $(5 + 3) - 3 = 5$

Similarly: $5 - 3 = 2$ and $2 + 3 = 5$ so $(5 - 3) + 3 = 5$

It is important that children realise that subtraction 'undoes' addition and vice versa. There is a similar inverse relationship between multiplication and division.

For example: $6 \times 3 = 18$ and $18 \div 3 = 6$ so $(6 \times 3) \div 3 = 6$

or $15 \div 3 = 5$ and $5 \times 3 = 15$ so $(15 \div 3) \times 3 = 15$

One way of thinking of multiplication is as repeated addition, and similarly division may be thought of as repeated subtraction (see Chapter 5).

So $4 \times 5 = 4 + 4 + 4 + 4 + 4 = 20$

and $20 \div 5$ can be thought of as 'How many times can 5 be taken away from 20?'

So $20 - 5 = 15$ 1
$15 - 5 = 10$ 2
$10 - 5 = 5$ 3
$5 - 5 = 0$ 4

Five has been subtracted 4 times so $20 \div 5 = 4$. The relationships of the basic operations can be summarised in the following diagram.

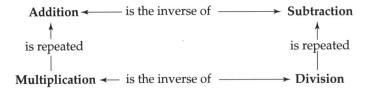

Mathematicians tend to develop specialised and often very abbreviated ways of writing down their ideas. This has already been seen in the symbols for the four basic operations.

Index notation

The index notation is another example of such brevity. It is used to represent repeated multiplication by the same number. So instead of writing $2 \times 2 \times 2 \times 2 \times 2 \times 2$

(i.e. 2 multiplied by itself 6 times) this is written as 2^6. The 6 is smaller and lifted up off the general line of writing. This notation can only be used if the same number is to be multiplied by itself several times. This way of writing makes it easier to read the operation quickly and it leads to some particularly convenient methods of calculation. For example, if two powers of any number are multiplied together then it is sufficient to add the indices.

For example: $3^2 \times 3^3 = (3 \times 3) \times (3 \times 3 \times 3)$
$$= 3 \times 3 \times 3 \times 3 \times 3 = 3^5 = 3^{(2+3)}$$

In a similar way if two powers of a number are divided, then the indices can be subtracted.

For example: $2^5 \div 2^3 = \dfrac{2 \times 2 \times 2 \times 2 \times 2}{2 \times 2 \times 2} = 2 \times 2 = 2^2$
$$= 2^{(5-3)} = 2^2$$

This leads to a meaning being established for a negative index. If we consider the problem of $3^2 \div 3^5$, we can represent it in two ways.

by writing it out in full:

$$= \frac{3 \times 3}{3 \times 3 \times 3 \times 3 \times 3}$$
$$= \frac{1}{3 \times 3 \times 3}$$
$$= \frac{1}{3^3}$$
so $3^{-3} = \dfrac{1}{3 \times 3 \times 3} = \dfrac{1}{3^3}$

or using index notation, and subtracting indices for division:

$$3^2 \div 3^5$$
$$= 3^{(2-5)}$$
$$= 3^{-3}$$

This convention maintains the useful rules of indices for multiplication and division and extends their range. Having defined the meaning of positive and negative indices, the question arises as to whether a number to the power 0 has any meaning and if so what that is. By following the same pattern as before, we can investigate what happens if 2^2 is divided by 2^2.

In the longer notation it means

$$\frac{2 \times 2}{2 \times 2}$$
$$= 1$$

In index notation, following the above rules, it becomes

$$2^{2-2}$$
$$= 2^0$$

so 2^0 is equivalent to 1. In fact any number (except 0) to the power 0 is 1. This is not intuitively obvious for there is no clear physical representation, but the fact is needed to complete the pattern so that the rules (or laws) of indices always work consistently. These laws of indices lie behind the use of logarithms or slide-rules as easy ways of doing complex multiplication and division problems before the days of calculators. Even with calculators it is necessary to understand indices, as very large and very small numbers are recorded in standard form, which involves them (see Chapter 5).

Check 3.2

1 What is the value of:
$2^3, 5^2, 3^4, 4^{-2}, 2^{-3}, 3^0$

2 Find the value of:

$2^3 \times 2^4$	$3^3 \div 3^2$
$3^2 \times 3^3$	$4^4 \div 4^1$
$4^2 \times 4^{-1}$	$2^3 \div 2^{-2}$
$2^5 \times 2^{-2}$	$5^2 \div 5^{-2}$

3 Using the digits 1, 2, 3 create as many new numbers as you can, e.g. 2^3, 12^3, 31^2. Which is the largest you can make without repeating a digit?

Precedence

Just as it was necessary to understand the meaning of the symbols used by mathematicians, it is also essential to know the unwritten rules or conventions within which they are applied. In particular, there is a recognised order in which the operations are worked out in a complicated expression. For example, look at the following:

$$6 + 3 \times (4 - 2) + 8 \times 3 - 14 \div 2$$

Depending on the calculator, and the way in which the numbers and operations are entered, various answers might be obtained. If the expression is read from left to right the answer might be 32. This comes from $6 + 3 = 9$; $9 \times (4 - 2) = 9 \times 2 = 18$; $18 + 8 = 26$; $26 \times 3 = 78$; $78 - 14 = 64$; $64 \div 2 = 32$. However, there is a standard way to work out such an expression.

Order of operations		expression $6 + 3 \times (4 - 2) + 8 \times 3 - 14 \div 2$
The operations inside brackets are carried out first	$(4 - 2) = 2$	$6 + 3 \times \quad 2 \quad + 8 \times 3 - 14 \div 2$
Next the multiplication and division operations are worked out	$3 \times 2 = 6$ $8 \times 3 = 24$ $14 \div 2 = 7$	$6 + \quad 6 \quad + 24 \quad - \quad 7$
Finally the addition and subtraction calculations are completed		29

The rules of precedence state that:

first, operations inside brackets or root signs should be completed (or the brackets removed by expanding them) **(B)**;

second, all indices, multiplication (including 'of') and division operations should be calculated **(IDM)**;

finally, addition and subtraction operations **(AS)** should be carried out. This can be summarised as **BIDMAS**. It does not matter how it is remembered, but it is essential that the operations be carried out in the correct order. Although these rules of precedence are necessary to read mathematical writing correctly, in practical problem solving they may not be used greatly because parts are worked out separately.

 ## Check 3.3

Work out the value of the following expressions:

1 $10 \div 2 + 14 - 3 \times 7 + 6$
2 $7 + 4 \times 3 - 5 \times (6 - 3) + 10$
3 $26 - 2 \times 7 + 12 \div 3 - 4$
4 $3 + 5 \times 2^3 - 4 + 3 \times (7 + 2)$
5 $(10 - 2) \div 2^2 + 5 \times 3$

Laws

In addition to these conventions, there are some basic rules about the way in which the operations interact with each other. These laws have complicated sounding names, which children do not need to know, but it is essential that they are aware when they may be used and when it is wrong to use them.

Commutative law

When numbers are linked by operations, does it matter if they change places or commute? For example, is $3 + 4$ the same as $4 + 3$ and is 4×5 the same as 5×4?

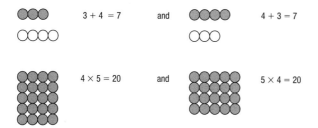

The results are the same whichever number is first. Addition and multiplication are said to be commutative. This can be expressed in general as:

$a + b = b + a$ and $a \times b = b \times a$ where a and b can represent any numbers.

This property is very useful as it halves the quantity of number facts (addition bonds and times tables) to be learned. It also permits the rearrangement of numbers into convenient pairs when adding up or multiplying more than two numbers.

For example $6 + 3 + 4 + 7 + 5$ and $5 \times 3 \times 2$ can be rearranged as shown below

$$6 + 3 + 4 + 7 + 5 \qquad \text{and} \qquad 5 \times 3 \times 2$$
$$= 6 + 4 + 7 + 3 + 5 \qquad\qquad\qquad = 5 \times 2 \times 3$$
$$= \quad 10 \ + \ 10 \ + 5 \qquad\qquad\qquad = \quad 10 \ \times 3$$
$$= 25 \qquad\qquad\qquad\qquad\qquad\quad = 30$$

This is particularly useful when adding or multiplying a lot of numbers, for example in column addition.

Knowing this fact about addition and multiplication, children often extend it to subtraction and division; but, unfortunately, it is not true in these cases, for

$$5 - 2 \quad \text{and} \quad 2 - 5 \qquad\qquad 6 \div 3 \quad \text{and} \quad 3 \div 6$$
$$= 3 \qquad\qquad\quad = {}^{-}3 \qquad\qquad\quad = 2 \qquad\qquad\qquad = \tfrac{1}{2}$$

The well-documented 'smaller from larger' bug in column subtraction is the result of this misunderstanding or mal-rule. For example:

$$\begin{array}{r} 54 \\ -28 \\ \hline 34 \end{array}$$
A child might think '4 take away, 8, can't do it, so $8 - 4 = 4$, then $5 - 2 = 3$'

So it is necessary to discuss explicitly with children both the usefulness and limits of the commutative rule (although you would not use this word with them).

Distributive law

In the section on precedence, it was stated that the operations inside any brackets must be carried out first. Sometimes this can be avoided by 'removing the brackets' or splitting the numbers up to make the calculations easier. For example, if you were working out 24×18 mentally you would probably work out 20×18 first ($= 360$), then 4×18 ($= 72$) then add the two answers to make 432. This is shown symbolically below.

$$24 \times 18 \qquad\qquad\qquad 24 \times 18$$
$$= 432 \text{ (using a calculator)} \qquad = (20 + 4) \times 18$$
$$= (20 \times 18) + (4 \times 18)$$
$$= \quad 360 \ + \ 72$$
$$= \qquad 432$$

In this case multiplication is said to be distributive over addition. The examples below show how 'brackets can be removed'.

$$2 \times (7 - 2) \quad \text{or} \quad 2 \times (7 - 2) \qquad (6 + 8) \div 2 \quad \text{or} \quad (6 + 8) \div 2$$
$$= 2 \times \quad 5 \qquad = 2 \times 7 - 2 \times 2 \qquad = 14 \quad \div 2 \qquad = 6 \div 2 + 8 \div 2$$
$$= 10 \qquad\qquad = 14 \quad - 4 \qquad\qquad = 7 \qquad\qquad = \quad 3 \ + \ 4$$
$$= 10 \qquad\qquad\qquad\qquad\qquad = 7$$

So multiplication and division are distributive over addition and subtraction. In general this may be written as

$$a \times (b + c) = a \times b + a \times c \text{ and } (a - b) \div c = a \div c - b \div c$$

where a, b, c can represent any number. In fact all written methods of long multiplication use this law (see lattice multiplication in Chapter 5).

However, the reverse is not true; addition is not distributive over multiplication.

For	$2 + (3 \times 5)$	whereas	$(2 + 3) \times (2 + 5)$
	$= 2 + 15$		$= 5 \quad \times \quad 7$
	$= 17$		$= 35$

Associative law

Consider adding up three numbers, such as $4 + 3 + 7$.

starting with first two numbers	starting with second two numbers
$(4 + 3) + 7$	$4 + (3 + 7)$
$= 7 \quad + 7$	$= 4 + \quad 10$
$= 14$	$= 14$

It does not matter whether we add the first two then the third, or whether we add the second and third, then add the first; the result will be the same. In symbols this can be represented as follows:

$$(a + b) + c = a + (b + c) \text{ where } a, b, c \text{ can represent any number.}$$

Because it does not matter in which order the addition is carried out, addition is said to be associative. Similarly, multiplication is associative. This might be expected since it can be thought of as repeated addition.

For example, consider $2 \times 5 \times 3$

start with first two numbers	start with second two numbers
$(2 \times 5) \times 3$	$2 \times (5 \times 3)$
$= \quad 10 \quad \times 3$	$= 2 \times \quad 15$
$= 30$	$= 30$

However, not all operations are so obliging. Consider subtraction and division and the examples $8 - 5 - 2$ and $24 \div 6 \div 2$

start with first two numbers	start with second two numbers	start with first two numbers	start with second two numbers
$(8 - 5) - 2$	$8 - (5 - 2)$	$(24 \div 6) \div 2$	$24 \div (6 \div 2)$
$= \quad 3 \quad - 2$	$= 8 - \quad 3$	$= \quad 4 \quad \div 2$	$= 24 \div \quad 3$
$= 1$	$= 5$	$= 2$	$= 8$

It can be seen that the results are not the same. Subtraction and division are not associative. In both cases if there are no brackets then it is correct to start with the first two numbers.

 Check 3.4

Try working each of these out in two different ways without using a calculator:

1 $7 + 6 + 3 + 4 + 5$
2 $2 \times 3 \times 5 \times 4$
3 $3 \times (2 + 5)$
4 $(9 - 6) \div 3$
5 27×13

Patterns in natural numbers

In the primary school, children are also introduced to various names for particular natural numbers. Most of these refer to a pattern made when such a number is represented by pebbles, stones, or counters arranged in a particular way. So odd and 'even' numbers can be depicted as two lines of counters (see Chapter 2). Examples of even numbers are 2, 6, 28, 104. If a number is divisible by two (i.e. 2 is a factor of it), then it must be even. If a number is not divisible by 2 then it must have a remainder of 1 when divided by 2 and it is odd.

More complicated patterns can be made, for example, squares.

Square numbers

The first few square numbers are 1, 4, 9, 16, 25. They can also be arranged to show the relationship between one square number and the next.

☐ ☐ ☐ ☐	1	
○ ○ ○ ☐	$4 = 3 + 1$	
☐ ☐ ○ ☐	$9 = 5 + 4$	$= 5 + 3 + 1$
○ ☐ ○ ☐	$16 = 7 + 9$	$= 7 + 5 + 3 + 1$

A discussion of 'hollow squares' or picture frames is given in Chapter 8.

Cube numbers

If we allow patterns in three dimensions then there are cube numbers; for example, 1, 8, 27, 64.

Counters or pebbles can be arranged in other shapes such as triangles and rectangles.

Triangles can be made on a square or triangular grid, but the numbers with a triangular shape are the same. The first few triangular numbers are 1, 3, 6, 10.

Triangular numbers

Many numbers can be represented as rectangles (with two or more equal rows of counters), for example, 6, 10, 14, 28. Some such as 12 can be arranged in more than one rectangle. From the example it can be seen that the number of counters along each side must be a factor of the total number. Many numbers can be represented by several different rectangles because they have several pairs of factors. The main point of interest is that numbers which cannot be represented as rectangles are prime. A prime number has only two factors, itself and 1, so it cannot be represented as a rectangular array.

Rectangular numbers

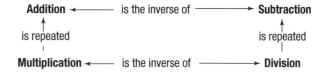

 ## Check 3.5

1 Classify the following numbers as odd, even, square, triangular, rectangular or cube. (Note: some numbers may belong to more than one type.)

   4   1   12   15   27   8   64   21

2 Draw diagrams to represent the 3rd and 4th triangular numbers. Predict the 5th and 6th.

3 Can you say anything about the result if two consecutive triangular numbers are added together? Try a few examples. Then try drawing pictures of them.

Summary

- There are several types of number including: natural numbers, integers, rational numbers (fractions) and real numbers.

- There are fundamental relations between the four basic operations of addition, subtraction, multiplication and division.

Addition ⟵ is the inverse of ⟶ **Subtraction**

is repeated   is repeated

Multiplication ⟵ is the inverse of ⟶ **Division**

- Index notation can be used to represent a number multiplied by itself several times.

- It is necessary to know the order of precedence of operations in complicated expressions. This can be summarised as BIDMAS.

- Addition and multiplication are commutative and associative, but subtraction and division are neither.
- Multiplication and division are distributive over addition and subtraction.
- Numbers can be described by the patterns they make, e.g. even, odd, square, cube, triangular numbers.

Links with the classroom

1 What would you do with a child who argued that $1/4$ was bigger than $1/3$ because 4 was bigger than 3?

2 What classroom activities might help children to understand the inverse relation of addition and subtraction?

3 How would you demonstrate that multiplication does not necessarily make a number bigger?

4 What classroom activity might persuade children that $12 \div 3$ is not the same as $3 \div 12$.

5 How and why would you introduce index notation to able pupils in Year 6?

Challenges!

1 By drawing, investigate pentagonal, hexagonal numbers. What other types can you find?

Pentagonal numbers

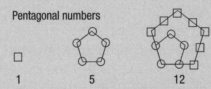

| 1 | 5 | 12 |

2 Find out about other types of number, e.g. complex numbers, transcendental numbers.

3 What do fractional indices mean, e.g. what is $16^{1/2}$?

References

Haylock, D. (1995) *Mathematics Explained for Primary Teachers*. London: Paul Chapman.

Jacobs, H. R. (1994) *Mathematics, A Human Endeavor*, 3rd edn. New York: A. H. Freeman and Company.

Record, R. (1557) *The Whetstone of Witte*, reproduced in Fauvel, J. and Gray, J. (1987). Open University course book, MA290, Topics in the History of Mathematics.

Counting, place value, addition and subtraction

Starter

TWO PEOPLE START counting at the same time and the same speed. One starts at 1 and counts in 8's, the other starts at 25 and then counts in 5's. Will they ever reach the same number at the same time?

Counting

From the earliest times counting has been a universal activity among people – probably developed as a way of checking possessions. It involves matching a series of objects (such as sheep) to a standard sequence of names or marks. Most children learn to count reliably by the time they are seven years old, but it is actually a complicated activity with several subskills. Children need to know the standard name sequence. They must then match each number name to one and only one of the objects being counted. This is often supported by pointing or touching. Finally they should realise that the last number name used also refers to the size of the set being counted. This is the cardinal aspect of number. Sometimes children interpret the instruction 'count' as telling them to point to the objects and recite the number sequence. They do not think of it as an activity to answer the question 'How many?' They may even write 1, 2, 3 to represent the size of a set of three blocks. The ordinal aspect of number depends on the fact that numbers are always in the same order. This means that they can also be used to order objects or events, so we can talk about the first or second day of the holidays or the first child to finish a race. By the time they complete Key Stage 1 most children should also be conserving numbers reasonably well. This means that they understand that the number of objects in a set remains the same even when the objects are moved around or counted in a different order. Although researchers such as Piaget did a great deal of work on this, it seems that children's understanding of this develops slowly and depends both on context and the size of the numbers involved.

Mathematicians call these numbers used in counting (1, 2, 3, . . .) 'natural numbers'. They are used whenever a 'How many?' type of question arises. This may happen in simple situations, such as laying the table and asking, 'How many cups do we need today?', or in more complicated ones such as 'How many people live in the borough?'

The Hindu-Arabic number system which we use has a decimal (denary or ten) base which shows both in the oral and written form. When saying numbers we start with the largest part and proceed to smaller ones, using the first ten digits as a 'reference'. Each 'part' is ten times the size of the next smaller part. For example, two hundred and thirty-four means two lots of a hundred and three lots of ten and four units (or ones) and is written (200 + 30 + 4) or 234. In English the naming between ten and twenty is irregular, with the smaller unit name coming first from thirteen to nineteen; this can cause children some difficulties, especially when moving from the spoken to the written form. Both our naming and written forms are basically additive, i.e. forty-six means four tens and (add) six units (ones). It is interesting to note however, that neither the base ten nor the additive principle is universal. Two examples of other systems will be considered briefly. Welsh has a twenty rather than ten base, and Yoruba not only has a twenty base but also uses a subtraction principle.

The traditional Welsh names for the first twenty numbers are given below.

1 Un	11 Un ar ddeg (one and ten)
2 Dau	12 Deuddeg (two ten)
3 Tri	13 Tri ar ddeg (three and ten)
4 Pedwar	14 Pedwar ar ddeg (four and ten)
5 Pump	15 Pymtheg
6 Chwech	16 Un ar bymtheg (one and fifteen)
7 Saith	17 Dau ar bymtheg (two and fifteen)
8 Wyth	18 Deunaw (two nines)
9 Naw	19 Pedwar ar bymtheg (four and fifteen)
10 Deg	20 Ugain

By looking at the names for the numbers from 11 to 20, it is clear that 10 and 15 are used as 'stepping stones'. For larger numbers 20 rather than 10 is used as a base, so 30 is deg ar hugain (ten and twenty). Up to 60 the smaller units are usually placed first, 41 is un a deugain (one and two twenties); 55 is pymtheg a deugain (fifteen and two twenties). Above this the larger units are often said first, so that 65 is trigain a phump (three twenties and five); 95 is pedwar ugain a phymtheg (four twenties and fifteen). 100 is cant. Interestingly in school arithmetic the number names are sometimes made completely regular, corresponding to the decimal notation. So 11 is un deg un (one ten one or onety one); 12 is un deg dau (one ten two); 55 is pum deg pump (five tens five).

The Yoruba people of south-west Nigeria also use a base 20 counting system, but use both addition and subtraction principles. There are different words for the numbers up to ten. Then (in translation) 11 is one and ten; 12 = 2 + 10; 13 = 3 + 10; 14 = 4 + 10; but at 15 the subtraction form starts so that 15 is five less than twenty,

16 is 4 less than 20 and so on. With larger numbers it can become quite complicated. For example, 35 is five less than two twenties and 50 becomes ten less then three twenties. This means that 46 would be four less than ten less than three twenties. There is no single word for 100: it is called 'five twenties'; but there is a special word for 200.

Symbols

Before looking more closely at our Hindu-Arabic written number notation, it is worthwhile considering the advantages and disadvantages of a few other systems, as these may illuminate the strengths and difficulties of our own system. One of the simplest is the early Egyptian hieroglyphs, where a separate symbol is used for units, tens, hundreds, etc., and the appropriate number of each (in standard layout/pattern) is drawn. The place of the Egyptian 'rope stretchers' is shown in the symbols used. The symbol for one was a single stroke (a short piece of rope when drawn in detail); that for ten was a longer piece of rope bent into a horseshoe; and the symbol 99 ∩∩∩ |||| for a hundred was a stylised coil of rope. So 234 is represented by

There are several advantages in this. It does not matter in which order the symbols are placed or whether they are vertical or horizontal. The value they represent is 999 ||| quite clear. So there is no confusion in writing numbers which do not have some parts, such as 303.
One disadvantage is the laborious nature of writing large numbers and the care needed to read them.

The Chinese overcame this problem by using the first nine digits as a 'reference' and simply writing them with the name of the unit size underneath (or to the right), so that 312 becomes

三百一十二

where 百 means 'hundreds' and 十 means 'tens'.

Before the abacus, the Chinese used a different form of representation for calculations. Rods were laid out so as to represent the numbers and moved around as the calculation proceeded. The basic numbers 1–9 are shown here.

The use of 5 as a 'stepping stone' means that the patterns are easier to discriminate, as the largest number of rods in one direction is five. To represent tens the arrangements are rotated, so 46 is shown as ☰ 丅

The hundreds, tens thousands etc., are written as the units, and the thousands, hundred thousands etc. as the tens. A few examples will illustrate the system.

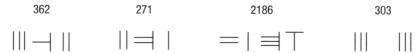

As this is not a written form, the problem of showing a number such as 303 is minimised, as whoever laid out the rods would know where the gap was. It is amazing to realise that complex calculations (including ratios and solutions of simultaneous equations) could be carried out with these rods.

The Roman system of writing numbers also used a 'semi-base' of 5 with the symbols being repeated. The convention was to put the higher units to the left of the smaller ones and to add them together. If a single smaller unit was placed to the left of a higher one, then it should be subtracted from that higher unit. This means that a single symbol is only repeated a maximum of three times. The number 1–10 are shown below, together with the symbols for some higher values.

I II III IV V VI VII VIII IX X
L = 50   C = 100   D = 500   M = 1000

A few examples will show the way the system works.

| 362 | 449 | 1998 | 2000 |
| CCCLXII | CDXLIX | MCMXCVIII | MM |

While it is not necessary to teach children any convention other than our standard one, they often enjoy the Egyptian and possibly the Roman form. If the Yoruba or Chinese rod numerals seem difficult, remember it is only because they are unfamiliar, and that young children may find our own system just as confusing initially.

Check 4.1

1 What numbers are represented by the following?

二百三　∩∩9||||||　三十二　∩∩∩∩|

2 Write each of these numbers in at least three different ways:
25 67 17 88 32

Place value

Our decimal place value system probably developed in India and came to us via the Arabs. It consists of two essential elements:

a nine different symbols for the natural numbers 1 to 9 and a symbol for 0 used as a placeholder;

b the convention that the lowest value digit is on the right and the value of each digit is ten times the value of the digits on its immediate right.

The number zero and its symbol 0 is a very important part of the number notation. It probably came from India via the Arabs. Zero itself has been described by David Wells (1986) as 'a mysterious number, which started life as a space on a counting board, turned into a written notice that a space was present, that is to say that something was absent, then confused medieval mathematicians who could not decide whether it was really a number or not, and achieved its highest status in modern abstract mathematics in which numbers are defined only by their properties, and the properties of zero are at least as clear, and rather more substantial, than those of many other numbers.' There is evidence that the use of a symbol to represent zero and to act as a placeholder arose independently in different cultures. It has a double function. It represents 'nothing'. In this role it represents no objects (e.g. there are no or 0 apples on the table) and it makes no difference when added to another number (4 + 0 = 4). The second role is that of a placeholder. In the number 403 (four hundred and three) it indicates there are no tens and forces the 4 into the hundreds place.

Except for the numbers between 11 and 19, we say the numbers in the same order as they are written from left to right, applying an addition principle throughout. So for three-digit numbers the columns are hundreds, tens and units (ones) and a number such as three hundred and forty-five is written 345 = 300 + 40 + 5. The zero as a placeholder is necessary to write numbers such as six hundred and two unambiguously 602 = 600 + 2. The relation between the standard notation and the extended notation can be illustrated by suitable cards aligned on the right hand edge (the 'tab' on the right allows children to hold and align the cards).

So: 3 0 0 $\rangle$ + 4 0 $\rangle$ + 5 $\rangle$ = 3 4 5 $\rangle$

and   6 0 0 $\rangle$ + 2 $\rangle$ = 6 0 2 $\rangle$

It is worth noting that children often have difficulty in saying and reading numbers beyond the thousands. They may read the number 62,308 as six million, two thousand, three hundred and eight instead of sixty-two thousand, three hundred and eight. In reading large numbers, it is useful to have commas or spaces to mark off the thousands and millions. For example it is more difficult to read 83695471 than 83,695,471 or 83 695 471. The latter two make it easier to see that there are 83 millions, 695 thousands and 471. A billion usually means one thousand million (10^9). In the USA it has always had this meaning and it is used in this way on the international money markets. Originally in the UK it meant a million million (10^{12}). Although not used as much, trillion can mean either 10^{12} (USA) or 10^{18} (UK), again the first meaning is more common. Children sometimes like to play with such words and invent terms such as 'zillions' meaning 'lots and lots of millions'. Altogether this system is a particularly clear and efficient notation, as has been shown by a brief look at one or two other systems. A wide range of numbers can be written quickly and clearly and the notation also supports calculations, as in the standard algorithms.

Although we use a decimal (base 10) system, the same principle of recording can be used with any numbers for its base. For example, most computers use a binary (base 2) system. In this there are only two numerals (1 and 0 or 'on' and 'off' in switches) and the successive columns from right to left are powers of 2, i.e. 1, 2, 4, 8, . . . Counting in binary is illustrated below:

Binary	1	10	11	100	101	110	111	1000	1001	1010
Decimal	1	2	3	4	5	6	7	8	9	10

Some further examples will illustrate the principle.

in binary

column values	2^4	2^3	2^2	2^1	2^0	
	16	8	4	2	1	
			1	0	1	$= 4 + 1 = 5$
		1	1	0	1	$= 8 + 4 + 1 = 13 = 10 + 3$
	1	1	0	1	0	$= 16 + 8 + 2 = 26 = 20 + 6$

in decimal

10^2	10^1	10^0
100	10	1
		5
	1	3
	2	6

It is possible to write numbers in any base. Ants would probably choose base 6, using numerals 0 to 5 and the columns being powers of 6. So:

in base 6

column values	6^2	6^1	6^0	
	36	6	1	
		2	4	$= (2\times6) + (4\times1) = 12 + 4 = 16$
	3	5	0	$= (3\times36) + (5\times6) + (0\times1)$
				$= 108 + 30 + 0 = 138$

in decimal

10^2	10^1	10^0
100	10	1
	1	6
1	3	8

If this looks complicated, remember it is only because it is unfamiliar and young children may find our standard notation just as difficult at first. It is probably unnecessary to introduce children to different bases, although working in several illuminates the underlying principles.

✎ Check 4.2

1 Change these numbers from binary into decimal form:

101   1011   11011   111   10011

2 Write the following in binary notation:

8   15   27   10   20

3 Try doing a few calculations in binary:

1010	101	1111	1010
+ 111	+ 11	− 100	− 101

You may well find that question 3 challenges your understanding of place value to an extreme. Try discussing what you are doing with another student or tutor.

Representing numbers

To learn the principles of our place value system, children need considerable experience, preferably using various models or representations of number. In particular they need to understand the principle of grouping into ten. For example, when counting a large number of straws it is easier and more accurate, to count ten and make them into a bundle; repeating this procedure until almost all the straws have been counted. Then it is easy to count the bundles, which gives the number of tens, then count on the single straws. Children need much experience of such activities and, if possible, the next stage of making bundles of ten bundles, which will be one hundred straws. If counters (or other objects) are used, they can be arranged in lines (or groups) of ten. With Unifix (or Multilink) the lines can be fixed together in rods of 10.

Represents 1 ten and
4 units = 14

The ready-made tens and units apparatus (or MAB, multi-base arithmetic blocks) provides small cubes for units, rods for tens, flats (squares) for hundreds and large cubes for thousands. These can be used to demonstrate the equivalence of, for example, 1 ten (rod) and 10 units (little cubes) and provide children with something concrete to model numbers and perform operations on. The use of overlapping cards (as shown earlier) and the extended written notation may be of some assistance. In a Chinese abacus there are five beads below the central bar (which count as ones) and two above it (which count as fives). The position of the beads in relation to the central bar shows whether they are active (when touching it they are counted) and their value depends on position (i.e. which wire they are on). Some different ways of representing 125 are shown.

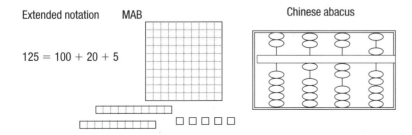

Extended notation   MAB   Chinese abacus

$125 = 100 + 20 + 5$

Some other models for numbers do not show the place value principle clearly, but emphasise other aspects of our number system. The number line illustrates the ordering of numbers, but does not show the relation between tens and units.

0	1	2	3	4	5	6	7	8	9
10	11	12	13	14	15	16	17	18	19
20	21	22	23	24	25	26	27	28	29
30	31	32	33	34	35	36	37	38	39
40	41	42	43	44	45	46	47	48	49
50	51	52	53	54	55	56	57	58	59
60	61	62	63	64	65	66	67	68	69
70	71	72	73	74	75	76	77	78	79
80	81	82	83	84	85	86	87	88	89
90	91	92	93	94	95	96	97	98	99

The number square does reflect both the ordering and the importance of the ten base in our number system. It is probably better to start with 0 as this makes the pattern of digits particularly clear and assists later extension.

Problems with money are often given as practice for arithmetic; but coins are an imperfect model for place value. If only £1, 10p and 1p coins are used then they do reflect the decimal place value system; but in practical situations children must also handle 2p, 5p, 20p and 50p coins as well.

Tallies may be a useful way of recording a count; but they do present several problems. Firstly children often omit to count the 'cross' stroke; secondly they may forget that the bundles only have five in them and count them as ten; and finally there is no symbol for 'bundles of bundles'.

Represents 16

Arguably one of the most useful representations is the number line. However, children find this one of the most difficult to understand and yet it is used to illustrate some methods of calculation. This means it is necessary to discuss it throughout the primary school and check the children's perceptions. An added complication is that two different models are used with the assumption that children will be able to move from one to the other.

In Key Stage 1 the image of stepping stones or numbered tiles is used. In this model it is the spaces between the dividing marks which are numbered.

1	2	3	4	5	6

Number track

Of course only whole numbers can be represented on such a number track. In Key Stage 2 it is usual to use a number line on which whole numbers are shown by points or ticks and it is possible to represent fractions and decimals.

Number line

Often the ticks for the tens and fives are longer to help in reading the value of a specific point. This convention should be pointed out to children if they are to be able to use it.

It is often assumed that using concrete and visual representations will help children to understand our number system. Because we understand the system, we can see how different aspects of it are illustrated by different representations. However, it is not clear whether using apparatus or representations necessarily helps children construct the abstract concepts. Discussion and negotiation of meaning are probably necessary as well. It has been suggested that moving from one representation to another might help this abstracting.

On the CD, there is a simple demonstration program which illustrates 15 different ways of representing tens and units. This is intended to be a stimulus for discussion about the strengths and limitations of various representations. It could be used with a group or a whole class. After a number has been selected on the first screen, two representations can be chosen on the second, then, on the third screen, the chosen number will be shown in those representations. For example, if 87 were selected to be shown in counters and number line 1 (the traditional number line) the screen would show:

Please note that the counters are arranged in lines of 10, with a small gap between the 5th and 6th counters (this makes it easier to see there are 7 in the last line as there are 5 + 2). Also there is small gap between 50 and 60. The drawing is too small to show the unit marks on the number line, but even

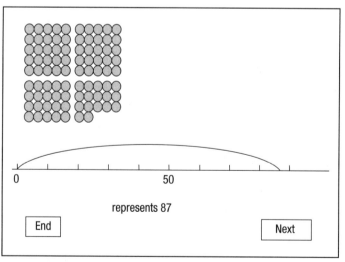

when they are visible children have difficulty in interpreting this form of the number line.

Although counting and representing numbers in different ways helps children understand the principles of place value, the real tests and opportunities for deeper learning come from using number in problem solving and calculations.

Addition and subtraction problems

Recent research (Carpenter *et al.* 1999) suggests that children entering school (at 4 or 5 years of age) can solve addition and subtraction problems by direct modelling. This involves using counters or blocks to represent the problem and then manipulating them to find the answer. Children can also develop their own counting strategies which are often closely linked to direct modelling. Later as their knowledge of number facts and relationships increases they are able to solve problems in a wider variety of ways. Carpenter identifies four basic types of simple one step addition and subtraction problems depending on the actions or relationships specified. The four types are as follows, although the names have been slightly altered (Carpenter's terms are given in brackets):

> Add (join)
> Take away (separate)
> Partition (part-part-whole)
> Compare (compare)

The first two are usually introduced to children first. Examples of each of the four basic types are given below with some indication of how children might solve such problems. It will be noticed that the examples are not really set in the children's world, but are contrived to illustrate different relationships.

Add

> There are 4 model cars on the table. Two more are placed beside them. How many are there altogether?

Young children may place 4 model cars, or 4 counters to represent them, on the table; then add 2 more; then count them all, so arriving at the answer 6. Later they may use a more abstract counting strategy, for example: saying 4 (pause); putting up two fingers; then saying 5, 6 as they put down their fingers; then stating that there will be 6 cars. The relation with the direct modelling of the problem is clear. If, however, the unknown is in a different position, it may be more difficult for the children to solve. For example:

> There were some model cars on the table, 2 more are added and now there are 6. How many cars were there on the table at the beginning?

Here it is difficult to model the problem directly as the starting number is not known. A determined child might start, say, with 3 cars (or counters), add 2 and find there were too few and so try again. Similarly the counting strategy is difficult for the same reason; but it is possible by trial and improvement. A more efficient method of solution involves understanding the inverse relation between addition and subtraction. For, if there are 6 cars at the end, the 'adding 2' can be 'undone' by taking away 2 from the 6, which leaves 4 cars. This clearly involves a much higher level of abstraction than the earlier direct modelling or simple counting strategies.

Take away

> There are 5 apples in a bowl. Two are eaten. How many are left?

A child who is modelling this problem directly may put 5 blocks (to represent the apples) on the table; take away 2; then count the remaining blocks, so reaching the answer 3 apples. A more 'advanced' counting strategy might involve a child in putting up 2 fingers to represent the 2 apples eaten; then saying 5 (pause), 4 (dropping one finger), 3 (dropping the other finger); then knowing that there would be 3 apples left. (Putting up 5 fingers, dropping 2, then counting the remainder is really a direct modelling strategy.) Some children may be able to give the answer 3 straight away explaining 'because I know that 2 and 3 makes 5'. Here they are drawing on their knowledge both of the number fact $2 + 3 = 5$ and also the inverse relation between addition and subtraction, so if $2 + 3 = 5$ then $5 - 2 = 3$. Again for problems with a take away structure the difficulty is greater if the starting number or the number to be taken away is unknown.

Partition

> There are 4 red model cars and 2 blue model cars on the table. How many are there altogether?

In this case the two parts of the set are known and the total size can be found by adding them. Again direct modelling or counting strategies can be used as for the active 'Add' problems. The other type of partition problem occurs when one part and the total size of the set is known. For example:

> There are 6 apples in the bowl, some are red and 2 are green. How many are red?

Children can model this directly by putting 6 blocks on the table; then moving 2 away; and counting the remainder, which is very like modelling a take away problem. In fact most children have little difficulty in transferring the methods they used for the active 'add' and 'take away' structures to static partition problems.

Compare

Children often find this type of problem more difficult to manage. Sometimes this comparison or 'difference' structure is treated as a second root meaning of subtraction, although this has its dangers as the operation involved may be either addition or subtraction depending on the position of the unknown. For example:

> Jane has 6 sweets and Alice has 4. Who has the most sweets and how many more than the other girl has she?

A child modelling the problem directly would put 6 counters in one line and 4 counters in another line underneath as shown in the diagram.

They could then see that there were 2 counters in the top line with no corresponding counter in the lower line, so the top line has 2 more counters than the lower line. An appropriate counting strategy might be to count on from 4 to 6. Indeed this can be viewed as a subtraction calculation, namely $6 - 4$. But consider another example:

> There is a collection of model horses and cows on the table. There are 4 horses and 2 more cows than horses. How many cows are there?

Here the structure is still a comparison '2 more cows than horses', but the operation to find the answer directly would be addition.

Enough has been said to show that solving apparently simple addition and subtraction problems can actually be quite complicated. To help children develop efficient and effective ways of solving problems, it is probably best to allow them plenty of time for discussion (both explaining what they are doing and listening to other methods). Although the examples used belong fairly clearly to one type, it is perfectly possible to model a problem in more than one way and use all the methods to arrive at a correct solution. For example:

> I have 12 mugs altogether. There are 4 in the dishwasher. The rest are in the cupboard. How many were in the cupboard?

This could be viewed either as a take away structure '12 mugs in the cupboard, then 4 are taken away (to be used and put in the dishwasher)' or as a partition problem '12 mugs altogether, 4 in the dishwasher, the rest in the cupboard'. Either model gives the answer of 8 mugs in the cupboard.

Check 4.3

How do you think about each of these problems? Try to analyse your own strategies and then compare these with an analysis of problem structure and the position of the unknown as shown above.

1 Twelve glasses were sent through the post. Only 8 arrived intact. How many were broken?
2 I was given 2 rings for my birthday. I now have 8 rings altogether. How many did I have before my birthday?
3 I have 4 more first class stamps than second class ones. If I have 8 second class stamps, how many first class ones do I have?
4 If there are 14 pieces of fruit in the bowl and 6 are apples, how many are not apples?

Methods of calculation

It is important for children to be able to do an appropriate calculation to solve a problem. This may involve writing it down or using a calculator, but the 'first stop' should be a mental method or a mental approximation. These three methods require different skills. In the Numeracy Strategy, there is considerable importance attached to helping children develop robust methods of mental calculation before they are introduced to formal written methods. So several mental methods may be presented and discussed. The children should be encouraged to choose the most suitable in a given circumstance. This should help the children become confident in their own ability to solve problems. However, there may be difficulties in moving towards written methods of calculation. Different mental methods lead towards different written methods and the most common mental methods do not lead to the traditional algorithms. Also, the most appropriate mental method may depend on the nature of the problem and the particular numbers involved. For example, if the sum is 45 + 29, it is quite likely that children might choose to add 30 then subtract 1, so getting the answer 74. This is quite unlike the traditional written method which starts by adding the units, namely 5 + 9. Certainly children need to learn reliable and efficient written methods, but these may not necessarily be the standard algorithms.

Children who have difficulty with written algorithms are frequently encouraged to use tens and units apparatus (see Chapter 3) to support their work. They may become quite proficient with this but are unable to transfer to the written form. There may be several reasons for this: manipulating the physical apparatus may not model the stages of the written form (e.g. you can perfectly well do the tens first); the visual and tactile clues are absent in writing; abstracting principles from physical actions may be difficult.

To use a calculator appropriately, children need to understand not only how to enter the numbers so that the correct operations are carried out, but they should also be able to make a rough approximation of the answer to guard against gross errors in keying. The most common methods of approximation are more closely linked to mental methods of calculation than to written ones. For example, some children were trying to use their calculators to work out $\frac{25 + 36 \cdot 9}{7 \times 44}$. They obtained three different answers, namely: 256·943; 0·201; 4·410. Who could not possibly be correct? What may the others have done wrong?

Addition

Mental methods

The National Numeracy Strategy suggests that, from the reception class on, children should be encouraged to explain how they solved a problem or did a calculation. If the work by researchers such as Carpenter, referred to above, is taken into account, then we should expect early counting strategies to reflect problem structure. At first this will involve counting objects (counters, blocks, fingers) in ones, but it is useful, even at the beginning of Key Stage 1, to encourage children to remember number bonds. They usually start with 'doubles', especially $5 + 5 = 10$, and 'one more', e.g. $6 + 1 = 7$.

When children start using larger numbers, involving place value notation, then new concepts and techniques are involved. Simply counting in ones is no longer adequate, as it is too time-consuming and provides too many opportunities for errors. If children understand the grouping principle behind the place value notation and if they know most of the number bonds, then they may develop their own mental methods of adding 'tens and units'. Although some children invent individual and highly idiosyncratic methods, the most common ones can be put into three groups, namely:

a first number unaltered, second number partitioned (split up);
b both numbers partitioned;
c near doubles.

To illustrate the difference between the main two types consider $35 + 28$.

In type *a* this might be seen as:
$$35 + 28 = 35 + (20 + 8)$$
$$= (35 + 20) + 8$$
$$= \quad 55 \quad + 8$$
$$= 63$$

In type *b* both numbers are split up and might be seen as:
$$35 + 28 = (30 + 5) + (20 + 8)$$
$$= (30 + 20) + (5 + 8)$$
$$= \quad 50 \quad + \quad 13$$
$$= 63$$

Clearly type *c* can only be used in certain circumstances (when the numbers are close together), whilst the other two could be used for any pair of numbers. One version of the second method leads to a traditional written algorithm.

There are many variations within these types and some of the more common are illustrated on the CD. In the demonstration program 'Mental methods' seven methods are shown. Type *a* methods are shown either on the number line or number square, while those of type *b* are illustrated either by counters or tens and units blocks. After a calculation is selected, a method must be chosen (in two steps) and finally a representation selected. The program is highly structured, going through the method in distinct steps (click on the 'Step' button). The representation is animated to illustrate each step and the answer to each must be completed correctly before it is possible to proceed. Numbers *must* be entered through the on-screen number pad and *not* via the keyboard. Such a program might again be used as a scaffold for class or group discussion. Of course there are many other methods and many other ways of representing them. For example, Lacey (1998) suggests that the number square could be extended (in all directions) to maintain the image of adding tens by moving down the appropriate number of rows and adding units by moving to the right.

−22	−21	−20	−19	−18	−17	−16	−15	−14	−13	−12	−11	−10	−9
−12	−11	−10	−9	−8	−7	−6	−5	−4	−3	−2	−1	0	1
−2	−1	0	1	2	3	4	5	6	7	8	9	10	11
8	9	10	11	12	13	14	15	16	17	18	19	20	21
18	19	20	21	22	23	24	25	26	27	28	29	30	31
28	29	30	31	32	33	34	35	36	37	38	39	40	41
38	39	40	41	42	43	44	(45)	46	47	48	49	50	51
48	49	50	51	52	53	54	55	56	57	58	59	60	61
58	59	60	61	62	63	64	65	66	67	68	69	70	71
68	69	70	71	72	73	74	(75)	76	77	78	79	80	(81)
78	79	80	81	82	83	84	85	86	87	88	89	90	91
88	89	90	91	92	93	94	95	96	97	98	99	100	101
98	99	100	101	102	103	104	105	106	107	108	109	110	111
108	109	110	111	112	113	114	115	116	117	118	119	120	121

Now calculations such as 45 + 36 can be thought of as 45 add 30 (move down 3 rows to 75) then add 6 (move 6 squares to the right) to 81. It will be noted that the same number appears in more than one place and negative numbers are now included.

Written methods

The National Curriculum and the Numeracy Strategy state that children must know a suitable written method for adding 2- and 3-digit numbers. One problem is that the traditional written method does not follow from the more common mental methods. So if children are to build on their mental work, then it will be useful to present several written methods. As examples we will use 35 + 28 for 2-digit numbers and 456 + 275 for 3-digit numbers.

If the first group of mental methods have been used, then a written form using an extended notation might be appropriate, so

35 + 28 could be written as $35 + 20 + 8$
$= 55 + 8$
$= 63$

and   456 + 275 becomes   456 + 200 + 70 + 5

$$= 656 + 70 + 5$$

$$= 726 + 5$$

$$= 731$$

It can be seen that this follows the steps in the mental method quite closely but is usually written horizontally.

In the second group where both numbers are partitioned, it is possible to use the extended notation written either horizontally or 'vertically' as shown below.

35 + 28 could be written as $30 + 5$

$$+\ 20 + 8$$

$$\overline{50 + 13} = 63$$

and   456 + 275 becomes $400 +\ 50 +\ 6$

$$200 +\ 70 +\ 5$$

$$\overline{600 + 120 + 11} = 731$$

A good grasp of the principles of place value is necessary to carry this out successfully.

The traditional method for multicolumn addition partitions both numbers, but starts at the right hand side with the units. In mental calculations, children usually start with the left hand side, so in the example above it would be the hundreds. The traditional method is shown below together with the usual 'patter' despite its dubious value.

Step 1   (looking at the units column)   4 5 6
         6 + 5 = 11,   + 2 7 5
         put down 1 in units column, carry 1 $_1$1

Step 2   (looking at the tens column)   4 5 6
         5 + 7 = 12   + 2 7 5
         12 + 1 = 13, $_1$3$_1$1
         put 3 in tens column, carry 1

Step 3   (looking at the hundreds column)   4 5 6
         4 + 2 = 6   + 2 7 5
         6 + 1 = 7   7$_1$3$_1$1
         put 7 in hundreds column

Note: the 'carried' digits can be placed in many different positions in the same column, but this does not alter the actual method.

Clearly any of the written methods above can be generalised for larger numbers. Although it is necessary for children to have a written method which will work for larger numbers, it is more important for them to be able to use a calculator reliably and be able to estimate the rough size of the answer as a check. Children should be encouraged, possibly through games, to estimate the size of an answer before entering it into a calculator. Estimation depends on a 'feel for numbers'; but there are techniques which can be discussed to help children develop this skill. For example, to estimate the result of 5,232 + 3,928, first look at the size of the largest digits in each number; in this case they are both thousands, so the answer will be a number of thousands, or possibly ten thousands. Secondly, look at the first one or two digits of each number; in this case 52 + 39 ≈ 50 + 40 = 90. So the first digit will probably be 9 and the answer will be around 9,000.

 Check 4.4

1 Find the answer to each of these sums in at least three different ways. Do your own mental methods correspond to the way you do written calculations?

a 46 + 77   **c** 789 + 436
b 121 + 344   **d** 872 + 128

2 Write in the missing digits

```
a    2 □ 8        b    □ 4 1
   + 2 9 □            7 □ 4
     5 5 5         + 6 2 □
                    □ 7 3 4
```

Subtraction

Mental methods

As explained earlier, children are usually introduced to the 'take away' root of subtraction first, and this is often illustrated by taking objects off the end of a display, which models a counting-back strategy for calculation. Even with small numbers some children encounter difficulties with counting back. For example, when given 6 − 3, they may put up 3 fingers, then say 6, 5, 4 (putting down one finger each time) and give the answer as 4. For larger numbers it is cumbersome and frequently inaccurate. For example, in trying to solve 63 − 35 an 8-year-old child started to count 63, 62, 61, 60 (long pause) 59 . . . she was trying to keep track of the 35 by using her fingers but got completely confused and failed. If a counting-back method is to be used, then it must be more sophisticated, for example counting back in tens then ones: so 63, 53, 43, 33 (counting back 3 tens) then 33, 32, 31, 30, 29, 28 (counting back in ones, supported by fingers if necessary).

There are other ways of solving this. Perhaps one of the simplest is counting-on, or 'complementary addition' or 'shopkeeper's method'. To use this method with confidence, it is necessary for children to understand that it does not matter whether concrete objects are taken off at the beginning or the end of a display.

So, in illustrating $8 - 3$ with counters we may draw

In both cases the answer is 5. With larger numbers it is often easier to count on from the subtrahend (the number to be taken away) to the original number.

> Note: Please excuse the technical terms. It is easier to use a single word (subtrahend) rather than 'the number to be taken away'. Similarly it is quicker to write 'minuend' rather than 'the number we started with'. It is clearly not necessary to introduce these terms to children in school.

As with addition, there are two main groups of mental methods for subtraction:

a those in which the first number is unaltered and the second number is partitioned;
b those in which both numbers are split up.

As an example, consider $63 - 35$. In type a, it is possible to count back from the minuend (63) or count on from the subtrahend (35).

counting back	$63 - 35$ becomes	$63 - 30 - 5$
		$= 33 \quad - 5$
		$= 28$

counting on	35 to 40	$= 5$
	40 to 60	$= 20$
	60 to 63	$= 3$
	then	$5 + 20 + 3 = 28$

or using a number line (conveniently marked in tens) for the counting-on method

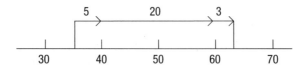

From the diagram $5 + 20 + 3 = 28$. This is a popular and robust method among adults and children. It is very similar to the traditional shopkeeper's method of giving change: for example, if a £5 note was offered for an article costing £3.45. The shopkeeper might say:

£3.45	cost of article
£3.50	giving 5p coin
£4.00	giving 50p coin
£5.00	giving £1 coin

So change received is £1.55 (£1.00 + 50p + 5p).

Other ways of counting on can be used, for example: (counting in tens) 35, 45, 55 (i.e. 20) (then in ones) 55, 56, 57, 58, 59, 60, 61, 62, 63. (8) so the answer is 28.

If both numbers are partitioned, type b, it is necessary to notice whether the units of the minuend are greater or less than the units of the subtrahend.

As $63 = 60 + 3$ and $35 = 30 + 5$ then
$$63 - 35$$
$$= 60 + 3 - 30 - 5$$
$$= 60 - 30 + 3 - 5$$

It is easy to say $60 - 30 = 30$, but it is difficult to know how to treat $3 - 5$. Only if children understand negative numbers can they proceed saying $3 - 5 = {}^-2$ then $30 - 2 = 28$.

The problem is exacerbated by the fact that if the number of units in the minuend is greater than or equal to the number of units in the subtrahend, then it is simple to treat them separately, so, for example:

$$65 - 33$$
$$= 60 - 30 + 5 - 3$$
$$= \quad 30 \quad + \quad 2$$
$$= 32$$

Children frequently find it difficult to distinguish between the two cases.

There are many variations within these types and some of the more common are illustrated on the CD. In the demonstration program 'Mental methods' eight methods of subtraction are shown. Type a are shown either on the number line or number square, while type b are illustrated either by counters or tens and units blocks. After a calculation is selected, a method must be chosen (in two steps) and finally a representation selected. The program is highly structured, going through the method in distinct steps (click on the 'Step' button). The representation is animated to illustrate each step and the answer to each must be completed correctly before it is possible to proceed. Such a program might again be used as a scaffold for class or group discussion.

There are many other ways of partitioning or 'chunking' numbers, for example:

as $35 = 33 + 2$ or   as $63 = 60 + 3$

$$63 - 35$$
$$= 63 - 33 - 2$$
$$= \quad 30 \quad - 2$$
$$= 28$$

$$63 - 35$$
$$= 60 - 35 + 3$$
$$= \quad 25 \quad + 3$$
$$= 28$$

The range of mental methods for subtraction is probably greater than those for addition, but again it is more common to start with the tens (or hundreds). Robust mental methods are frequently personal and depend on a good grasp of place value and a sound knowledge of number bonds.

Written methods

As with addition, the problem is that mental methods do not easily lead to the traditional written algorithms. There are at least two standard written algorithms, both starting with the units. These can be done mechanically, although knowing why they work requires considerable conceptual understanding. One of the main problems is that the routine differs according to whether the unit digit of the subtrahend is greater or smaller than the unit digit of the minuend (the number at the beginning). Other possible methods which can be developed from mental methods will be shown first. As examples we will consider $63 - 35$ and $502 - 37$.

a) A written version of counting on

35 and 5 = 40	5	37 + 3 = 40	3
40 and 20 = 60	20	40 + 60 = 100	60
60 and 3 = 63	3	100 + 400 = 500	400
63 − 35	5 + 20 + 3 = 28	500 + 2 = 502	2
		502 − 37	3 + 60 + 400 + 2 = 465

Children might just write down $5 + 20 + 3 = 28$ or use a number line as shown earlier.

b) 'Optimisation' addition

In this case the amount to be added to both the subtrahend and the minuend is chosen to make the calculation easy. This usually means that the subtrahend is made up to the next ten or hundred.

$$63 \xrightarrow{+5} 68 \qquad 502 \xrightarrow{+63} 565$$
$$-35 \xrightarrow{+5} -40 \qquad -37 \xrightarrow{+63} -100$$
$$\overline{\quad 28 \quad} \qquad \overline{\quad 465 \quad}$$

c) Another method invented by a bright 9-year-old who understood negative numbers is:

Step 1 $60 - 30 = 30$

$$\begin{array}{r} 63 \\ -35 \\ \hline 30 \end{array}$$

Step 1 $500 - 30 = 470$

$$\begin{array}{r} 502 \\ -37 \\ \hline 470 \end{array}$$

Step 2 $3 - 5 = {}^-2$

$$\begin{array}{r} 63 \\ -35 \\ \hline 30 \\ -2 \end{array}$$

Step 2 $2 - 7 = {}^-5$

$$\begin{array}{r} 502 \\ -37 \\ \hline 470 \\ -5 \end{array}$$

Step 3 $30 - 2 = 28$

$$\begin{array}{r} 63 \\ -35 \\ \hline 30 \\ -\ 2 \\ \hline 28 \end{array}$$

Step 3 $470 - 5 = 465$

$$\begin{array}{r} 502 \\ -37 \\ \hline 470 \\ -5 \\ \hline 465 \end{array}$$

d) Using extended notation

63	$60 + 3$	$= 50 + 13$
-35		$= 30 + \ 5$
		$20 + \ 8 = 28$

502	$500 + 2$	$= 400 + 90 + 12$
-37		$=\qquad\quad 30 + \ 7$
		$400 + 60 + \ \ 5 = 465$

The two standard written algorithms are 'decomposition' and 'equal addition'. The labels do not matter but they summarise the principle used in each case. 'Decomposition' is the most frequently used method in schools today, but 'equal addition' was taught widely 50 years ago. Decomposition is certainly less complicated conceptually but can look quite messy, especially if there are more than two columns. The traditional 'patter' for each method is given although these are not always helpful.

e) 'Decomposition' method of subtraction

In this method, 63 is broken into 50 and 13 or 5 tens and 13 units, then the subtraction is possible within the units, then within the tens.

Step 1   (looking at the units column)

$3 - 5$ (can't do it)

so 'change' $60 + 3$ into $50 + 13$

writing 1 near 3 (units) and 5 near 6 (tens)

$$\begin{array}{r} {}^5 6 {}^1 3 \\ -3\ 5 \\ \hline \end{array}$$

Step 2 $13 - 5 = 8$

write 8 in units column

$$\begin{array}{r} {}^5 6 {}^1 3 \\ -3\ 5 \\ \hline 8 \end{array}$$

Step 3 $50 - 30 = 20$

or 5 (tens) $-$ 3 (tens) $= 2$

write 2 in tens column

$$\begin{array}{r} {}^5 6 {}^1 3 \\ -3\ 5 \\ \hline 2\ 8 \end{array}$$

Now look at $502 - 37$:

Step 1	$2 - 7$ (can't do it)	$4^5 9 0^1 3$
	so 'change' $500 + 2$ into $490 + 12$	$-\ \ 3\ 7$
	writing 4 near 5, 9 near 0 and 1 near 2	

Step 2	$12 - 7 = 5$	$4^5 9 0^1 2$
	write 5 in units column	$-\ \ 3\ 7$
		5

Step 3	$9 - 3 = 6$ in tens column	$4^5 9 0^1 2$
	write 6 in tens column	$-\ \ 3\ 7$
		$6\ 5$

Step 4	Write 4 in hundreds column	$4^5 9 0^1 2$
		$-\ \ 3\ 7$
		$4\ 6\ 5$

The first step of 'changing' 500 into $490 + 10$ is often found difficult.

f) 'Equal addition' method of subtraction

This rests on the principle that the difference between two numbers is unaffected by adding the same amount to both numbers. For example, if my mother is 25 years older that I am, this will still be the case in 10 years' time when we are each 10 years older.

Considering the problems $63 - 35$ and $502 - 37$

Step 1	(looking at the units column)	$6^1 3$
	$3 - 5$ 'can't do it. Borrow a ten'	$-3\ 5$
	put 1 near 3 (units) making it 13	

Step 2	$13 - 5 = 8$. Write down 8 in units column	$6^1 3$
		$-3\ 5$
		8

Step 3	'Pay it back'	$6^1 3$
	(Write 1 near 3 (tens), so making it 4)	$-_1 3\ 5$
		8

Step 4	(looking at the tens column)	$6^1 3$
	$6 - 4 = 2$. Write 2 in tens column	$-_1 3\ 5$
		$2\ 8$

The word 'borrow' used in the traditional 'patter' is somewhat misleading. Nothing has been borrowed and even if it had it is 'paid back' somewhere else. In fact ten has been added to both numbers. It has been counted as 10 units in the minuend and one ten in the subtrahend. The main advantage of this method is that it can be written quite neatly, even if there are many columns of digits.

Step 1   2 − 7 can't do it. Borrow a ten. $50^{1}2$

12 − 7 = 5   − 3 7

write 5 in units column   5

Step 2   'Pay it back' writing 1 near 3 making it 4 $5^{1}0^{1}2$

0 − 4 can't do it. Borrow a ten (hundred)   − $_{1}$3 7

10 − 4 = 6 write 6 in tens column   6 5

Step 3   'Pay it back' writing 1 under 5 in hundreds $5^{1}0^{1}2$

column $-_{1\,1}$3 7

6 5

Step 4   5 − 1 = 4 write 4 in hundreds column $5^{1}0^{1}2$

$-_{1\,1}$37

4 6 5

Needless to say, all this 'borrowing and paying back' often became confused, especially in cases like the second example where there was 0 in the tens column. With both of these written methods there is a complicated sub-routine which must be followed if the unit of the minuend is less than the unit of the subtrahend; but which is unnecessary if this is not the case. Many children find it difficult to discriminate between the two cases, especially as they are frequently given the more straightforward one to practise alone first. This can lead to the classic 'smaller from larger' 'buggy' algorithm. So 63 − 35 becomes

Step 1   (looking at the units column)   63

3 − 5 'can't do it'   −35

so 5 − 3 = 2   2

Step 2   (looking at the tens column)   63

6 − 3 = 3   −35

32

Few adults (other than teachers) use either of these methods in everyday life.

Clearly any of the written methods above can be extended to larger numbers with more columns of digits. It is also important to help children develop methods of estimation of the result of subtraction, and similar methods to those used for addition can be used. Again, if a calculator is used with large numbers, it is important to be able to estimate the answer. This can be discussed in a similar way to that suggested for addition. Consider 6,348 − 2,856. First look at the size of the largest digits. In this case there are thousands in both numbers. Secondly, look carefully at the first one or two digits in each number. So it could be thought of as 6 thousands − 3 thousands which is roughly

3,000. It is important to realise that this is only an approximate answer, the actual result might be up to a thousand above or below; but it could not be 30,000 or 300.

Check 4.5

1 Find the answer to these subtraction problems in at least three ways. Discuss your methods with friends.

    a 84 − 52
    b 367 − 245
    c 542 − 376
    d 1002 − 549

Summary

- We normally read numbers from left to right, but the naming of the 'teens is irregular.
- The decimal place value system is very powerful. It is essential that children's understanding of it is developed (and checked) throughout the primary school.
- There are many different representations of number, each with its own strengths and limitations.
- The basic structure of a problem and the calculation necessary to solve it may be different.
- Robust mental methods of calculation must be developed.
- There are many ways of writing down addition and subtraction calculations. Children should be encouraged to use the ones they understand and can use with confidence.
- Estimation methods should be discussed in primary school.

Links with the classroom

1 How would you tell a child that eighteen is not written as 81?
2 A child wrote 5007 for the number five hundred and seven. How would you try to develop his or her understanding of place value?
3 What activities would you give a child who showed the 'smaller from larger' bug in subtraction calculations?
4 Which method of 2 digit subtraction would you introduce first?
5 Can you develop a sequence of written methods of subtraction?
6 'The traditional written algorithms are past their sell-by date.' Discuss with friends.

Challenges!

1 Try doing some addition and subtraction with a Chinese abacus.
2 Do some written calculations using Egyptian, Roman or Chinese rod notation.
3 Collect mental methods of 2-digit (tens and units) subtraction.
4 Use MAB or other apparatus to carry out subtraction problems. Can a written method be developed which mirrors the actions necessary?

References

Askew, M. (1997) 'Mental methods of computation', *Mathematics Teaching*, **160**, 7–8.

Carpenter, T. P., Fennema, E., Franke, M. L., Levi, L. Empson, S. B. (1999) *Children's Mathematics*. Portsmouth NH: Heinemann.

Fuson, K, D. (1992) 'Research on whole number addition and subtraction', in Grouws, D. A. (ed.) *Handbook of Research on Mathematics Teaching and Learning*, 243–75. New York: Macmillan Publishing Company.

Joseph, G. G. (1991) *The Crest of the Peacock*. Harmondsworth: Penguin Books.

Lacey, P. (1998) *Building Numeracy*. Stafford: Robert Powell Publications.

Plunkett, S. (1979) 'Decomposition and all that rot', *Mathematics in School*, **8**(3), 2–7.

Thompson, I. (1993) 'Thirteen ways to solve a problem', *Mathematics Teaching*, **144**, 27–30.

Wells, D. (1986) *The Penguin Dictionary of Curious and Interesting Numbers*. Harmondsworth: Penguin Books.

Multiplication and division

Starter – 79th problem on the Rhind Papyrus (1650 BC)

SEVEN HOUSES EACH have seven cats. The seven cats each kill seven mice. Each of the mice would have eaten seven ears of wheat. Each ear of wheat would have produced seven measures of flour. How many measures of flour did the cats save?

Early meanings

When children are first introduced to multiplication in school the problem is usually in the form of 'lots of'. For example, there are six children in a group and they each have a pair of shoes. How many shoes are there altogether? This can be solved by repeated addition, that is $2 + 2 + 2 + 2 + 2 + 2$, which equals 12. The children might simply count all the actual shoes, or they might model it as 6 pairs of blocks and then count the blocks one by one. One possible counting strategy might be to count in twos saying 2, 4, 6, 8, 10, 12, keeping track of the number of twos by raising a finger each time up to 6. The shoe problem can be thought of as 6 lots of 2

In this case the number of groups (6) and the number of elements (or objects) in each group (2) is known and the total number of elements in all the groups is required. This is $2 \times 6 = 12$. Strictly the first number is the size of one of the groups and the second number is the number of groups, so 2×6 is 2, six times or 6 lots of 2. As multiplication is commutative, in practice it does not matter if 6 lots of 2 is written as 6×2.

Division is often first presented to children as 'sharing'. For example, if 12 sweets are shared equally between three children, how many sweets will each child have? With concrete objects, this can be solved by the simple procedure of giving the sweets out one by one and moving around the three children; the number each child has at the end is then counted. The physical act of sharing is quite straightforward, and if sweets are involved, the participants have a vested interest in making sure it is done correctly. The only problems that may arise are remainders. In the early stages of primary school, when they are using concrete objects to support their calculations, children often find division problems simple to solve, because it is a situation with which they are familiar outside school. This may be a good introduction to division, but it has serious limitations if it is the only way division is presented. Firstly the meaning of 'sharing' is difficult to apply to fractions or decimals later. Secondly the inverse relation to multiplication is not apparent. Thirdly it only models one type of basic division problem, i.e. when the total number of elements and the number of groups are known. But there are other types of structure some of which lead to simpler methods of calculation with large numbers.

Problem structure

In fact the whole field of multiplication and division problems is very complex. Four main types can be identified (adapting the work of Greer (in Grouws) and Carpenter *et al*. 1999).

> Simple groups
> Rectangular products
> Prices, rates, conversions
> Ratio and proportion

Simple groups

In this type the numbers are usually positive integers (whole numbers). There are three numbers involved: the number of groups (G), the number of elements in each group (N) and the total number of elements in all groups (T). The basic relationship is $G \times N = T$. There are three types of problem depending on the position of the unknown.

1 *'Lots of'* model for multiplication (unknown T)

e.g. If there are 5 sweets in each pile, how many sweets are there in 4 piles?

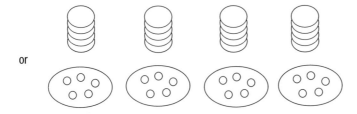

or

This model leads to the concept of multiplication as repeated addition. The total number (T) is 4 lots of 5 or $5 \times 4 = 5 + 5 + 5 + 5 = 20$.

2 *Sharing* model for division (unknown *N*)

e.g. If 20 sweets are shared equally between 4 children how many sweets will each child get?

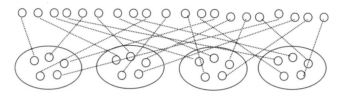

With concrete objects the final number in one of the groups can be counted (5). So $20 \div 4 = 5$. This model does not lead easily to counting strategies.

3 *Grouping* model for division (unknown *G*)

e.g. If 20 sweets are put into tubes with 5 sweets in each tube, how many tubes can be made?

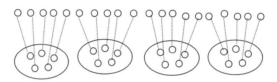

Young children might model this problem by counting out 20 blocks. From this 20 they would count 5 and put them in one group, then 5 in another group, until all the 20 counters are used up. Then they would count how many groups, in this case 4. The counting strategy closest to this model is repeated subtraction, which can be shown as:

$$20 - 5 = 15 \qquad 1$$
$$15 - 5 = 10 \qquad 2$$
$$10 - 5 = 5 \qquad 3$$
$$5 - 5 = 0 \qquad 4$$
$$\text{So } 20 \div 5 = 4$$

The underlying question is 'How many lots of 5 are there in 20?', showing the inverse relation to the 'lots of' model for multiplication and possibly leading to a method for long division (see later).

So there are three basic types of simple (group) multiplication and division problems (Carpenter's terms are given in brackets).

	Number of groups (*G*)	Number of elements in each group (*N*)	Total number of elements in all groups (*T*)
lots of (multiplication)			$T = G \times N$
sharing (partitive division)		$N = T \div G$	
grouping (measurement division)	$G = T \div N$		

In fact, by thinking of the 'sharing' model in a slightly different way, it too can be solved by repeated subtraction. In the problem of 20 sweets shared between 4 children, the sweets can be removed 4 at a time and then distributed one to each child. The number of sweets each child receives is the same as the number of times 4 sweets can be removed.

Rectangular products

There are three main subtypes which can all be illustrated by rectangular displays.

1 *Arrays*

The number of elements in an array can be found by multiplying the number of rows by the number of columns, for example, the total number of boxes in 4 piles each of which contains 3 boxes.

Number of columns (4)

Number of rows (3)

2 *Cartesian product*

The Cartesian product is used when there are two sets and the number of different ways of choosing one from each set is required. For example, consider the number of different sandwiches that can be made if there are 3 types of bread and 4 different fillings. The diagram below illustrates the problem.

	Cheese	Ham	Egg	Salad
White				
Brown				
Wholemeal				

From the diagram it can be seen that there are $3 \times 4 = 12$ possibilities. The similarity with finding the area of a rectangle 3 cm by 4 cm is clear.

3 *Area*

To find the area of a rectangle the length is multiplied by the width (see Chapter 11).

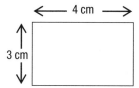

If the lengths are known then the area can be found by multiplication (in the example, 3×4), and if the area and one length are known, then the other length can be found by division.

Prices, rates, conversions

In many ways the structure of these problems is very similar to that of simple groups. However, the contexts are different and the numbers may involve decimals.

1. *Prices*

Problems involving price have a very similar structure to rate problems. Children often find these simpler, partly because they are familiar with the situation, and partly because the multiplier (the number of units) is nearly always a whole number, even if the price per unit is a decimal (e.g. £4.99).

> If one book costs £14, how much will 5 books cost?

This multiplication problem can be modelled as 'leaps along the number line' (rates) or 'lots of' (simple groups). There are several strategies for finding 14 × 5, some of which will be discussed later. If the unknown is the cost per book or the number of books, then a division strategy must be used, like 'sharing' or 'grouping'.

> If 5 books cost £70, how much does one book cost?
> How many books at £14 each can be bought for £70?

2. *Rates*

Problems involving rates are found more difficult by many children. Look at a simple example first.

> e.g. A car is travelling at 12 m/sec. How far will it travel in 3 seconds?

This problem can be illustrated as 'leaps along the number line'.

The relation to '3 lots of 12' is obvious. Indeed the number line can be used to illustrate 'simple group' problems too. The units in which the rate is given actually state the relationship between the quantities. In the above case the speed is given in 'metres per second', that is the distance travelled in each second, so the formula must be.

$$\text{Speed} = \frac{\text{distance}}{\text{time}}$$

This means speed × time = distance. So the distance travelled in 3 seconds is 12 × 3 = 36 m. If the unknown is the speed or the time, then a form of division must be used. This is just like sharing or grouping in the 'simple group' model. The car problem is a fairly straightforward rate problem. However, consider the following problem which has the same structure.

> A mouse can run at 1·5 m/sec. How far can it run in 0·8 seconds?

Greer reports that in a test children were simply asked to choose the correct operation for several problems, some of which were like the two given above. When the multiplier (in this case the time) changed from an integer to a decimal less than one, the number of correct answers decreased by over 40%. The distance the mouse can run should be $1.5 \times 0.8 = 1.2$ m, but many children chose $1.5 \div 0.8 = 1.875$ m. One possible explanation for this is the application of a 'mal-rule' (an incorrect intuition). This might be that as the operation is multiplication, then the answer must be larger than 1.5. If a diagram of 'leaps along the number line' had been drawn, this might have helped to show why the mouse must go less than 1.5 m if the time is less than 1 second. In examples of division, the number of errors increased by over 60%. In such cases a common 'mal-rule' seemed to be that the larger number must be divided by the smaller number.

Although rates are often given with reference to time (e.g. heart beats per minute, miles per hour, litres per second) other situations have similar structures, for example:

If the density of lead is 11·3 g/cm³, what is the mass of 5 cm³?

Here the rate is density, which is mass per unit volume. This means that every cm³ of lead has a mass of 11.3 g, so density $= \frac{\text{mass}}{\text{volume}}$ and mass $=$ density $\times$ volume.

$$\text{mass} = 11.3 \times 5$$
$$= 56.5 \text{ g}$$

3. *Conversion*

Changing from one unit to another (e.g. changing currency) is another type of rate problem, although the information is usually given as an equation.

e.g. **1** If £1=$1.50, how many dollars would I get for £5?

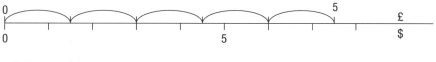

$$£5 = 5 \times \$1.50$$
$$= \$7.50$$

If a dress costs $100, how much would that be in pounds?

£1 = $1·50   or how many lots of 1·5 are there in 100?

dividing both sides by 1.5 $£\frac{1}{1.5} = \$1$ $£\frac{100}{1.5}$

$100 = £100 \times \frac{1}{1.5}$ $= £66.67$

$= £66.67$

2 If 1 litre $= 1.75$ pints, how many pints in 5 litres?

5 litres $= 5 \times 1.75$ pints
$= 8.75$ pints

How much is 1 gallon (8 pints) in litres (to the nearest litre)?

1 pint $= \frac{1}{1 \cdot 75}$ litres

8 pints $= 8 \times \frac{1}{1 \cdot 75}$

$\qquad = 4 \cdot 57$

$\qquad \approx 5$ litres (to the nearest litre)

Ratio and proportion

There are many situations in which ratio and proportion occur. A ratio is a comparison between two quantities, which are measured in the same units. There are three common situations in which such comparisons are made:

1 *Ratio* (part–part)

This is a comparison between parts of a whole and is usually written as, say, 1:4 and read as 'one to four'. For example, the instructions might be 'mix one part of concentrated orange with 4 parts of water'. This means that the ratio of concentrated orange to water is 1:4. It is important to note that in this case two parts are being compared. If 100 ml of concentrated orange is mixed with 400 ml of water, then there will be 500 ml of orange drink.

2 *Proportion* (part–whole)

'Proportion is used to describe the relationship of some part of a whole to the whole itself and is usually given as a fraction' (QTS Skills Test support material). This means, for example, the orange drink is made up of ⅕ concentrated orange and ⅘ water. The proportion of concentrated orange is ⅕. Proportion can also be expressed as percentages so, in the example above, 20% of the drink is concentrated orange and 80% water.

3 *Scaling* (whole–whole)

It is also possible to compare two separate wholes, e.g. the scale of the map is 1:25,000, i.e. 1 cm on the map represents 25,000 cm (or 0·25 km) on the ground.

A wide variety of language is used to describe ratios and proportion problems, which can be a source of difficulty. For example:

8 out of every 10 owners said their cats preferred it.

The vote was 3 to 1 in favour.

There was a 15% reduction in price during the sale.

Enlarge the rectangle with a scale factor of 3.

The first statement compares part with the whole and so might be called a proportion. It could be expressed as 4 out of 5 or ⅘ or 80% of the cat owners. The statement about votes is a ratio, i.e. it is a comparison of two parts (those who were in favour and those who were against). For every 3 votes in favour, there was one against. As this is a ratio comparing parts, the number of parts must be added to find the number in the whole. This means ¾ of the group voted in favour and ¼ against. The third statement is a proportion as the reduction (part) is compared to the whole (pre-sale price) and expressed as a percentage. A diagram might help to clarify this.

If a music centre costs £250 and there is a 15% reduction in a sale, what will its sale price be?

So the ratio of the sale price (£S) to £250 = 85 to 100. This can be expressed in the equation

Let £S be sale price then

$S : 250 = 85{:}100$

or $\frac{S}{250} = \frac{85}{100}$

$S = \frac{85 \times 250}{100}$

$S = 212{\cdot}50$

The sale price would be £212·50

or 100% = £250

so 10% = £25

and 5% = £12.50

so 85% = £(8 × 25) + £12.50

= £200 + £12.50

= £212.50

This diagram is similar to a thermometer on which there are two scales, one for Centigrade and one for Fahrenheit.

In this case a change of 100°C = a change of 180°F or a change of 1°C = a change of 1·8°F or the ratio of °C:°F is 5:9.

The last example above, about enlarging a rectangle, is a scaling problem involving a comparison of one whole to another whole, i.e. the original to the new, so each length in the new rectangle should be 3 times that of the corresponding length in the original. In such cases of enlargements and reductions it is useful to ask whether the resultant shape is similar to the original (see Chapter 18).

One of the common mistakes in ratio and proportion problems is the use of addition and subtraction to calculate the unknown quantities. For instance, when making pastry the ratio of flour to fat is usually 2:1. The recipe may have 8 ounces of flour and 4 ounces of fat, but if there are only 6 ounces of flour left, how much fat is needed?

Flour	Fat
8 oz	4 oz
6 oz	?

A common mistake would be to think that as there are 2 ounces less flour then there should also be 2 ounces less fat, so 4 − 2 = 2 ounces of fat are needed. It might help if the problem is recast in terms of proportions expressed as fractions. So as 2 parts of flour and 1 part of fat are needed, there are 3 parts altogether. So ⅔ is flour and ⅓ is fat. If ⅔ is 6 ounces, then ⅓ will be 3 ounces. Interestingly, there is a commonly used strategy in many ratio problems, which on the face of it looks like an additive strategy. If a recipe for 4 people is to be changed to one for 6 people, many people would take each quantity and 'add half as much again'. So, if 500 g of chicken is needed for 4 people, then $500 + 250 = 750$ g will be needed for 6 people. This is correct because, in effect, the quantities are being multiplied by 1½ or 1·5 and using the distributive law:

$$1·5 \times 500 = 1 \times 500 + 0·5 \times 500$$

As illustrated earlier, the difficulty in solving multiplication and division problems depends not only on their structure but also on the type of numbers involved. Problems only involving positive integers are the simplest. The difficulty increases if decimals greater than 1 are present, but the cases which cause most misunderstandings are those where one or both numbers are less than 1. So to extend ideas of multiplication and division to decimals, especially numbers less than 1, children must have plenty of practical experience and discussion over many years. Two simple examples with numbers less than one are given as illustrations (see Chapter 7 for more examples).

First consider multiplication, for example, $0·25 \times 0·5$. If we can think of 5×4 as '4 lots of 5' then $0·25 \times 0·5$ or $\frac{1}{4} \times \frac{1}{2}$ could be 'half of a quarter'. The diagrams below illustrate this.

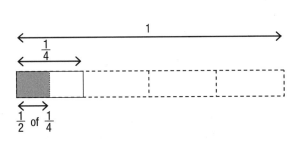

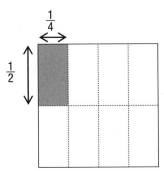

This diagram suggests a piece of cloth ¼ m long which is to be divided into half.

This diagram suggests a tile with part shaded.

In both cases the fraction ½ is thought of as an operator.
Then $\frac{1}{2}$ of $\frac{1}{4}$ is $\frac{1}{8}$ or $0·25 \times 0·5 = 0·125$.

The answer is smaller than both of the initial fractions.

An example for division might be $0·75 \div 0·2$. A suitable context for this could be:

How many glasses each holding 200 ml (0·2 l) can be filled from a ¾ (0·75) litre bottle?
    1 glass holds 0·2 litres
    2 glasses hold 0·4 litres
    3 glasses hold 0·6 litres

So 3 glasses can be filled and there will be 0·15 l left. This would make a fourth glass ¾ (0·75) full. So 0·75 ÷ 0·2 = 3·75.

In this case the answer is larger than the two starting numbers.

For more examples see Chapters 7 and 11.

Check 5.1

Solve these problems

1 In a class of 32 children, each child needs 4 exercise books. How many books should be ordered?

2 There are three children aged 9, 6 and 5 years old in a family. If the children receive pocket money in proportion to their ages, and £10 is put aside, how much does each child get?

3 The exchange rate is 2.6 DM to the £1. If £50 is changed, how many DM will be obtained? If at least 800 DM are required, what is the smallest number of £s to be changed?

4 In a dancing class there are 5 boys and 6 girls. How many different couples (1 boy and 1 girl) could be formed?

5 The government imposed a 15% luxury tax. If a diamond ring costs £350 before the tax was introduced, what should be its price afterwards?

6 If a car is travelling at 45 mph how far will it go in 20 mins?

7 If a car can travel 35 miles per gallon of petrol, how much petrol (to the nearest gallon) would it need to go 100 miles?

A selection of questions from National Test papers

8 A bus company has 62 minibuses. On average, each minibus travels 19 miles on a gallon of fuel and goes 284 miles each day. The company says it needs about 1000 gallons of fuel every day. Approximate these numbers and make an estimate to show whether what the company says is about right.

9 A and B are two chain wheels on a bike.

For every 2 complete turns that wheel A makes, wheel B makes 5 complete turns. If wheel A makes 150 turns, how many turns will wheel B make? If wheel B makes 90 turns, how many turns will wheel A make?

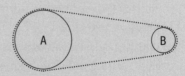

10 Here are the ingredients for fish pie for two people.

Fish pie (for 2 people)   250 g fish
                                  400 g potato
                                  25 g butter

Omar makes fish pie for 3 people. How many grams of fish should he use?

11 Children were asked to choose between a safari park and a zoo for the school trip. They had a vote. The result was a ratio of 10:3 in favour of going to a safari park. 130 children voted in favour of going to a safari park. How many children voted in favour of going to the zoo?

12 If ☐ represents any digit, investigate what they might be in the following:
   a ☐☐ × 3 = 8 ☐
   b ☐☐ × ☐ = 3 7 1

13 a Nigel pours 1 carton of apple juice and 3 cartons of orange juice into a big jug. What is the ratio of apple juice to orange juice in Nigel's jug?
   b Lesley pours 1 carton of apple juice and 1½ cartons of orange juice into another big jug. What is the ratio of apple juice to orange juice in Lesley's jug?
   c Tandi pours 1 carton of apple juice and 1 carton of orange juice into another big jug. She wants only half as much apple juice as orange juice in her jug. What should Tandi pour into her jug now?

14 a Use £1 = 9.60 francs to work out how much 45p is in francs. Show your working.
   b Use 240 pesetas = £1 to work out how much 408 pesetas is in pounds. Show your working.
   c Use £1 = 9.60 francs and £1 = 240 pesetas to work out how much 1 franc is in pesetas. Show your working.

15 The ship *Queen Mary* used to sail across the Atlantic Ocean. The ship's usual speed was 33 miles per hour. On average, the ship used fuel at the rate of 1 gallon for every 13 feet sailed. Calculate how many gallons of fuel the ship used in one hour of travelling at the usual speed (there are 5280 feet in one mile). Show your working and write down the full calculator display. Then write your answer correct to two significant figures.

Now some TTA (QTS Skills) type questions

16 On the internet, a German bookshop prices its books in Deutsche Mark (DM). I wish to buy two books and pay with a cheque in sterling. The books cost 55 DM and 45 DM and there is a charge of 25 DM for postage and packing. The exchange rate is £1 = 3.4 DM.
What is the cost in pounds (£) rounded up to the nearest 10p?

17 1 mile = 1·609 km
How far is 15 kilometres in miles?
How far is 25 miles in kilometres?
Give your answers correct to two decimal places.

18 In a given school there are 450 pupils at Key Stage 3 and 325 at Key Stage 4. What is the ratio between them?

19 Each week pupils should have 5 hours of Maths and 1·5 hours of PE. What is the ratio of Maths lessons to PE lessons? If there are 25 hours of lessons in the week, what percentage of time is spent on Maths?

20 An infant school has 120 pupils. 20 go home for lunch. What proportion stay at school for lunch?

Note: before considering various methods of calculation, it is necessary to discuss the meanings of some terms:

a A factor is a number which divides another number exactly, e.g. 1, 2, 3, 6 are all factors of 6.

b A multiple is a number that is the product of a given number and an integer, so 6 is a multiple of 2 and 3.

c A prime number is a whole number greater than 1 which is divisible only by 1 and itself. The first few prime numbers are 2, 3, 5, 7, and 13. Any whole number can be written as a product of primes, so $4 = 2 \times 2$; $12 = 2 \times 2 \times 3$; $15 = 3 \times 5$.

As explained in Chapter 3, multiplication and division are each the inverse of the other. This means that division problems are often solved by converting them into the equivalent multiplication form. For example, $56 \div 8$ can be thought of as 'What number must 8 be multiplied by to make 56?' or, in symbols, $8 \times ? = 56$, where ? is the number wanted.

Representing multiplication

In discussing different types of multiplication problems, various diagrams have been used. Such representations can be divided into four main types, namely:

a 'lots of' or 'groups of' or 'sets of' e.g. plates of fruit, bunches of flowers;
b arrays of counters;
c number line e.g. hops on a number line, groups of beads;
d sets in a number square.

On the CD there is a demonstration program 'Multiplication' showing these. After choosing a multiplication sum, select two representations. The chosen product will then be shown on the screen in these two ways, which could provide a stimulus for discussion. The 'lots of' model seems to be understood most easily by children, but it offers no assistance in finding out the answer. The array, especially if it is subdivided at 5, not only shows the two numbers, but also provides some help in finding the answer; so 7×8 is shown by

which can be seen as
$5 \times 5 \ (25) + 2 \times 5 \ (10) + 3 \times 5 \ (15) + 2 \times 3 \ (6) = 56$
This calculation depends on the distributive law which was discussed in Chapter 3. It appears that initially many children see the separate parts as dominant and need help to see it as also representing a multiplication sum.

The hops on the number line or beads are particularly appropriate for illustrating rates, but many children cannot interpret the clues leading to the answer. The sets in the number square show the answer more clearly; but the actual multiplication sum is less obvious.

Methods of calculation

To be able to use multiplication and division to solve problems children must know most if not all their 'times table' facts and be able to derive new ones from known facts. They need to understand how the tables can be obtained from first principles (repeated addition or counting arrays), to recognise patterns (especially in the units digits in some tables) and to be aware of the commutative nature of multiplication (which reduces the number of facts to be memorised). They also need repeated practice, possibly including games, so that the facts are 'known by heart' and are available for use rapidly.

It is also crucial that they know the results of multiplying and dividing by powers of 10. This involves not only knowing that $10 \times 10 = 100$ and $10 \times 6 = 60$, but also being aware that $10 \times 100 = 1,000$; that $10 \times 5,000 = 50,000$; that $30 \times 40 = 1,200$ not 120. Understanding this fully involves a thorough grasp of our denary (base 10) place value system. If a number is multiplied by 10, each digit is worth ten times the amount it was before and this is shown by moving it one place to the left so, for instance, the units become tens and the tens become hundreds. e.g. $24 \times 10 = 240$. Similarly if a number is divided by 10, then the digits are worth a tenth of the original value and they move one place to the right, so $24 \div 10 = 2.4$.

On the CD there is a demonstration program, 'Powers of ten', which shows what happens when a 6-digit number is multiplied or divided by multiples of ten. It will be noticed that the digits move and the decimal point (which identifies the units column) remains stationary. It is frequently said that 'to multiply by ten move the decimal point one place to the right'. Clearly this gives the same result as leaving the point stationary

	0·01	0·02	0·03	0·04	0·05	0·06	0·07	0·08	0·09
	0·1	0·2	0·3	0·4	0·5	0·6	0·7	0·8	0·9
	1	2	3	4	5	6	7	8	9
	10	20	30	40	50	60	70	80	90
	100	200	300	400	500	600	700	800	900
	1 000	2 000	3 000	4 000	5 000	6 000	7 000	8 000	9 000
	10 000	20 000	30 000	40 000	50 000	60 000	70 000	80 000	90 000

and moving the digits one place to the left; but it does not reinforce the place value concept. Other traditional 'short cuts' may be even more misleading, for example 'to multiply by 10, just add a nought' is not even always true, for example, $4 \cdot 36 \times 10$ is not 4·360. What it should say is 'to multiply a whole number by ten, the digits must move one place to the left and a 0 must be placed in the units column to hold them there'. Using the word 'add' is doubly misleading as adding 0 to any number leaves it unchanged. The 'Gattegno tens chart' can be used to illustrate and discuss this.

So if 35 is seen as $30 + 5$ (the extended notation and illustrated in the diagram), then to multiply 35 by 100, the outline is simply moved down two lines and becomes 3,500. To divide by 10 it is moved up a line and becomes 3·5. Knowing the structure of the number system, perhaps supported by this image, allows multiplication and division of any numbers of powers of ten to be accomplished.

Multiplication

Mental methods

The range of methods used by children is surprising. A few are illustrated by considering 34×7. Many of these involve splitting the numbers, operating on them then recombining them and so could be regarded as 'chunking'. There is no reason why some stages should not be written down.

a) Using a tens first method (extended notation) i.e. splitting the multiplicand

$$
\begin{aligned}
34 \times 7 &= (30 + 4) \times 7 \\
&= (30 \times 7) + (4 \times 7) \\
&= \quad 210 \quad + \quad 28 \\
&= 238
\end{aligned}
$$

b) Using doubles

as $7 = (2 \times 2 \times 2) - 1$
$34 \times 2 = 68$
$(34 \times 2) \times 2 = 68 \times 2 = 136$
$34 \times 2 \times 2 \times 2 = 34 \times 8 = 136 \times 2 = 272$
but we only want 34×7 so subtract 34
$272 - 34 = 238$

c) Splitting the multiplier and using addition

as $7 = 1 + 2 + 4$
$$
\begin{aligned}
34 \times 7 &= (34 \times 1) + (34 \times 2) + (34 \times 4) \\
&= \quad 34 \quad + \quad 68 \quad + \quad 136 \\
&= 238
\end{aligned}
$$

Written methods

As shown above, some mental methods can be developed to provide written algorithms for simple multiplication.

2-digit by 1-digit

A traditional algorithm has been set out with the 'patter' usually associated with them. At times this obscures rather than clarifies what is happening.

Step 1	Units first	3 4
	$4 \times 7 = 28$	$\times\ 7$
	Put 8 in units column,	$_2 8$
	carry 2 in tens column	
Step 2	Tens next	3 4
	$3 \times 7 = 21$ Add 2 tens carried	$\times\ 7$
	$21 + 2 = 23$	$2\ 3_2\ 8$
	Put 3 in tens column and 2 in hundreds column	
	so $34 \times 7 = 238$	

Note: exactly where the 'carried' digit is placed in the column is unimportant.

2-digit by 2-digit

Again there are many methods, most of them depending on a thorough understanding of place value and keeping figures in columns. The traditional units first algorithm may be the neatest and most concise, but it is not necessarily the best for children to start with. Consider ways of calculating 87×36.

(a) 'Building up'

$$
\begin{array}{rcl}
87 \times 10 & = & 870 \\
87 \times 10 & = & 870 \\
87 \times 10 & = & 870 \\
87 \times\ 6 & = & \underline{522} \\
 & = & 3132
\end{array}
$$

(b) Splitting multiplier and using distributive law

$$
\begin{array}{rcl}
87 \times 36 & = & 87 \times (30 + 6) \\
 & = & 87 \times 30 + 87 \times 6 \\
 & = & 2610\ +\ \ 522 \\
 & = & 3132
\end{array}
$$

(c) 'Cabbage patch' sums

The problem can be thought of as how many cabbages would there be in a field with 36 rows with 87 cabbages in each row?

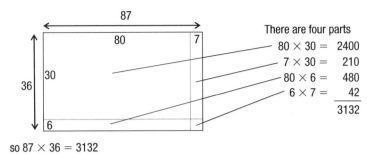

so 87 × 36 = 3132

(d) Traditional algorithm

The standard 'patter' is given, although this may not aid understanding.

Step 1	Multiply 87 by 6	8 7
	units first; 6 × 7 = 42; put down 2 (units) carry 4 (tens)	× 3 6
	tens next; 6 × 8 = 48; 48 + 4 (carry) = 52 (tens)	5 2$_4$ 2
	put down 2 in tens column and 5 in hundreds column	

Step 2	Multiply 87 by 30	8 7
	put 0 in units column	× 3 6
	3 × 7 = 21 (tens); put 1 in tens and carry 2 in hundreds	5 2$_4$ 2
	3 × 8 = 24 (hundreds); 24 + 2 (carry) = 26	2 6$_2$ 1 0
	put 6 in hundreds column and 2 in thousands	

Step 3	Add numbers found in Steps 1 and 2	8 7
	(traditionally units first as explained in Chapter 4)	× 3 6
		5 2$_4$ 2
		2 6$_2$ 1 0
		3$_1$ 1 3 2

There are several variations in this method, for example, Step 2 can be done before Step 1.

(e) Egyptian multiplication

This only requires knowledge of the 2 times table. It is probably the method used to solve the problem at the head of this chapter about houses, cats, mice, wheat and flour.

1	87
2	174
4	348
8	696
16	1392
32	2784

Each line is obtained by doubling the previous one. Now, looking at the numbers in the left hand column, choose those which add up to 36 (the number required):

32 + 4 = 36

Add up those numbers in the right hand column opposite the selected numbers:

2784 + 348 = 3132

This works because:

$$87 \times 36 = 87 \times (32 + 4)$$
$$= 87 \times 32 + 87 \times 4 \text{ (multiplication is distributive)}$$
$$= 2784 + 348 \text{ (from table)}$$
$$= 3132$$

(f) *Lattice (Chinese) multiplication*

$$30 \times 80 = 2400$$
$$30 \times 7 = 210$$
$$6 \times 80 = 480$$
$$6 \times 7 = 42$$
$$3132$$

In this method the numbers to be multiplied are written along the top and down the right hand side of a square (or rectangle). In each small square write the result of multiplying the digit above with the one on the right of that square. If the result is more than 10, write the tens digit in the upper left triangle and the units digit in the lower right part of the square. If the result is less than 10 simply write it in the lower right of the square. So, considering the top left square, 8 × 3 = 24. Put 2 in the upper left part and 4 in the lower right part of the square. When all the squares are filled, add the digits diagonally, starting at the lower right and carrying as required. Go around the corner and up the left hand side. This gives the required answer. So 87 × 36 = 3132. The table at the right illustrates what is happening. Children may enjoy making and using the simpler form called Napier's bones (or rods). They can be used to multiply any number by a single digit, or, if paper and pencil are used as well, by any other number.

In general children should not be expected to do 2-digit by 2-digit multiplication without writing anything down. However, it is useful to discuss some special cases, such as multiplying by 25 or 60. The first of these can be thought of as multiplying by 100 then dividing by 4 and the second as multiplying by 6 then by 10.

✎ Check 5.2

Try doing the following multiplication calculations in different ways, so that you have tried each of the methods given at least once.

1 46 × 8
2 83 × 26

3 72×39

4 67×25

5 17×74

Large numbers

Very large numbers can be fascinating and awe inspiring. For example, the speed of light in empty space $\approx 301,000,000$ m/s. Stars are so far away that their distance from the Earth is measured in terms of how long the light has taken to reach us. The light from our nearest star, Alpha Centauri, takes 4·3 years to reach us. The following calculation must be carried out to find how far this is in metres:

4·3 light years =	4·3	× 365	× 24	× 60	× 60	× 301,000,000
	number	days	hours	mins	secs	speed
	of years	in year	in day	in hour	in mins	of light

When this is put into a calculator, the answer shown is 4·08 ^{15}. The full answer would be 4,080,000,000,000,000 metres but the calculator display means $4·08 \times 10^{15}$ i.e. 4·08 multiplied by 10 fifteen times. This way of writing numbers is called standard form. To enter such a number into a calculator, first put in 4·08 in the usual way, then press the EXP key and enter 15, the power of ten.

It may clarify what is happening if children are shown several intermediate steps with simpler numbers, for example:

$$123 = 123 \times 1$$
$$= 12·3 \times 10 \qquad = 12·3 \times 10^1$$
$$= 1·23 \times 100 \qquad = 1·23 \times 10^2$$

In moving from one line to the next, the first part of the number is divided by 10 and the second part multiplied by 10. This is equivalent to multiplying by $^{10}/_{10} = 1$, which does not alter the value. So $123 = 1·23 \times 10^2$.

Standard form is useful for writing very small numbers as well. A number such as 0.0000000736 is quite difficult to read. It can also be expressed in two parts. First a number between 1 and 10, in this case 7·36 then the number of tens it must be divided by, in this case 8. So the number becomes $7·36 \times 10^{-8}$. As explained in Chapter 3, the negative index means that the number must be multiplied by $^1/_{10}{}^8$ or divided by 10^8. To enter such a number into a calculator first put in 7·36, then press EXP then press ± then 8. The display should look like 7·36 $^{-8}$.

Before children use a calculator, particularly with large numbers, they should be able to make a reasonable estimate of the answer. This is more complicated than for addition or subtraction. For example, consider 546×384. One way is to approximate the numbers e.g. to 500×400 (rounding one down and the other up) which is 200,000. The other is to note that it is hundreds × hundreds, so the answer will be at least tens of thousands and $5 \times 3 = 15$, so it will be greater than 150,000.

Division

The different ways of thinking about division have already been considered. Written methods of division never model the one by one sharing process, but some follow the repeated subtraction model, while others use the fact that division is the inverse of multiplication. The standard algorithms depend on the latter and assume a secure knowledge of 'times tables'.

Mental methods

Almost all of these rely on the fact that division is the inverse of multiplication. As an example take $42 \div 7$. This can be read as 42 divided by 7. It is frequently rephrased as 'How many times will 7 go into 42?' This is equivalent to asking 'What number when multiplied by 7 will make 42?' So $42 \div 7$ is changed to $? \times 7 = 42$. By searching through the 7 times table (on paper or in memory) it is discovered that $6 \times 7 = 42$, so $42 \div 7 = 6$. This procedure depends on a good understanding of the relation of multiplication and division as well as recall of 'times tables'.

If the dividend is not an exact multiple of the divisor, then there will be a remainder. The nature of the problem from which the calculation arose should suggest the most appropriate way of handling this. If only whole numbers are being used, and the context gives no guidance, it is usual to state both the quotient and the remainder, so $75 \div 8 = 9$ remainder 3, because $9 \times 8 = 72$ and $72 + 3 = 75$. In the sharing model, if 75 sweets are divided equally between 8 children each will get 9 sweets and there will be 3 left over.

Written methods

Simple cases (3 or more digit numbers divided by 1-digit numbers)

These problems can be solved in several ways including a traditional algorithm. Consider as an example, $735 \div 4$.

(a) Building up

$$4 \times 100 = 400$$
$$4 \times 40 = 160 \qquad 400 + 160 = 560$$
$$4 \times 40 = 160 \qquad 560 + 160 = 720$$
$$4 \times 3 = 12 \qquad 720 + 12 = 732$$

Then $100 + 40 + 40 + 3 = 183$ and $735 - 732 = 3$
so $735 \div 4 = 183$ remainder 3.

(b) Repeated subtraction

It would be possible, but tedious, to subtract 4 from 735 repeatedly and count how many times this was possible. A quicker and more reliable way is to write:

$735 \div 4$

$$4 \times 100 = 400 \qquad 735 - 400 = 335$$
$$4 \times 40 = 160 \qquad 335 - 160 = 175$$
$$4 \times 40 = 160 \qquad 175 - 160 = 15$$
$$4 \times 3 = 12 \qquad 15 - 12 = 3$$

So $735 \div 4 = 100 + 40 + 40 + 3 = 183$ remainder 3.

These may seem like long-winded methods if you are used to the traditional method; but they can be extended to larger numbers (see later). A traditional method is included here, but the difficulty of explaining clearly what is happening shows the complexity of the ideas underlying this algorithm. As the extension to larger numbers is even more complicated, it is doubtful whether it is useful to try to teach it to children.

(c) A traditional algorithm (written in long method)

The difficulty experienced in trying to explain exactly what is happening reflects the complexity of the ideas underlying this algorithm.

Step 1   Starting with the hundreds, how many 4s in 7?
(really how many hundred times will 4 go into 700?)
Answer 1 (hundred) write 1 in hundreds column on top
Subtract 4 from 7 (really 400 from 700)
'Bring down' 3 (really 30) from dividend

$$\begin{array}{r} 1 \\ \hline 4\,|\,7\ 3\ 5 \\ -\ 4 \\ \hline 3\ 3 \end{array}$$

Step 2   Looking at tens column (i.e. 33)
How many 4s in 33?
(really how many ten times will 4 go into 330?)
Answer 8 (tens). Put 8 in tens column on top
Subtract 32 from 33. 'Bring down' 5 from dividend

$$\begin{array}{r} 1\ 8 \\ \hline 4\,|\,7\ 3\ 5 \\ -\ 4 \\ \hline 3\ 3 \\ -\ 3\ 2 \\ \hline 1\ 5 \end{array}$$

Step 3   Look at units column (i.e. 15).
How many 4s in 15?
Answer 3 and 3 remainder

$$\begin{array}{r} 1\ 8\ 3 \\ \hline 4\,|\,7\ 3\ 5 \\ -\ 4 \\ \hline 3\ 3 \\ -\ 3\ 2 \\ \hline 1\ 5 \\ -\ 1\ 2 \\ \hline 3 \end{array}$$

so $735 \div 4 = 183$ remainder 3.

(d) Short division

This is the same method as shown above, but the writing is much abbreviated, with the remainders at each stage being written as small figures in front of the next column:

$$\begin{array}{r} 1\ \ 8\ \ 3\,\text{r}3 \\ \hline 4\,|\,7^3\ 3\ ^15 \end{array}$$

Check 5.3

1 $478 \div 7$

2 $2{,}356 \div 6$

3 $6{,}437{,}109 \div 9$

4 $32{,}064 \div 4$

More complicated cases (3 or more digit numbers divided by 2-digit numbers)

The traditional algorithm for long division can be tedious and difficult to remember, so it may be better to develop other written ways. As with short division, it is possible to either build up to the required amount (i.e. changing it to a multiplication problem) or take away from it (thinking of it as repeated subtraction). Consider the calculation $56{,}435 \div 73$. It is probably helpful to work out $73 \times 2 = 146$ and $73 \times 5 = 365$ first in both methods.

a) Building up

$73 \times 500 = 36{,}500$

$73 \times 200 = 14{,}600 \qquad 36{,}500 + 14{,}600 = 51{,}100$

$73 \times 50 = 3{,}650 \qquad 51{,}100 + 3{,}650 = 54{,}750$

$73 \times 20 = 1{,}460 \qquad 54{,}750 + 1{,}460 = 56{,}210$

$73 \times 2 = 146 \qquad 56{,}210 + 146 = 56{,}356$

$73 \times 1 = 73 \qquad 56{,}356 + 73 = 56{,}429$

Then $500 + 200 + 50 + 20 + 2 + 3 = 773$ and $56{,}435 - 56{,}429 = 6$

So $56{,}435 \div 73$ is 773 remainder 6.

b) Repeated subtraction

Look at the first 2 digits, $56 < 73$			$56{,}435$
so look at first 3 digits (564)	$73 \times 500 = 36{,}500$		$-36{,}500$
			$19{,}935$
	$73 \times 200 = 14{,}600$		$-14{,}600$
Look at first 2 digits of 5335, $53 < 73$			$5{,}335$
So look at first 3 digits	$73 \times 50 = 3{,}650$		$-3{,}650$
			$1{,}685$
	$73 \times 20 = 1{,}460$		$-1{,}460$
Look at first 2 digits of 225, $22 < 73$			225
So look at all 3 digits	$73 \times 2 = 146$		-146
			79
	$73 \times 1 = 73$		-73
			6

So $56{,}435 \div 73 = 500 + 200 + 50 + 20 + 2 + 1 = 773$ remainder 6.

Before using a calculator for division problems, children must be aware that division is not commutative (see Chapter 3) and be able to make a reasonable estimate of the answer. Possibly because they are thinking only of the sharing model of division, some children feel that the larger number must be divided by the smaller one, however they are written. So when confronted with, say, $24 \div 486$, they will enter 486 then $\div$ then 24 into a calculator; but this is $486 \div 24$, quite a different problem. Similar methods of approximation can be used for division as for multiplication. For example, $486 \div 24 \approx 500 \div 20$, or, as it is hundreds divided by tens, the answer will be in tens and as $4 \div 2 = 2$ it will be 2 tens or near 20. Similarly $24 \div 486$ could be approximated to $25 \div 500$ which is approximately $0 \cdot 05$. Some children may find it easier to write this as a fraction. So $\frac{25}{100} = \frac{1}{20}$.

Summary

- Multiplication is usually introduced as 'lots of' and division as 'shares'.
- A great range of practical situations give rise to multiplication and division calculations.
- Rate, ratio and proportion are difficult concepts.
- Common misunderstandings occur when multiplication and division are applied to decimals, especially numbers less than 1.
- There are many ways of writing down multiplication and division calculations. Children should be encouraged to use those they understand.
- Mental methods of approximation should be discussed in primary school.
- Very large and very small numbers are usually written in standard form.

Links with the classroom

1 Which models or diagrams would you use to introduce ideas of ratio and proportion?
2 Which method of recording long multiplication would you introduce first? Why?
3 How would you introduce standard form to older pupils?
4 Which method of division would you introduce first?

Challenges!

1 Investigate Russian multiplication, e.g. 27×43.

Write the numbers side by side at the top of two columns. Divide the number in the left column by 2, ignoring halves, and multiply the right number by 2:

27	43	*
13	86	*
6	172	
3	344	*
1	688	*

Add the numbers in the right hand column opposite odd numbers in left hand column (*)

$43 + 86 + 344 + 688 = 1161$

Does this always work? If so why?

2 A multiplication was set out as shown:

```
            5  6
         ×  2  4
5 × 2 → │ 1  0 │ 2  4 │ ← 6 × 4
        │ 2  0 │       ← 5 × 4
        │ 1  2 │       ← 6 × 2
         1  3  4  4
```

Does this always work? Why or why not?

It is very like the Vedic method of 'vertically and crosswise'. Can you extend the pattern to numbers with more digits? Find out about other methods of Vedic multiplication.

3 Collect mental methods of approximating answers to multiplication and division problems.

4 The standard paper sizes provide a useful resource for studying proportion. Find the ratio of length to width. Using a calculator investigate several other relationships, e.g. length of A4 to length of A3; length of A5 to width of A4; length of A4 × ? = length of A3.

References

Carpenter, T. P., Fennema, E., Franke, M. L., Levi, L. and Empson, S. B. (1999) *Children's Mathematics*. Portsmouth NH: Heinemann.

Dobson, K. (1991) *The Physical World*. Walton-on-Thames: Thomas Nelson and Sons.

Greer, B. (1992) 'Multiplication and division as models of situations', in Grouws, D. A. (ed.) *Handbook of Research on Mathematics Teaching and Learning*. 276–95. New York: Macmillan Publishing Company.

Joseph, G. G. (1991) *The Crest of the Peacock*. Harmondsworth: Penguin Books.

Lacey, P. (1998) *Building numeracy*. Stafford: Robert Powell Publications.

Integers

Starter

THE SUM OF two integers is 8 less than the sum of their squares. Can you find a solution? Are there any more possibilities?

Definitions

In Chapter 3 the need for different types of numbers was discussed. In practical situations, such as measuring height above and below sea level, or temperature above or below freezing point (0°C), or bank balances in credit or debit it is necessary to have numbers which not only have size (magnitude) but also sign or direction (we need to know whether they are above or below 0). Such numbers form an extension of the natural number system below or to the left of 0. Their direction or the side of zero on which they are situated is indicated by a sign. This sign (+ or −) is raised up and written immediately in front of the number. The negative numbers are ordered to the left of 0 and the positive numbers to the right of 0.

The diagram illustrates the negative numbers as 'mirror images' of the positive ones.

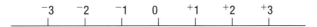

It can be seen that $^-1$ is the same distance from 0 as $^+1$ and $^-3$ is the same distance from 0 as $^+3$. This means that $^-3$ can be defined as that number which when added to $^+3$ makes 0 or in symbols $^+3 + {}^-3 = 0 = {}^-3 + {}^+3$.

Models

The practical situations in which integers were needed provide useful ways of imagining them. So one model for directed numbers is like a thermometer or a ladder in a mine or a lift in a department store.

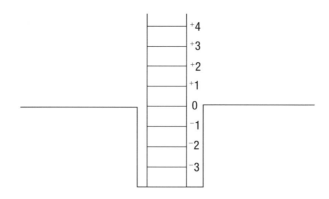

A more satisfactory, but more abstract, way of thinking of integers is as arrows lying along the number line.

A more common visualisation is of 'Sentry Sam' marching back and forth along a number line, with zero in the middle.

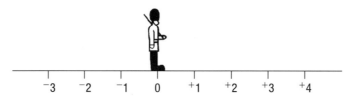

A further way of representing the integers involves a field in which heaps (like molehills) represent positive integers and holes represent negative integers. For example:

$^+5$ could be represented as

and $^-3$ as

The concept of directed numbers is abstract, but children need to have some intuitive feeling for the way they behave and this is facilitated by a grasp of some (preferably more than one) models for them.

Addition and subtraction

Having defined integers and established some situations in which they might be useful, it is necessary to discover how they are affected by the standard mathematical operations. As the positive integers have such a close relation with the natural numbers, they should behave in the same way when added, subtracted, multiplied and divided.

So as $\quad 2 + 3 = 5 \quad$ then $\quad ^+2 + {}^+3 = {}^+5$

and as $\quad 5 - 2 = 3 \quad$ then $\quad ^+5 - {}^+2 = {}^+3$

The question is what happens when negative integers are introduced. What does something like $^+5 + {}^-2$ equal?

First we need some ground rules (although the examples below show specific numbers, the statements can be generalised for all numbers):

(a) $^+3 + {}^+2 = {}^+5$ $\qquad$ (see above)

(b) $^+5 - {}^+2 = {}^+3$ $\qquad$ (see above)

(c) $^+5 + 0 = {}^+5$ $\qquad$ (meaning of zero)

(d) $^+2 - {}^+2 = 0$ and $^-2 - {}^-2 = 0$ $\qquad$ (meaning of subtraction)

(e) $^+2 + {}^-2 = 0 = {}^-2 + {}^+2$ $\qquad$ (meaning of negative number)

These definitions and relationships can be used to develop a reasonable answer. This may appear to be simply 'fiddling with symbols', but in fact we are trying, with small but valid steps, to change what at the moment we cannot do, into something that we know how to manipulate. Although this may be difficult to follow, it is a good example of how deductive argument can help us. Two possible versions are given. The letters on the right show which of the ground rules are being used.

$$
\begin{array}{llll}
& ^+5 + {}^-2 & & \\
= & ^+5 + {}^-2 + \quad 0 & \text{(c)} \\
= & ^+5 + {}^-2 + {}^+2 - {}^+2 & \text{(d)} \\
= & ^+5 + \quad 0 \quad - {}^+2 & \text{(e)} \\
= & ^+5 \qquad\qquad - {}^+2 & \text{(c)} \\
= & ^+3 & \text{(b)} \\
\text{so} & ^+5 + {}^-2 = {}^+3 &
\end{array}
$$

$$
\begin{array}{llll}
\text{As } ^+5 = {}^+3 + {}^+2 & \text{(a)} \\
^+5 + {}^-2 & \\
= {}^+3 + {}^+2 + {}^-2 & \text{(a)} \\
= {}^+3 + \quad 0 & \text{(e)} \\
= {}^+3 & \text{(c)}
\end{array}
$$

This leads to the rule that adding a negative integer is equivalent to subtracting the corresponding positive integer, for example $^+10 + {}^-6 = {}^+10 - {}^+6 = {}^+4$ or $^+3 + {}^-8 = {}^+3 - {}^+8 = {}^-5$.

In a similar way we can look at subtraction. What does $^+3 - {}^-2$ equal? Again we try to replace the part we do not understand with something we can do.

$$
\begin{array}{llll}
& ^+3 \qquad\qquad - {}^-2 & \\
= & ^+3 + \quad 0 \quad - {}^-2 & \text{(c)} \\
= & ^+3 + {}^+2 + {}^-2 - {}^-2 & \text{(e)} \\
= & ^+3 + {}^+2 + \quad 0 & \text{(d)} \\
= & ^+3 + {}^+2 & \text{(c)} \\
= & ^+5 & \text{(a)} \\
\text{so} & ^+3 - {}^-2 = {}^+5. &
\end{array}
$$

$$
\begin{array}{llll}
\text{As } ^+3 = {}^+5 + {}^-2 & \text{(from above)} \\
^+3 - {}^-2 & \\
= {}^+5 + {}^-2 - {}^-2 & \\
= {}^+5 + \quad 0 & \text{(d)} \\
= {}^+5 & \text{(c)}
\end{array}
$$

This leads to the rule that subtracting a negative integer is equivalent to adding the corresponding positive integer e.g. $^+3 - {}^-2 = {}^+5 = {}^+3 + {}^+2$. This is counter-intuitive, so children need some form of explanation or justification.

The discussion above is very close to the formal proof from definitions, but is not suitable for most primary children. A demonstration can be constructed by looking at patterns in subtraction. For example, start with $^+3 - {}^+3$ and construct a table so that the number being subtracted from 3 decreases by one in each line.

$$^+3 - {}^+3 = 0$$
$$^+3 - {}^+2 = {}^+1$$
$$^+3 - {}^+1 = {}^+2$$
$$^+3 - \phantom{{}^+}0 = {}^+3$$
$$^+3 - {}^-1 = {}^+4$$
$$^+3 - {}^-2 = {}^+5$$

If this is worked through for several pairs of numbers, then a pattern can be extracted. It appears that as the number being taken away decreases by one, so the answer increases by one, and this can be adopted as a rule of thumb.

Another approach is to look at some of the models suggested. In each case, actions must be specified which correspond to addition and subtraction, and which model the answers obtained by calculation following the rules derived above. The following four calculations will be illustrated throughout:

$$^+3 + {}^+2 = {}^+5 \quad {}^+3 + {}^-2 = {}^+1 \quad {}^+3 - {}^+2 = {}^+1 \quad {}^+3 - {}^-2 = {}^+5$$

First consider the integer number line and the arrow representation. In all calculations the first arrow is placed with its back at zero. For addition, the back of the second arrow is placed at the point of the first arrow and the position of the point of the second arrow gives the answer. This is like travelling along the arrows to find the answer.

This works well for addition of both positive and negative numbers. To use this model for subtraction new rules for manipulating the arrows must be developed. The point of the second arrow is placed beside the point of the first arrow, then the position of the back of the second arrow gives the answer (this is like moving backwards along the arrow to take away or undo its effect).

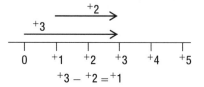 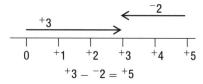

It could be argued that this is pushing the model too far and that it creates more problems than it solves.

We can try another model and a different way of viewing subtraction. Consider the points on the number line as representing integers and think of the difference aspect of subtraction. To start with positive integers where we know the answer, $^+5 - {}^+2$ can be represented as the distance between $^+2$ and $^+5$. This is rather like the 'counting on' strategy for subtraction mentioned in Chapter 5. We know that $^+5 - {}^+2 = {}^+3$ and it is represented as three steps to the right on the number line in the diagram.

It will be noted that this is like standing at the second number and moving to the first. We know that $^+2 - {}^+5 = {}^-3$. This is represented by the distance from $^+5$ to $^+2$ as shown in the diagram.

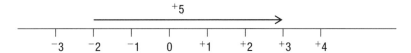

Now looking at $^+3 - {}^-2$. In the model this is represented by the distance from $^-2$ to $^+3$.

From the diagram it is clear that this is five steps to the right, so $^+3 - {}^-2 = {}^+5$.

These representations are somewhat abstract, so what happens in the other models? The other models will not be worked through completely, but a brief indication of how they represent subtracting negative numbers is given. With Sentry Sam the integers tell him the number of steps to take and whether they are to be forwards (+) or backwards (−) and the operations tell him whether to face to the right (addition) or left (subtraction). To model $^+3 - {}^-2$, Sentry Sam starts at $^+3$, turns to face the left, then takes two steps backwards, finishing at $^+5$.

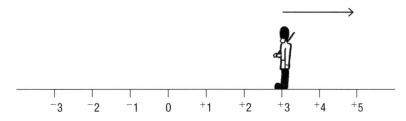

In the same way as subtracting a negative number appears to be equivalent to adding a positive number, so for Sentry Sam facing left and going backwards has the same result as facing right and going forwards. Although it is not necessary for primary children to learn how to manipulate integers, they quite enjoy acting as Sentry Sam (all together as a line of soldiers across the hall), following instructions.

 ## Check 6.1

Try working these out. Use both the rules and the models.

1 $^+10 + {}^-6$

2 $^+15 - {}^+20$

3 $^-4 - {}^-10$

4 $^+6 - {}^-4$

5 $? + {}^-2 = {}^+3$

6 $^+6 - ? = {}^+9$

Some questions from National Tests

7 Here is a table of temperatures at dawn on the same day.

Temperature	°C
London	−4°
Moscow	−6°
New York	−9°
Paris	+6°
Sydney	+14°

What is the difference in temperature between London and Paris?

At noon the temperature in New York has risen by 5°C. What is the temperature in New York at noon?

8 Here is a list of numbers

$^-7 \quad ^-5 \quad ^-3 \quad ^-1 \quad 0 \quad 2 \quad 4 \quad 6$

You can choose some of the numbers from the list and add them to find their total.
For example:

$6 + {}^-1 = 5$

a Choose two numbers from the list which have a total of 3

$\ldots + \ldots = 3$

b Choose two numbers from the list which have a total of $^-1$

$\ldots + \ldots = {}^-1$

Choose two other numbers from the list which have a total of $^-1$

$\ldots + \ldots = {}^-1$

c What is the total of all eight numbers on the list?

d Choose the three numbers from the list which have the lowest possible total. You must not use the same number more than once.

$\ldots + \ldots + \ldots =$

If directed numbers are used, then there must be some consideration of how to enter them into a calculator. Calculators vary. It is impossible to enter negative numbers in some simple ones. In most school calculators the number is entered first, then, if it is negative, the ± (not the −) pressed. This should alter the display, so that a negative number is shown. In more complicated calculators, the negative sign may be entered before the number. Rules for multiplying and dividing integers can be deduced from the axioms or illustrated by looking at the models. Suffice it to say that when multiplying or dividing two numbers, the magnitude of the result is found by multiplying or dividing the numbers as if they were natural numbers, and the sign will be positive if the two original numbers were either both positive or both negative, while it will be negative if they were different. It seems fine that the product of two positive integers should be a positive integer; but there is a problem with the product of two negative integers. The result is often remembered as the rule 'Two minuses make a plus'. At times this statement can be very misleading. For example in the expression $^-5 + {}^-3$, the two minuses do not make a plus, as the answer is $^-8$. It is only when two negative numbers are multiplied together that the rule applies, for example $^-5 \times {}^-3 = {}^+15$.

 ## Check 6.2

Work out these both without and with a calculator.

1 $^+26 - {}^+32$
2 $^-15 - {}^-21$
3 $^+10 - {}^-5$
4 $^-5 + {}^-13$
5 $^+15 - {}^-5$

Summary

- The need for integers can arise in practical situations, where numbers less than zero are required.
- Consistent rules for addition and subtraction can be developed intuitively from patterns and rigorously from definitions.
- Models for directed number and operations on them are commonly used.

Links with the classroom

1 How might the need for negative numbers arise in primary school?
2 How would you persuade able Year 6 pupils that taking away a negative number was equivalent to adding a positive integer?

Challenges!

1 Work out how the rules for addition and subtraction of integers are modelled in the thermometer (or ladder in a mine, or a lift in a department store) or the heaps and holes model.

2 How can the models be extended to cover multiplication and division?

3 Try developing (either by pattern or from definitions) the rules of signs for multiplication and division of integers.

4 Fill in the missing numbers in this grid:

Make up some more grids with integer entries like this and try them out on a friend.

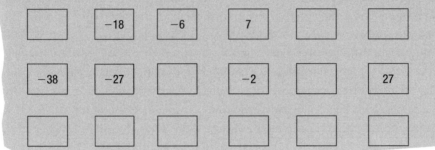

References

Chilvers, P. (1985) 'A consistent model for operations on directed numbers', *Mathematics in School*, **14**(1), 26–8.

7

Fractions, decimals and percentages

Starter

An Arabian sheikh had 3 sons and 17 camels. In his will he left ½ of his camels to his oldest son, ⅓ to his middle son and ⅑ to his youngest son. When their father died the young men were troubled by what they should do. They couldn't see how to carry out their father's will without killing the camels and cutting them up. A stranger came along with 1 camel. He offered to solve their problem. He put his own camel with the other 17, then told the oldest son to take 9 camels (½ of 18); the middle son to take 6 camels (⅓ of 18) and the youngest son to take 2 camels (⅑ of 18). The visitor then claimed his own camel and went on his way. Why did the trick work?

Practical need for numbers smaller than one

The need for some other type of number between the integers arises in two main ways. First when measuring, it is often desirable to state the quantity (e.g. length) to a greater degree of accuracy than the nearest whole unit. For example, when measuring the height and width of a door, it is not sufficient to give it to the nearest inch or centimetre, if it is to fit well. So a smaller unit (usually tenths of the standard unit) can be used.

Secondly in 'sharing' situations, frequently the number of objects (e.g. sweets) to be shared out is not a multiple of the number between which the sharing is to take place, so there is a remainder. Another way to cope with this is to subdivide the whole units in the remainder and distribute the parts.

There are three main ways of thinking about and writing these parts, namely fractions (rational numbers see Chapter 3), decimals and percentages. The same sized part can be written in all three ways, so a half is shown by ½, 0·5 and 50%. But each way of writing involves a different way of looking at the part and has different advantages and difficulties, so they will be discussed separately.

Rational fractions

Although children meet the symbols of ½ and ¼ early and learn to read them accurately, this form can be difficult. Both the notation and basic concepts are complex. The Egyptians only used unit fractions, that is fractions with a numerator of 1 such as ⅓ or ½, and this is the form to be introduced earliest in the National Numeracy Strategy. Children need to realise that this symbol, apparently with two numbers, actually refers to one bit. So ¼ can be thought of as 1 whole one divided into 4 equal parts and just one of those parts is selected. A suitable model might be an apple or a pizza which is divided between 4 children. A little practical experience will show that the larger the number of people sharing the pizza, the smaller the piece each one will get. Hence the larger the denominator, the smaller the size of a unit fraction, so ⅕ is smaller than ¼.

After their experience with natural numbers, many children find this counter intuitive and confusing. The link with division (or sharing) should be stressed.

If a square pizza or cake is divided into, say, 4 parts, it is quite possible to take more than one part and this can be shown as a fraction where the numerator is greater than one, for example, ¾ means 3 parts each of which is the size of a whole one divided into 4 parts. Alternatively ¾ can be thought of as 3 divided by 4 (3 ÷ 4), that is 3 cakes each of

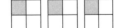

which is divided into 4 and one quarter from each is taken.

Of course, if there are two pizzas, each divided into 4 parts, it would be possible to take 5 pieces, which could be written as ⁵⁄₄ (an improper fraction) or 1¼ (a mixed number).

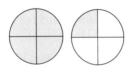

Although the model of a pizza has been used to introduce the concepts of fractions, it is not the only model and indeed has certain shortcomings. Other possibilities include a bar (of chocolate), coloured balls, jugs and the number line. So ¾ could be shown as:

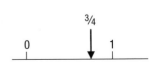

On the CD there is a program which shows fractions (up to 3 whole ones) in various representations. First choose a fraction, then select two representations. The given fraction will be shown in the two styles. The number line representation shows the link with decimals (sometimes called decimals fractions), which will be discussed more fully later.

Fractions as operators

If 20 sweets are divided equally between 4 children, each will get 5 sweets (see Chapter 5). We could say that one child's share is ¼ of the total number of sweets. So ¼ of 20 is 5. In this case the model of coloured balls (or marbles) is probably appropriate. The link with division is very clear in this example. And the fraction (¼) behaves like an operator (i.e. it tells us to do something with 20). So what would ⅝ of 32 mean? ⅝ tells us that the whole (32) is to be divided into 8 equal parts, so each part will be 4; and of these parts, 5 are selected; that is 5 lots of 4 which makes 20. So ⅝ of 32 is 20. This can be illustrated with marbles as:

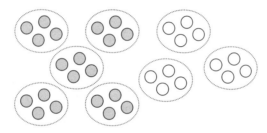

Check 7.1

1 What is ¼ of 12?
2 What is ½ of 28?
3 What is ⅗ of 50?
4 What is ¾ of 24?
5 What is 5⁄7 of 14?

Equivalent fractions

Consider two identical pizzas A and B. A is divided into 8 equal slices and B into 4 equal slices.

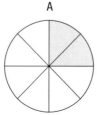

A

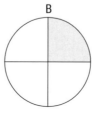

B

If Anna has 2 slices of A (²⁄₈) and Basil has 1 slice of B (¼), who has the bigger piece? Assuming the cutting is accurate and no crumbs are lost, it is apparent from the diagram that they both have the same amount. So ²⁄₈ is equivalent to ¼. This idea of being able to write the same amount in many different ways is difficult for many children to grasp. With natural numbers and integers each number can be written in one unique way, such as 2 or ⁺3 or ⁻1, but with fractions the same amount can be written in many ways, so ¼ is equivalent to ²⁄₈ and also to ³⁄₁₂, ⁵⁄₂₀, ¹⁰⁄₄₀, ²⁵⁄₁₀₀ and so on. Even when they acknowledge that a half can be written as ⁵⁄₁₀ or ⁶⁄₁₂ they may still not be able to generalise to more complicated fractions. So they may write ³⁄₇ = ⁶⁄₁₄ but then say that ⁶⁄₁₄ is bigger because the numbers are bigger. Much discussion and practice are necessary to help them see that a larger number of smaller pieces can be equivalent to a smaller number of larger pieces. A similar concept arises in measurement: for example, if a distance is measured in metres (a large unit) it may be, say, 2 metres; but if the same distance is measured in centimetres (a small unit), then there will be a large number of units, namely 200. Two metres and 200 centimetres represent the same length (see Chapter 10). The concept of equivalent fractions is very important later when children have to add and subtract fractions, so care must be taken to present it well.

If any fraction can be written in any number of ways, then it is pertinent to ask whether one form is preferable to another. This depends on what is being done with them, but if a fraction is standing alone, for example as an answer, then it is usual to write it in its 'lowest form', for example, ¾ is better than ⁹⁄₁₂. Children can be taught how to do this as a mechanical routine, called cancelling (which is how more experienced practitioners do it) but it should also be illustrated as grouping together slices or parts, so

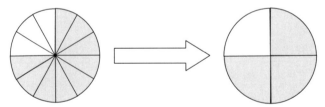

Once the idea of equivalent fractions has been grasped, it is possible to answer questions such as, which is bigger, ¾ or ⅔? It is possible to guess or estimate on a diagram, but to be quite sure, it is necessary to change their form so that the amount stays the same, but their denominators are equal (i.e. the pieces are the same size). In this case we can change each fraction into twelfths.

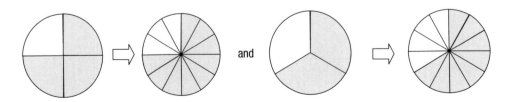

and

So ¾ becomes ⁹⁄₁₂ and ⅔ becomes ⁸⁄₁₂. Clearly ⁹⁄₁₂ is larger than ⁸⁄₁₂ (by ¹⁄₁₂) so ¾ is bigger than ⅔. Another way to answer such a question is to change both fractions to decimals (which will be discussed later).

Operations on and with fractions

Although the National Curriculum for primary schools does not include adding, subtracting, multiplying or dividing fractions, it is desirable for teachers to understand how these basic operations are carried out so they see where ideas of equivalence can be used. Fortunately they do not have to cope with the multiple misapprehensions which can (and do) arise.

Addition and subtraction

It is probably best to start with concrete situations, so that there is a ready-made model available. For example, if Yusef eats ½ of a pizza for lunch, then later has another ⅓ of the original pizza, is it possible to say how much he has had as a single fraction?

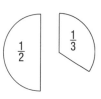

It is possible to put the two parts together, but the result cannot be represented as a single fraction as yet. In order to do this it is necessary to convert each part into an equivalent form which can be manipulated. This means that each piece must be subdivided into parts which are the same size. So, in our example, if each pizza is divided into small slices each $\frac{1}{6}$ of a whole pizza, then Yusef eats $\frac{3}{6}$ and $\frac{2}{6}$ of the pizza. It is then possible to add the parts, so $\frac{3}{6} + \frac{2}{6} = \frac{5}{6}$. Of course this only works in an ideal world where each part is equal and no crumbs are wasted. Subtraction is handled in the same way.

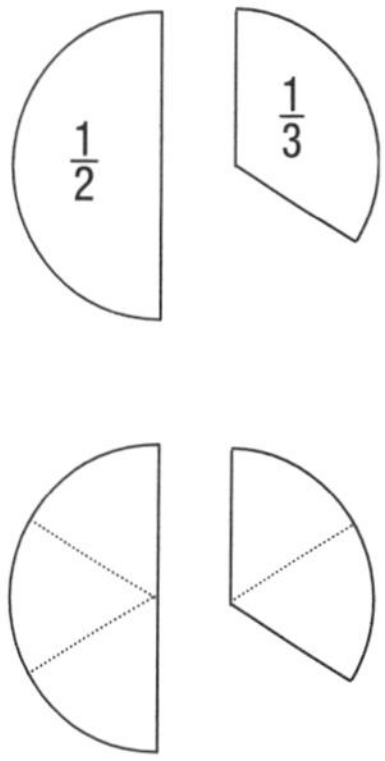

A cake is being shared between some children. Alex takes ⅓ and Jane takes ¼. How much of the cake is left? There are two ways of thinking about this. Either the total amount of cake taken can be found (by adding ⅓ and ¼) then the result is taken away from 1; or first ⅓ is taken away from 1 and then ¼ subtracted from the result. In the first method when adding ⅓ and ¼, it is necessary to subdivide each piece, regarding them as groups of small pieces, each ¹⁄₁₂ of the whole cake.

$$\text{Then } \frac{1}{3} = \frac{1 \times 4}{3 \times 4} = \frac{4}{12} \quad \text{and} \quad \frac{1}{4} = \frac{1 \times 3}{4 \times 3} = \frac{3}{12} \quad \text{so} \quad \frac{1}{3} + \frac{1}{4} = \frac{4}{12} + \frac{3}{12} = \frac{7}{12}.$$

If the whole cake were divided into twelfths and 7 parts were taken away there would be 5 parts left.

$$1 - \frac{7}{12} = \frac{12}{12} - \frac{7}{12} = \frac{5}{12} \quad \text{so} \quad \frac{5}{12} \text{ of the cake is left.}$$

In the second method, first ¼ is taken away from 1 leaving ¾.

i.e. $1 - ¼ = ¾.$

To take away ⅓ from ¾ it is necessary to change both into twelfths;

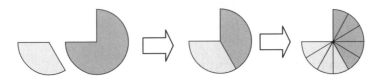

As $\dfrac{3}{4} = \dfrac{3 \times 3}{4 \times 3} = \dfrac{9}{12}$ and $\dfrac{1}{3} = \dfrac{1 \times 4}{3 \times 4} = \dfrac{4}{12}$

Then $\dfrac{3}{4} - \dfrac{1}{3} = \dfrac{9}{12} - \dfrac{4}{12} = \dfrac{9-4}{12} = \dfrac{5}{12}$

So ⁵⁄₁₂ of the cake will be left.

Multiplication and division

The procedure for multiplying fractions appears to be much simpler than that for addition, but the problem situations which give rise to such calculations are more difficult. Situations which might give rise to calculations involving fractions can be discussed using the 'lots of' or 'sets of' model of multiplication (see Chapter 5). If '3 sets of 4' can be found by 3 × 4 = 12, then 'half a set of 4' can be found by ½ × 4 = 2. This can be thought of in two other ways

First as a multiplication	4 × ½
	= 2
Second as division	4 ÷ 2
	= 2

The answer is the same in both cases. In the first method the structure of the problem as 'lots of' is dominant. In the second method the sharing or division aspect of the fraction is dominant with the fraction being regarded as an operator. For more complicated examples it is necessary to appreciate the structure.

If the area or Cartesian product model of multiplication is used, then $\frac{3}{4} \times \frac{2}{3}$ can be shown as

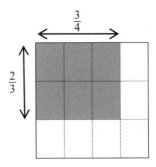

From the diagram it is clear that there will be 4×3 (=12) small rectangles altogether, and of these 3×2 (=6) are required. So $\frac{3}{4} \times \frac{2}{3} = \frac{6}{12} = \frac{1}{2}$.

It appears that to obtain the numerator simply multiply the two numerators (top numbers) and similarly multiply the two denominators (bottom numbers) for the denominator.

After learning the procedure for multiplication, some children try to use a similar one for adding fractions, so that $\frac{1}{2} + \frac{1}{3}$ is thought to be

$$\frac{1}{2} + \frac{1}{3} = \frac{1+1}{2+3} = \frac{2}{5}$$

This shows both a lack of understanding of fractions and the absence of any intuitive model for them. It is probably best to suggest the children go back to practical activities.

A practical situation which requires division by fractions is more difficult to find. The sharing model of division is inappropriate for we do not share objects between fractions of people. Another way to think of division is as repeated subtraction (see Chapter 4), so $10 \div 2$ can thought of as 'How many 2s in 10?' or 'How many times can 2 be taken away from 10?' This sort of problem can also have fractions in it. For example 'How many halves in 10?' could be written as $10 \div \frac{1}{2}$. As there are 2 halves in each unit there are $2 \times 10 = 20$. A more complicated example will be used to illustrate methods of solution. 'How many pieces, each $\frac{2}{5}$ metres in length, can be cut from a rope which is $\frac{9}{10}$ metres long?'

There are three possible ways to solve the problem. In all the methods, it is necessary to change the fractions to an equivalent form, in this case tenths.

a) Building up

Now $\dfrac{2}{5} = \dfrac{4}{10}$

Then $\dfrac{2}{5} + \dfrac{2}{5} = \dfrac{4}{10} + \dfrac{4}{10} = \dfrac{8}{10}$

So 2 pieces can be cut with a small piece ($\frac{1}{10}$) left over.

b) Repeated subtraction:

Rope left	Number of pieces
$\frac{9}{10} - \frac{4}{10} = \frac{5}{10}$	1
$\frac{5}{10} - \frac{4}{10} = \frac{1}{10}$	2

So 2 whole pieces can be cut and a piece $\frac{1}{10}$ m will be left, which is $\frac{1}{4}$ of the length of the other two pieces.

c) Division

$$\frac{9}{10} \div \frac{2}{5}$$

$\frac{2}{5}$ can be thought of as $2 \times \frac{1}{5}$ so the question can be tackled in two parts. First finding how many pieces $\frac{1}{5}$ m long can be cut, then dividing the result by 2.

As 5 pieces each ⅕ m long can be cut from 1 m of rope,

then $5 \times \frac{9}{10} = 4\frac{1}{2}$ pieces can be cut from $\frac{9}{10}$ m of rope.

i.e. 4 pieces each $\frac{1}{5}$ m long can be cut with $\frac{1}{10}$ m left over.

But each piece must be $\frac{2}{5}$ m, not $\frac{1}{5}$ m, so there will be half as many, namely $4\frac{1}{2} \div 2 = 2\frac{1}{4}$

So 2 pieces of $\frac{2}{5}$ m can be cut from the rope with a small piece ($\frac{1}{10}$ m) left over which is $\frac{1}{4}$ of $\frac{2}{5}$.

So $\dfrac{9}{10} \div \dfrac{2}{5} = \dfrac{9}{10} \times 5 \times \dfrac{1}{2} = \dfrac{9}{10} \times \dfrac{5}{2}$

This procedure is sometimes summarised as 'to divide by a fraction, turn it upside-down and multiply'. Another way to justify this is to write the calculation as a fraction i.e. $\frac{9/10}{2/5}$. Now if the numerator and denominator are multiplied by the same number its value will not be altered. ⁵⁄₂ is chosen because when it is multiplied by ⅖ it equals 1 (the denominator becomes 1).

$$\frac{9/10}{2/5} = \frac{9/10 \times 5/2}{2/5 \times 5/2} = \frac{9/10 \times 5/2}{1} = \frac{9}{10} \times \frac{5}{2} = \frac{9}{4} = 2\frac{1}{4}$$

 Check 7.2

Work out the following calculations, draw diagrams to illustrate them and make up stories from which they might have arisen.

1 $\frac{1}{2} + \frac{2}{5}$

2 $\frac{5}{6} - \frac{1}{2}$

3 $\frac{3}{4} \times \frac{2}{3}$

4 $\frac{7}{8} \div \frac{1}{2}$

Decimals (decimal fractions)

As discussed in Chapter 4, our number system uses a base 10, so that each column is ten times larger that the one on its right. This means we can extend the notation to include parts less than one, namely, tenths, hundredths, thousandths and so on. The decimal point is used to indicate the border line between whole numbers and the parts less than one. So 45·637 means $40 + 5 + \frac{6}{10} + \frac{3}{100} + \frac{7}{1000}$. It is important that this is read as 'forty five point six three seven'. Sometimes children read it as 'forty five point six hundred and thirty seven', probably because of the convention of showing money as £5.75 which is read as 'five pounds seventy five pence'.

Any rational fraction can be written in many ways, so that it is possible to express it in terms of tenths or hundredths. For example, ½ can be written as ⁵⁄₁₀ which would be 0·5 in decimal notation. In fact it is possible to change any fraction into a decimal and vice versa. For example, $\frac{1}{4} = \frac{25}{100} = 0\cdot25$.

This can be illustrated on a number line.

It can also be found on a calculator by entering 1 ÷ 4. There are two ways of visualising what is happening when doing such a division calculation. For both, consider a large square representing 1. In the first case imagine this subdivided into 100 little squares (each will be ¹⁄₁₀₀), then there will be 25 little squares (i.e. ²⁵⁄₁₀₀) in a quarter of it (as shown in the diagram below).

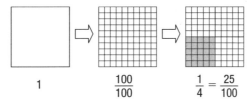

In the second case the large square is divided into tenths (as shown in the diagrams below). We can divide these tenths into 4 groups so that each group has ²⁄₁₀ with ²⁄₁₀ left over. This ²⁄₁₀ can be changed into hundredths and divided between the 4 groups so that there are ⁵⁄₁₀₀ in each group. Then

$$\frac{1}{4} = \frac{2}{10} + \frac{5}{100} = 0.25.$$

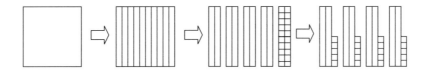

Then fractions like ¾ can be found in the same way by division, or by multiplication i.e. 3 × 0·25 = 0·75. Children should recognise some of the common fractions both as rationals and decimals.

To change a decimal to a rational fraction, it is sufficient to remember our place value system. This means that 0·6 = ⁶⁄₁₀ so ⁶⁄₁₀ is one possible fraction. But it is usual to express a fraction in its lowest terms; and as both numerator and denominator are divisible by 2, 0·6 = ⁶⁄₁₀ = ⅗. Similarly, more complicated decimals can be changed e.g. 0·85 = ⁸⁄₁₀ + ⁵⁄₁₀₀ = ⁸⁵⁄₁₀₀ = ¹⁷⁄₂₀.

Operations on and with decimals

In many ways the rules for adding, subtracting, multiplying and dividing decimals are similar to those used for whole numbers, so most children find them much easier to cope with than fractions (see Chapters 3 and 4).

Addition and subtraction

Once the importance of setting out addition and subtraction calculations correctly has been realised, then the rules developed for hundreds, ten and units can be extended to tenths and hundredths. The vital first step is to align the numbers so that the decimal points are under each other, in order to ensure that equal sized units are aligned. So 1·4364 + 0·67 should be written as

$$
\begin{array}{r}
1{\cdot}4364 \\
+\ 0{\cdot}67 \\
\hline
2{\cdot}1064 \\
\hline
\end{array}
$$

Similarly, in subtraction calculations units of the same size must be directly under each other, so 10·68 − 2·956 should be set out as follows:

$$
\begin{array}{r}
10{\cdot}68 \\
-\ 2{\cdot}956 \\
\hline
7{\cdot}624 \\
\hline
\end{array}
$$

Multiplication and division

It is vital that children understand how to multiply and divide decimal numbers by powers of 10. This is often taught as a rule, e.g. 'to multiply by 10 move the point to the right' and 'to divide by 10, move the point to the left'. Although this gives correct results it is more accurate to think of the decimal point as remaining still while the digits move, so:

$$4{\cdot}621 \times 100 \qquad \text{or} \qquad 56{\cdot}16 \div 10$$
$$= 462{\cdot}1 \qquad\qquad\qquad = 5{\cdot}616$$

i.e. in the first example, the 4 units when multiplied by 100 becomes 400 etc.
in the second example, the 5 tens when divided by 10 becomes 5 units etc.

 The demonstration program 'Powers of ten' on the CD illustrates this very clearly, as the decimal points are always directly underneath each other and the digit cards move to right and left.

All the models used for multiplication in Chapter 5 can be extended to decimals, although the language may have to be adjusted. For example, the 'lots of' model illustrated by leaps along the number line can be used for decimals. For example, to make a picture frame 4 pieces of wood each 0·45 m are needed. How much wood should be bought?

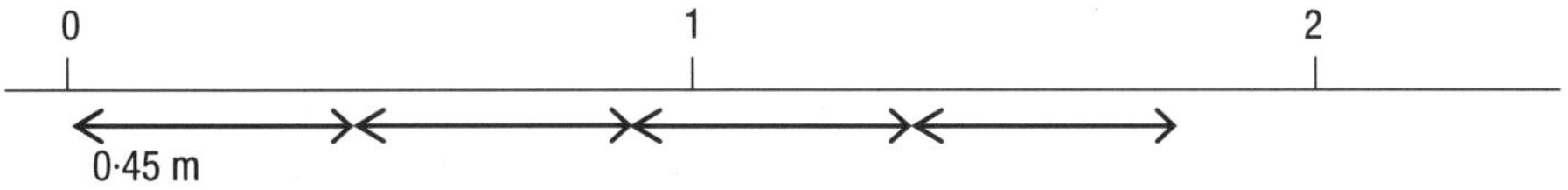

As illustrated in the diagram, 4 × 0·45 = 1·8 m is needed.

In a similar way, practical situations and models should be discussed for division. The fact that the result of a division calculation can be larger than the original numbers is perhaps appreciated more easily from the repeated subtraction view. If a 2-metre ribbon is cut into pieces each 0·25 m long, then it is possible to cut it into 8. Some children have difficulty in understanding that this can be represented by 2 ÷ 0·25.

It is also very important for children to learn to estimate the size of the answer in order to check the result from a calculator. The most common errors arise from transferring ideas from experiences with whole numbers, for example that multiplication always makes bigger and division always makes smaller. Children must be given plenty of experience of multiplying by decimals less than 1 and discussing the results. Again, practical situations and models can be useful. For example, if a quarter of a set of 12 apples is eaten, how many will be left? Most children can visualise this and will be able to say that 3 apples have been eaten, so 9 are left. The number eaten can also be represented as $\frac{1}{4}$ of 12 or $\frac{1}{4}$ × 12 or 0·25 × 12, and can be found on a calculator. Another useful introduction to multiplication and division of decimals is the 'Target game' on a calculator. The rules allow only certain keys to be used e.g. only × and ÷ operations or only certain numbers. A target number is set e.g. 50 and a starting point is given e.g. 91. The challenge is to reach the target with as few calculations as possible.

Check 7.3

1 Write the following as decimals: $\frac{3}{5}$, $\frac{5}{8}$, $\frac{7}{9}$, $\frac{5}{6}$, $\frac{3}{7}$

Find the results of the following calculations and write some word stories for them.

2 15·36 + 7·4
3 9·1 + 3·62
4 5·4 − 3·25
5 7·1 − 4·745
6 6·4 × 0·4
7 2·6 × 1·5
8 12·5 ÷ 2·6
9 5·4 ÷ 0·2
10 David thinks of a number. He uses his calculator to multiply the number by itself and then adds 10. His answer is 34·01. What is David's number? (SAT question)

Percentages

The third method of writing parts is by percentages. These give the number of parts out of a hundred that are required. They were first used in the sixteenth century by merchants who needed to compare parts of different sized quantities. So 40% means that 40 parts out of every hundred parts are selected. In all problems which use percentages, it is important to know exactly to what 100% refers. If there is a 15% tax we have no idea how much this will cost until we are told on what it is being levied. If it is on a book costing £20, then it will be £3, whereas if it is on a computer which cost £2,000, then it will be £300.

Operations on and with percentages

Although they are related to fractions and decimals, percentages are used and manipulated in different ways. It is best to think of them as operators. For example, one of the common practical situations in which percentages are used is in problems about discounts or tax (VAT) on items. So if a music centre was priced at £950 and there is a 15% reduction in a sale, what will the sale price be? There are two ways of solving this problem. The simplest is to find the actual reduction and subtract this from the original price; the quickest is to find the new price directly by calculating $(100 - 15)\%$ of the original price.

Discount = 15% of £950   Sale price = 85% of £950

$£\frac{15}{100} \times 950 = £142.50$ $£\frac{85}{100} \times 950 = £807.50$ or $£0.85 \times 950 = £807.50$

Sale price = £950 − 142.50

           = £807.50

Prices are sometimes given excluding VAT, so that this must be added to find the actual cost to the customer. For example, a computer might be priced at £2,000 + VAT (at 17·5%). The final price (P) will be £2,000 + 17·5% of £2,000.

The actual cost can again be found in several ways.

VAT = 17·5% of £2,000   or   Price = 117·5% of £2,000

$£\frac{17·5}{100} \times 2,000 = £350$ or $£0.175 \times 2,000 = £350$ $£\frac{117·5}{100} \times 2,000 = £2,350$

Final price = £2,000 + 350   Final price = £2,000 + 350

            = £2,350   = £2,350

As $17·5 = 10 + 5 + 2·5$

$$\text{Price (ex. VAT)} = £2,000$$

Then 10% of £2,000 = £ 200

5% of £2,000 = ½ of £200 = £ 100

2·5% of £2,000 = ½ of £100 = £ 50

so 17·5% of £2,000 = £ 350   Then final price = £2,000 + 350 = £2,350

The tricky case occurs when the final price is given and the original price is required. For example, if a suite was sold at £1,275 in the sale with a 15% reduction, what was the original price?

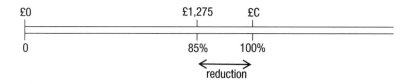

It is incorrect to find 15% of £1,275 and to add it on, because the reduction was 15% of the original price (C), not the final price. So there is only one method of finding the original price. The final price is 85% of the original price, so 85% of original price = £1,275.

Correct method

85% = £1,275

$1\% = £\frac{1,275}{100} = £15$

100% = £15 × 100

= £1,500

Incorrect method

$15\% \text{ of } £1,275 = £\frac{15}{100} × 1,275$

= £191·25

Original price = £1,275 + 191·25

= £1,466·25

Great care must be taken when adding percentages. For example, the numbers of boys and girls in two schools is given below.

	Boys	Girls	Total	Percentage girls
School A	160	140	300	47%
School B	95	70	165	42%

What is the average percentage of girls in the two schools? Because the percentages are of two different quantities (300 and 160) it is incorrect to find their average by adding them and dividing by 2. The only valid method is to find the total number of girls, the total number of pupils and then find the percentage of girls.

Total number of children in the two schools = 300 + 165 = 465

Total number of girls in the two schools = 140 + 70 = 210

So average percentage of girls in the two schools = $\frac{210 × 100}{465} = 45·16 \approx 45\%$

Check 7.4

1 Find 12% of £350.

2 How much VAT (at 17·5%) would be paid on a £750 (excluding VAT) suite?

3 A 20% reduction is offered in a sale. If the pre-sale price of a coat is £120, what would the sale price be?

4 In a restaurant, the bill is calculated by totalling the cost of the food and drink, then adding 10% service charge, then VAT (at 17·5%) is added. Would it make any difference to the customer if the VAT were calculated first, then the service charge? Which way would be best for the restaurant staff?

5 Linda buys a pair of trainers. She says, 'I bought this pair of trainers when there was 20% off the normal price. I paid £18 for them'. What was the normal price? (from National Tests)

6 The number of people going to a cinema increased from 52,000 in 1988 to 761,500 in 1992. Calculate the percentage increase in the number of people from 1988 to 1992.

A question from National Tests

7 A report on the number of police officers in 1995 said:
'There were 19 000 police officers. Almost 15% of them were women.'

   a The percentage was rounded to the nearest whole number, 15. What is the smallest value the percentage could have been, to one decimal place?

   b What is the smallest number of women police officers that there might have been in 1995? (Use your answer to part (a) to help you calculate this answer.) Show your working.

   c A different report gives exact figures:

Number of women police officers	
1988	12 540
1995	17 468

   Calculate the percentage increase in the number of women police officers from 1988 to 1995. Show your working.

   d The table below shows the percentage of police officers in 1995 and 1996 who were women.

1995	14.7%
1996	14.6%

   Use the information in the table to decide which one of the statements below is true.

1 In 1996 there were more women police officers than in 1995

2 In 1996 there were fewer women police officers than in 1995

3 There is not enough information to tell whether there were more or fewer women police officers

Explain your answer.

Some QTS skills test type questions

8 A pupil gains the following marks in 3 exams:

	English	Maths	Science
Pupil's mark	95	72	38
Maximum mark	120	100	60

In which exam did the pupil do best?

9 Look at the following table:

	1999	2000
Number of pupils staying on for Year 14	434	461
Total number of pupils	560	575

a By how many percentage points had the number of pupils staying on increased between 1999 and 2000?

b By what percentage did the numbers staying on increase between 1999 and 2000?

10 There are two papers for A-level Physics. Paper 1 is marked out of 80 and paper 2 out of 110. If a pupil gets 60 for paper 1 and 75 for paper 2, what is his overall mark, expressed as a percentage?

11 There are three elements to a music exam: theory, performance and history. The weighting is 1:2:1. If each is marked out of 100 and a pupil gets 60, 75 and 50, what is her final mark as a percentage? Give a formula for finding the final percentage for a student who gained a, b and c, in the three elements.

Summary

- Quantities with parts of units can be written as fractions, decimals or percentages.
- Fractions are written as an integer divided by an integer, e.g. ¾, ⅗.
- Decimals extend the place value system to parts of a whole, namely tenths, hundredths and so on. The decimal point shows the position of the units digit, e.g. 0·75, 1·6667.
- Percentages give the number of parts per hundred, e.g. 75%, 167%.
- Children should be introduced to various models for fractions.
- Percentages make comparisons of proportions in different cases easier.

Links with the classroom

1 How would you explain that 0·23 is not 'zero point twenty-three'? What might lead children to think this?
2 What activities and discussion might help children understand that $6 \times \frac{1}{3}$ is equivalent to $6 \div 3$?
3 What investigations or games might be used to show that 'multiplication makes bigger' is not true for numbers less than 1?
4 How would you set up an investigation into the relation between fractions and decimals?

Challenges!

1 Investigate Egyptian fractions. Are there any advantages to their notation?
2 Choose two numbers. Is their sum greater or less than their product? If the two numbers are x and y, under what conditions is $x + y > xy$? Investigate when $xy < x/y$? Can you find any numbers such that $x + y < y/x$ and at the same time $x + y < x/y$?
3 $\frac{50}{100} = 0·5$. Is $\frac{51}{101}$ more or less than 0·5? What happens if you go on adding 1 to the top and the bottom? What about subtracting 1? What about other numbers?
4 Choose a number (N) (say 8). Using a calculator, enter 1, * multiply by N (press =), take square root, take square root, record the result. Repeat from * until two consecutive results are the same, correct to two decimal places. What have you found? Can you make up other converging sequences?

References

Dickson, L., Brown, M. and Gibson, O. (1984) *Children Learning Mathematics*. Eastbourne: Holt, Rinehart and Winston, for Schools Council.

Kerslake, D. (1986) *Fractions: Children's Strategies and Errors*. Berkshire: NFER-Nelson.

Mason, K. and Ruddock, G. (1986), *Decimals Assessment at age 11 and 15*. Berkshire: Assessment of Performance Unit, NFER-Nelson.

8

Understanding algebra

Starter — card trick

ASK SOMEONE TO think of a playing card (not a King), then carry out the following calculation.

> Take the value of the card (spot value; Jack, Queen, King are 11, 12, 13)
>
> Add on next highest value (e.g. if 9 diamonds then add 9 and 10)
>
> Multiply the result by 5
>
> If the card is a club add 1, a heart add 2, a spade add 3, a diamond add 4.

Ask for answer. Subtract 5 from answer. The units digit gives the suit (as above), the tens and hundreds digits reveal the card value (e.g. if final total = 66, subtract 5 = 61, card was six of clubs).

Does this always work? If so why?

Nature of algebra

When asked what they think algebra is, students often say 'arithmetic with letters' or 'generalised arithmetic'. It is certainly true that the rules of manipulation in algebra and arithmetic are basically the same and that letters are used as well as numbers, but there are important differences. The word 'algebra' comes from a ninth century book by Al-Khwarizmi (an Arab mathematician) called *Hisab al-jabr w'al-muqabala* (Calculation by Restoration and Reduction). It was a blend of many mathematical traditions including Babylonian, Indian and Greek and included the solution of problems of inheritance and property division (among many others). The use of mathematical knowledge to solve practical problems is at the root of algebra. In fact it can be thought of as a highly compact and efficient set of tools for solving problems (practical and theoretical).

One of the initial difficulties in setting down a problem is how to represent the answer we are trying to find; this is called the unknown. In algebra if it is a number, it is often represented by a letter such as 'a' or 'x'. This can lead to misunderstandings.

In arithmetic letters are used as abbreviations for units of measurement, for example if the length of a garden is under consideration then 12 m means 12 metres. Sometimes expressions such as $3a + 4b$ are said to mean '3 apples and 4 bananas'. This is interpreting the letters in an arithmetic context and can be misleading. In an algebraic context, $3a + 4b$ means 3 times one number plus 4 times another, that is, 'a' and 'b' do not represent apples and bananas, they stand for unknown numbers. If 'a' was 5 and 'b' was 2 then:

$3a + 4b$ would be $3 \times 5 + 4 \times 2 = 15 + 8 = 23$.

In primary school it may be better to introduce other signs for the unknown at first. In some early maths books a box is used to represent an unknown number, for example $3 + \square = 7$ and the children are expected to put the appropriate number in the box. Other possible ways are to use a ? or a cloud symbol ⌒. These have the advantage of being less definite and suggesting the possibility of 'trial and improvement'.

At this point it should be mentioned that this use of letters or boxes to represent an unknown is not the same as the use of letters to represent variables in functions (see Chapter 9). In the statement $3 + \square = 7$ or $3 + a = 7$, the box or 'a' stand for a single number, in this case 4. However, in the statement $y = 3 + x$, x can take many values and depending on the value it takes y can be calculated. In this case x and y are called variables. Although x and y are often used to represent variables, other letters may also be used. For example, $p = 3 + q$ would represent the same function.

Many children regard the $=$ sign as a command to 'find the answer', that is to do something. It is read as 'makes'. This is sometimes called the 'calculator model' of $=$. So the statement $3 + 4 = 7$ is read as 'Three add four makes seven'. In algebra this reading does not make sense. Consider the algebraic statement $(x - y)^2 = x^2 - 2xy + y^2$. The $=$ sign should be read here as 'equals' or 'is equivalent to' or 'is the same as' because the statement is always true whatever value x and y may take. The picture (or model) of a beam balance, with the two pans containing different objects but with the same mass, is useful. Just as the two sides of the balance may look different but they are the same in one important respect, so the two sides of an algebraic equation may look different, but they represent the same amount, whatever numbers the letters represent.

Another difficulty is the convention that xy means $x \times y$. As explained in Chapter 3, children may be tempted to interpret this within the place value notation. However, the placing of letters next to each other and next to numbers should be read as involving multiplication, so $2x = 2 \times x$ and $2xy = 2 \times x \times y$. To avoid confusion, it is probably best to include the multiplication signs in any work done in the primary school. In fact symbolic manipulation is not appropriate for Key Stage 1 or 2. The use of brackets might be included for some Year 6s, but is probably best introduced through arithmetic.

It has been said the mathematics is the study of patterns. This is rather too general, but it includes an element of truth. Algebra is a very powerful way of expressing patterns concisely. It is concerned with generalities and finding equivalences among expressions. For example, when finding the perimeter of rectangles pupils may start by adding the lengths of all the sides, e.g. $2 + 7 + 2 + 7 = 18$ cm.

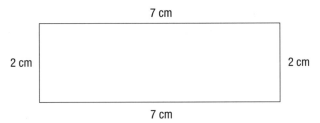

They may then realise they can find the distance more efficiently by either (a) adding the lengths and the breadth and doubling the answer or (b) doubling the length and breadth and then adding them. To show that either of these will always work, they can be expressed in algebraic form and the equivalence demonstrated.

(a) Perimeter	$= (l + b) \times 2$	$= l \times 2 + b \times 2$	$= 2l + 2b$
(b) Perimeter	$= l \times 2 + b \times 2$	$= 2l + 2b$	
Also perimeter	$= l + b + l + b$	$= l + l + b + b$	$= 2l + 2b$

This search for pattern and equivalences is a suitable (and can be an exciting) undertaking for primary children. The formal symbolic manipulation, which so many regard as algebra, is not.

Doing and undoing

This study of patterns can start in Key Stage 1. For example, children can be asked to predict the next number after 1, 3, 5, 7, and then to explain how they worked it out. This leads to the idea of doing the same thing each time, in this case 'add 2'. More difficult patterns could be attempted, for example 11, 15, 19, . . . this provides good practice in mental arithmetic. It is also useful to ask the children to 'undo' a pattern. For example, having established the rule 'add 4' for the second example, what would be the number before 15? and the number before 11? What is the 'undoing' rule? What is the relation between the 'doing' rule and the 'undoing' rule?

Another Key Stage 2 activity might be the game 'Guess my rule'. In this the teacher, or one group of children, decide on a 'rule' and the others try to discover it by asking for its effect on different numbers. For example, say the rule was 'multiply by 2 then add 4', then if 3 is offered, the answer after applying the rule would be $3 \times 2 + 4 = 10$. It is easier to spot the relation if the input and results are entered into a table, such as the one below.

input	3	1	0	20	12	0·5	−1
result	10	6	4	44	28	5	2

The practice in mental arithmetic is useful, as well as the discussion that might occur if more than one rule were suggested. For example in the above case the rule could be 'multiply by 2 then add 4' or 'add 2 then multiply by 2'. Do these two rules always give the same results? Algebraic notation can be used to clarify the position. First, a symbol to stand for any number (the input) must be agreed, say 'p'. Then the first rule can be written as:

Think of a number	multiply by two	then add four
p	$p \times 2 = 2p$	$2p + 4$

In this p stands for any number and $p \times 2 = 2p$ because multiplication is commutative (see Chapter 3).

In the same way the second rule can be written:

Think of a number	add two	then multiply by two
p	$p + 2$	$(p + 2) \times 2 = 2(p + 2)$

Again p is any number and $(p + 2)$ must be put in a bracket, so that it is done first. As multiplication is commutative $(p + 2) \times 2 = 2(p + 2)$.

The question 'are the two rules the same?' can now be written as 'Is $2p + 4 = 2(p + 2)$?' The rules of arithmetic and algebra can now be applied to the symbolic statement

$$2(p + 2) = 2 \times p + 2 \times 2 \text{ (multiplication is distributive over addition)}$$
$$= 2p + 4$$

This means that whatever number is put instead of the letter 'p', $2(p + 2)$ will give the same result as $2p + 4$. So, with algebra, it is possible to prove the equivalence of the two rules. It would be unsuitable and unnecessary to do this at primary level, but it could be shown that they gave the same results for all those numbers tried. It can also be interesting to discuss how this rule could be 'undone', that is how to get from answer to the input. In the above example, how can 'multiply by 2 and add 4' be undone? What rule will take 10 to 3, 6 to 1 and so on? A first attempt might be 'divide by 2 and take away 4', but this does not work. The order of the operations must also be reversed, so the 'undoing' or inverse rule is 'take away 4 then divide by 2'.

Another game which provides both good practice in mental arithmetic and an introduction to algebra is 'Think of a number' or THOAN for short. This can be introduced as a 'magic' trick or puzzle. For example, the instructions might be:

Think of a number, add 1, multiply by 2, divide by 2, take away the number you first thought of and the answer is (pause) 1.

Is this always true? And if so, why? Even in the written form it is possible to see what is happening. In the middle the 'multiply by 2, then divide by 2' cancel each other out (division is the inverse of multiplication). So the instructions could be simplified to 'Think of a number, add 1, take away the number you first thought of' and the result must be 1. This can also be shown with algebraic symbols. Choose a letter (or symbol) for the number thought of, say 'n', then write down what happens.

Think of a number	add 1	multiply by 2	divide by 2	take away the number you first thought of
n	$n + 1$	$2(n + 1)$	$\dfrac{2(n + 1)}{2}$	$\dfrac{2(n + 1)}{2} - n$

So if the first number is n, after applying all the instructions the result will be $\frac{2(n + 1)}{2} - n$. Now it is possible to simplify this expression using the rules of algebra. This can be thought of in two equivalent ways, both of which are shown below.

$$\frac{2(n + 1)}{2} - n$$

Divide top and bottom of
the fraction by 2.

$$= \frac{2^1(n + 1)}{2^1} - n$$

This is often referred to as 'cancelling'

$$= n + 1 + n$$

$$= 1$$

$$\frac{2(n + 1)}{2} - n$$

Multiply the bracket out,
write n as $\frac{2n}{2}$

$$= \frac{2n + 2 - 2n}{2}$$

$$= \frac{2}{2}$$

$$= 1$$

To do this it is essential to be aware of the conventions followed in writing algebraic expression and the basic rules for manipulation. It would be unsuitable to do this with the children, but discussion of the reason why it works would bring out the inverse nature of multiplication and division, and of addition and subtraction. These THOANs can become quite complicated, as can be seen in the puzzle invented by Fibonacci and given in the Challenges section at the end of this chapter.

✎ Check 8.1

1 Write down possible algebraic instructions for these 'rules':
  a add 4, multiply by 3
  b add 10, subtract 5
  c multiply by 2, add 6, multiply by 5, subtract 15
  d multiply by 4, add 8, divide by 2, take away 1

2 Try tracing what is happening in these THOANs. Do they always work?
  a multiply by 3, add 12, divide by 3, take away the number you first thought of, the answer is 4

b multiply by 2, add 4, multiply by 3, add 12, divide by 6, take away the number you first thought of, divide by 4, the answer is 1

c multiply by 2, add 4, multiply the result by 5, divide this result by 10, take away the number you first thought of, the answer is 2

3 Make up some THOANs of your own.

Sequences

Copying, continuing and inventing patterns is now part of the mathematics curriculum from the beginning of Key Stage 1 and can be fruitful throughout the primary school. The simple examples given at the beginning of the previous section (doing and undoing) are sequences, that is a succession of terms following some rule. As another example, consider 2, 4, 6, . . . there are two ways in which the rule can be given, both of which can be expressed in words or symbols. The above sequence can be written in a table as shown.

Number of term	1	2	3	4	5	6
Value of term	2	4	6	8	10	12

The rule for the sequence above might be given as 'add 2'. This means that to find the value of a term, 2 must be added to the value of the previous term. This is called a recursive formula for the value of a term is given in terms of the one before. It can be written as 'the value of a term' = 'the value of the previous term' + 2, or the value of the nth term is the value of the $(n − 1)$th term add 2. This is fine for finding out the value of terms early in the sequence, but if the value of, say, the 100th term is required, it would take some time to calculate.

In many cases it is possible and very useful to give a general formula which links the number of the term directly to its value. In the case above, if the number of the term is multiplied by 2 it gives the value of the term, e.g. $1 × 2 = 2$; $2 × 2 = 4$ and so on. This can be written as:

$$\text{'the value of the term'} = \text{number of term} × 2$$
$$= 2 × n$$
$$= 2n$$
$$\text{where } n \text{ is the number of the term}$$

Using this general formula it is quite simple to work out the value of the 100th term $= 2 × 100 = 200$.

In Year 3 or Year 4 the search for patterns may take the form of looking at several models and trying to find a rule which governs the relation between one model and the next. This type of investigation might be set up as follows:

Suppose some models are made of bricks (say Multilink) as shown:

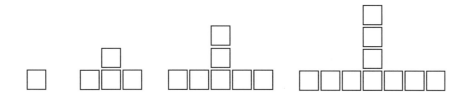

Make the next model. How many cubes are used in each model? If you made the sixth model, how many cubes would you need? What about the tenth model, or the hundredth?

There are several stages in this sort of investigation and not all children will manage to complete them all.

a   The models given must be studied and the relation between one model and the next spotted. In the above case it might be expressed as 'Add one cube to each arm'. There is usually more than one way of seeing what is happening.

b   The next model (in this case the fifth) is constructed.

c   The number of cubes in each model is counted and recorded. A table such as the one below is a neat way of doing this.

Number of term	1	2	3	4	5	6
Value of term	1	4	7	10		

d   The number of cubes in the sixth model can be found either by actually making the model or by extending the pattern in numbers in the bottom line or by both.

e   The challenge to find the number of cubes in the 10th model is intended to encourage the children to concentrate on what happens between one model and the next. This may refer to the model, e.g. 'put a block on each arm' or to the numbers in the table, e.g. 'add 3'. The children might then be able to extend the table to the 10th model and find the number of cubes by adding 3 to the previous number in the bottom line each time.

Number of term	1	2	3	4	5	6	7	8	9	10
Value of term	1	4	7	10	13	16	19	22	25	28

f   The final challenge to find the number of cubes in the 100th model could be found by extending the table to 100, but is intended to encourage the children to find a general relation. This relation is between the number of the model and the number of bricks in it or the numbers in the top and bottom lines of the table. The relation might be described as 'times the top number by 3 then take away 2'. Again there are several ways of seeing this relation and the 'guess' should be tested against all the results obtained so far.

Then the number in the 10th model is $10 \times 3 - 2 = 30 - 2 = 28$
and the number in the 100th model is $100 \times 3 - 2 = 300 - 2 = 298$.

Few children will reach the last stage, but most will be able to make the table and find the number in the sixth and perhaps the tenth model.

Because the study of sequences is an important part of mathematics, some special notation and conventions have developed. This notation is not suitable for primary school but may be encountered in mathematical texts. A particular sequence can be identified by a letter, for example 'u'. Each term of the sequence is identified by a small number written after the u and in the subscript position. So u_1 means 'the value of the first term', u_2 means 'the value of the second term'. Using this notation we can say, for the sequence above,

$$u_1 = 1 \qquad u_2 = 4 \qquad u_3 = 7 \qquad u_4 = 10$$

The recursive formula for the number of bricks needed in the nth model is, in words 'add 3 to the number in the previous model' or in symbols $u_n = u_{n-1} + 3$. This states that the number of bricks in the nth model is equal to the number of bricks in the previous [$(n-1)$th] model add 3. The general rule or formula is more difficult to see. It is rather like the 'Guess my rule' game. In this case it might be 'times the number of the model by 3 then take away 2'. In symbols this becomes $u_n = 3n - 2$, that is the number of bricks in the nth model is 3 times n take away 2.

To give another example of this type of investigation, consider making square picture frames from cubes such as Multilink.

The first few models are shown below. The number of cubes in each model is recorded in the table.

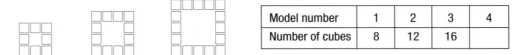

Model number	1	2	3	4
Number of cubes	8	12	16	

The recursive formula for the number of cubes in a given model seems to be 'add four to the number in the previous model' or $u_n = u_{n-1} + 4$. It is possible to give the general formula in several ways, which can be linked to ways of viewing the models. Taking the second model as an example:

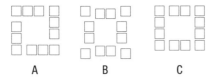

A   B   C

The first way (A) is 4×3, the second (B) is $4 \times 2 + 4$ and the third (C) is $2 \times 4 + 2 \times 2$. All these give the correct result of 12 cubes. These different ways of viewing a general formula are tabulated below for 2nd, 3rd, 4th and nth models.

Model number	A	B	C
2	4 × 3	4 × 2 + 4	2 × 4 + 2 × 2
3	4 × 4	4 × 3 + 4	2 × 5 + 2 × 3
4	4 × 5	4 × 4 + 4	2 × 6 + 2 × 4
n	4 × (n + 1)	4 × n + 4	2 × (n + 2) + 2 × n

The rules of algebra can be used to show that all three general expressions are equivalent.

A $\quad$ 4 × (n + 1) = 4n + 4 (multiplication is distributive over addition)

B $\quad$ 4 × n + 4 = 4n + 4

C $\quad$ 2 × (n + 2) + 2 × n $\quad$ = 2n + 4 + 2n (multiplication is distributive over addition)

$\qquad\qquad\qquad\qquad\qquad\qquad\quad$ = 2n + 2n + 4 (addition is commutative)

$\qquad\qquad\qquad\qquad\qquad\qquad\quad$ = 4n + 4

In all the sequences considered so far, one term has been found by adding a given number to the previous term. Of course there are similar sequences in which a given number may be subtracted from each term, for example, 10, 6, 2, ¯2, . . . Sequences in which a given number is added or subtracted from each term are called arithmetic sequences or progressions. But sometimes one term in a sequence is found by multiplying the previous term by a given number. These are called geometric progressions. For example, look at the following sequence:

Model number	1	2	3	4	5
Value	1	2	4	8	16

The recursive rule seems to be 'multiply by 2'. If the terms up to 10 are calculated, it will be appreciated that the value of the terms increase rapidly. The delightful story of the reward claimed for the invention of chess, given in the Challenges at the end of this chapter, involves this sequence.

This sort of investigation need not start with physical models; it can be applied to a sequence of numbers, as explained at the beginning of this section. One very interesting sequence starts 1, 1, 2, 3, 5, 8, 13. It is called a Fibonacci sequence after the man who first studied it and the numbers in it can be found in various natural phenomena. The recursive formula states that the number in a term equals the sum of the numbers in the two previous terms or in symbols $u_n = u_{n-1} + u_{n-2}$.

✎ Check 8.2

1 Look at the following diagrams of models:
Draw the next model. Make a table showing the numbers of cubes in each model. How many cubes will be needed for the 5th, 12th and 80th models?

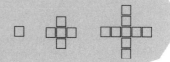

2 Look at the following number sequence: 3·5, 5, 6·5, 8,

What is the next number? Can you find a recursive formula (give it in words or symbols)? What about a general formula?

3 Look at this sequence: 9, 6, 3,

What is the next term? What about the sixth term?

Can you suggest a formula? Find the 20th term?

4 Examine this sequence: 16, 8, 4, 2,

What is the next term? Suggest a recursive rule for finding the next term.

Some questions from National Tests

5 Ann makes a pattern of L shapes with sticks:

Shape number	1	2	3
Number of sticks	7	11	15

Ann says 'I find the number of sticks for a shape by first multiplying the shape number by 4, then adding 3'. Work out the number of sticks for the shape that has shape number 10. Ann used 59 sticks to make another L shape. What is its shape number? Write a formula to work out the number of sticks for any L shape. Use S for the number of sticks and N for the shape number.

6 Here is a sequence of towers built from cubes:

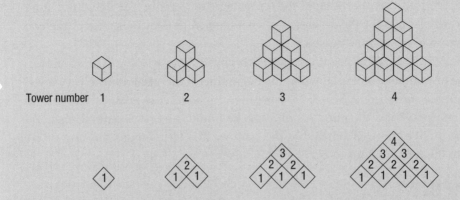

Tower number   1   2   3   4

These are the plans of each tower.

The numbers show how many cubes are in each vertical column.

How many cubes are required to build tower 5? What is the number of the tower in this sequence which uses 165 cubes?

7 Abdi starts a sequence of numbers. He begins with 10,000 and subtracts 7 each time. The first five numbers in his sequence are:

| 10,000 | 9,993 | 9,986 | 9,979 | 9,972 |

Abdi says 'If I continue my sequence, the first negative number in it will be ⁻3' Is Abdi correct? Explain how you know.

8 Fill in the empty boxes to complete the pattern:

$n + 6$		$7n + 6$
	$4n + 3$	$7n + 3$
n	$4n$	

Equations

One of the perennial complaints about children's maths is that they can carry out calculations with numbers but are unable to apply these to appropriate practical situations. There is a real difficulty in linking the problem structure with mathematical operations (see Chapters 4 and 5). The same problem arises in algebra because problems must be correctly formulated in algebraic terms before the powerful tools of algebraic manipulation can be used. The construction of algebraic statements to represent a problem is difficult. Consider an example.

In a café a cup of tea costs 50p and biscuits 25p each. How much would 2 cups of tea and 2 biscuits cost? How much would 5 cups of tea and 4 biscuits cost? If 6 people all had a cup of tea and the bill came to £4, how many biscuits were eaten? What would the cost of 'a' cups of tea and 'b' biscuits be?

It is sometimes helpful to make a table:

Number of cups of tea	Cost of tea		Number of biscuits	Cost of biscuits		Total cost	
2	2×50	£1.00	2	2×25	50p	£1.00 + 50	£1.50
5	5×50	£2.50	4	4×25	£1.00	£2.50 + 1.00	£3.50
a	$a \times 50$		b	$b \times 25$			
	$= 50a$			$= 25b$		$50a + 25b$	

From the table it is clear that 2 cups of tea and 2 biscuits costs £1.50 and 5 cups of tea and 4 biscuits would cost £3.50. The cost of tea was found by multiplying the number of cups by 50p. Similarly the cost of the biscuits was given by the multiplying the number by 25p. It is important that the operation is recognised as multiplication, whatever the number. The bottom line of the table shows the cost of 'a' cups of tea and 'b' biscuits. This is $50a + 25b$ pence. The final part of the question can either be solved by arithmetic or by algebra.

By arithmetic

> 6 cups of tea is cost $6 \times 50 = £3.00$
> Amount spent on biscuits is $£4.00 - 3.00 = £1.00$
> Number of biscuits $= {}^{100}\!/_{25} = 4$

Before solving the equation algebraically, we need to establish rules of manipulation. If the equation is thought of as a balance, then the equivalence is not destroyed if both sides are treated in the same way. This means the same amount may be added to or subtracted from both sides, or both sides may be multiplied or divided by the same number.

By algebra

> Let b = number of biscuits
> $50 \times 6 + 25b = 400$ (all costs in pence)
> $300 + 25b = 400$
> $25b + 300 = 400$ (addition is commutative)
> Subtract 300 from both sides
> $\qquad 25b = 400 - 300 = 100$
> Divide both sides by 25
> $\qquad$ and $b = {}^{100}\!/_{25} = 4$

Problems about the cost of food in a café may well occur in Years 5 and 6, but it may not be suitable to introduce the formal algebraic notation. It is important, however to discuss explicitly the structure of the problems and the relation to the mathematical operations.

If the general formula is given, for example, total cost $= 50a + 25b$, then the cost of any number of cups of tea and biscuits can be calculated.

e.g. if $a = 10$ and $b = 5$ (10 cups of tea and 5 biscuits)

> total cost $= 50 \times 10 + 25 \times 5$
> $\qquad = \quad 500 \quad + \quad 125$
> $\qquad = 625p = £6.25$

The formula linking temperatures in Fahrenheit (F) and Centigrade (C) is:

$$F = C \times {}^{9}\!/_{5} + 32 \qquad \text{or} \qquad C = (F - 32) \times {}^{5}\!/_{9}$$

e.g. **a** If the temperature is 15°C what is it in Fahrenheit?

> **b** If the temperature is 68°F what is it in Centigrade?

a $\quad 15 \times {}^{9}\!/_{5} + 32 \qquad$ **b** $\quad (68 - 32) \times {}^{5}\!/_{9}$

$\quad = \quad 27 \quad + 32 \qquad\qquad = \quad 36 \quad \times {}^{5}\!/_{9}$

$\quad = 59 \qquad\qquad\qquad\qquad = 20$

Some investigations, especially with calculators, challenge the children to solve equations by trial and improvement. For example, find a number which when multiplied by itself is equal to ten. This is really solving the equation $x^2 = 10$. The iterative method of making an estimate, calculating the result, then improving the estimate, is used widely these days, especially in computer programs, where the calculations are very rapid and will continue until the desired degree of accuracy is reached. When working on this type of investigation children should be helped to set out their findings in an orderly way, for example, by using a table.

	Estimate for x	x^2	
	3	9	Too small
	4	16	Much too large
	3·5	12·25	Too large
	3·2	10·24	Still too large
	3·15	9·9225	Slightly too small
	3·16	9·9856	Even better
	3·17	10·0489	Just over
	3·165	10·017225	
	3·164	10·010896	
	3·163	10·004569	Very close
	3·1625	10·00140625	
	3·1624	10·00077376	
	3·1623	10·00014129	Very close indeed
	3·1622	9·99950884	

This sort of challenge gives the children good practice in handling numbers and helps develop their understanding of decimals. For example, as 3^2 (9) is much closer to 10 than 4^2 (16), it might have been a good guess to try 3·2 instead of 3·5 and again as 3·16 was closer than 3·17, then 3·162 might have been the next guess.

Check 8.3

1 In a café the menu is:

Cup of tea	60p
Cup of coffee	70p
Ham sandwich	£1.20
Cheese sandwich	£1.00

Find the cost of the following:

a 2 cups of tea and 2 cheese sandwiches

b 2 cups of tea, 1 cup of coffee, 2 ham sandwiches and 1 cheese sandwich

c a cups of tea and b cups of coffee

d x ham sandwiches and y cheese sandwiches

e a cups of tea, b cups of coffee, x ham sandwiches and y cheese sandwiches.

2 Find the side of a square whose area is 20 cm² i.e. $x^2 = 20$

Some questions from National Tests

3 In this equation N stands for a number:

$5N - 2 = 3N + 12$

What is the value of N?

4 Find the value of x in this equation:

$6x - 27 = 0$

Summary

- There are several ways of representing unknown numbers or quantities; in algebra letters are often used.
- Games like 'Guess my rule' or THOANs can be used as introductions to algebraic thinking.
- Investigations into sequences of models or numbers encourage children to identify patterns and relationships in number.
- Constructing algebraic equations to represent problems is not easy.
- Some problems are best solved by trial and improvement.

Links with the classroom

1 What symbols to represent unknowns would you use in Key Stage 1?
2 What activities might clarify the difference between a letter or box used to represent an unknown and a letter used as a variable in a function?
3 What initial guidance would you give children who were investigating number sequences for the first time? What additional suggestions would you have ready in case the children became stuck?
4 Under what circumstances would you challenge Key Stage 2 children to construct general equations to represent problems?

Challenges!

1 Think of a number less than 300. Divide your number by 5, then by 7 and then by 9 and note the remainders. Multiply the first remainder by 126, the second by 225 and the third by 280; add these products; subtract 315 from the result as many times as possible. The remainder is your original number. (Fibonacci 1200 AD)

   Why does it work? Find simpler examples.
2 According to legend, an Indian King offered the inventor of chess anything he liked to ask for. He is reputed to have said 'Majesty, give me a grain of wheat to place on the first square, and two grains of wheat to place on the second square, and four grains of wheat to place on the third square, and eight grains of wheat to place on the fourth, and so, O King, let me cover each of the 64 squares of the board'. The King thought this a modest request. Do you agree?
3 Find out about Fibonacci sequences.

4 Use a hundred number square (only part is shown below):

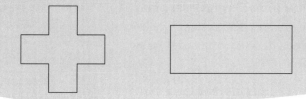

For the squares drawn above, calculate difference between diagonal sums:

e.g. $(12 + 23) - (13 + 22)$; $(5 + 16) - (6 + 15)$

What do you notice? Does this happen for any square? Why?

Try the difference between diagonal products, e.g. $(12 \times 23) - (13 \times 22)$

Investigate similar patterns in 3×3 or 4×4 squares.

What about crosses or rectangles?

References

Giles, G. (1984) The Dime Pre-Algebra Project, University of Stirling.

Booklets: Operations 1 *Flags*
Operations 2 *Pattern and Notation*
Number Mappings 1 *Number Machines*
Number Mappings 2 *Mappings and Graphs*
Number Patterns 1 *Simple Mappings*
Number Patterns 2 *Further Mappings*
(Available from Tarquin Publications, Stradbroke, Diss, Norfolk IP21 5JP.)

Mason, J., Graham, A., Pimm, D. and Gowar, N. (1985) *Routes to/Roots of Algebra*. Milton Keynes: Open University Press.

Graphs and functions

Coordinates

THERE ARE SEVERAL ways of describing the position of a point on a 2-D plane but the most common is by using Cartesian coordinates. This system grew out of the work of the French philosopher and mathematician Descartes who published a book entitled *La Géométrie* in 1637, which set out a new way of linking algebra and geometry. The system locates a point with reference to two lines or axes which define a grid.

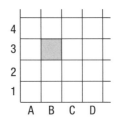

The National Numeracy Strategy suggests introducing a simplified introductory idea, that of 'addresses' on a square grid, in Year 3. The map (or paper) is divided into squares with the rows numbered and the columns labelled with letters as shown. It is then quite simple to specify any square, for example, B3.

It should be noted that a reference such as B3 specifies a whole square; it is not possible to use decimal numbers or refer to parts of a square. Because the columns are labelled with letters, not numbers, it does not really matter in which order the two references are given. It is clear that 3B means the same square as B3. This system of reference is used in games such as 'Battleships'.

When they reach Years 5 and 6, children are expected to use and understand the traditional Cartesian coordinate system. Usually two perpendicular lines called the *X*-axis and the *Y*-axis are used to define a grid upon which points are located. The grid may look very similar to the one above, but it is the lines and not the spaces between them that are numbered and there are no letters, both axes are numbered.

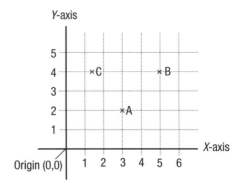

The point A is referred to as (3,2); it is placed 3 units to the right of the origin along the X-axis and 2 units above the origin along the Y-axis. Similarly the point B is (5,4). As the lines are numbered, it is now possible to have decimals, so a point such as C could have the coordinates (1·5, 4·2).

It should also be noted that the order of the numbers is important. (2,3) is not the same point as (3,2). It is purely conventional to put the x-coordinate first, but it is universal; so children must abide by it.

A similar system is used on the Ordnance Survey maps, where the position of a place is given by a National Grid Reference. When using maps such as 1:50,000 or 1:25,000 it is usual to give a 6-figure reference. For example, in a reference such as 236458, the first three figures (236) are the 'eastings' and the second three (458) are the 'northings'.

Line graphs

Using the system of Cartesian coordinates relationships between sets of numbers can be shown graphically. For example, consider numbers which add up to 10. A table can be made as shown below:

0	1	2	3	4	5	6	7	8	9	10
10	9	8	7	6	5	4	3	2	1	0

And these points can be shown on a grid as illustrated below on the left.

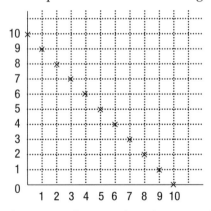
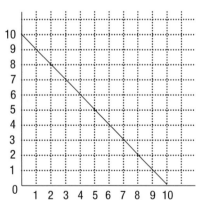

But there are other numbers between these such as 1·5 and 8·5 which also add up to 10. If all the points are joined with a straight line (as in the second diagram), then any point on this line represents a pair of numbers which add up to 10; (that is the x-coordinate and the y-coordinate add up to 10).

Graphs can be used as 'ready reckoners'. For example: if the exchange rate is £1 = 1.4 €, then a graph can be drawn.

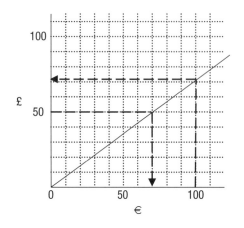

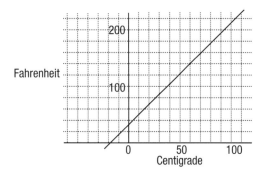

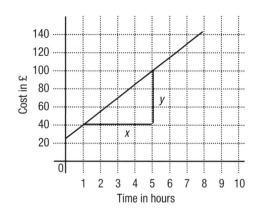

This can be used to find out how many euros are equivalent to a given number of pounds (for example, £50 = 70 €) or how many pounds are equivalent to a given number of euros (for example 100 € = £71).

A similar graph could be drawn to illustrate the relationship between temperatures measured in degrees Centigrade and Fahrenheit.

It will be noticed that the line does not go through the origin (0,0), because the freezing point of water is 0 °C and 32 °F.

A ready reckoner could also be constructed for a plumber who had a £25 call-out charge and whose hourly rate was £15.

Simple linear (straight-line) graphs such as those discussed above have certain characteristics; in particular they can be specified by their intercept and gradient. The intercept is the value of y when $x = 0$, that is the point at which the straight line cuts (meets) the Y-axis. In the example of the plumber's charges, it is 25, as the graph cuts the Y-axis at (0, 25). This is the call-out charge. The gradient is the amount by which the y-value increases, when the x-value increases by 1. This is often found by drawing a small triangle on the graph as shown, then the gradient is y/x. For the plumber's graph this is $60/4 = 15$, which is the hourly rate. The graph can also be specified by an equation; in the above case it is $y = 15x + 25$, where y is the charge in £, and x is the time in hours. It will be noted that the figure in front of the x is the gradient and the last figure (the constant term) is the intercept. In fact the equation for any straight line graph can be written in the form of $y = mx + c$ where m is the gradient and c is the intercept.

A very common graph is one showing distance–time on which the gradient is speed. However, children do not find it easy to interpret. For example, a graph could be drawn to illustrate this story.

'I went for a long walk today. The first part was fairly level so I could keep up a steady pace. Then there was a steep and uneven section which meant I had to slow down. Once I had reached the top, I had a rest, ate my sandwiches and admired the view. I had to hurry down as I could see cloud and rain approaching.'

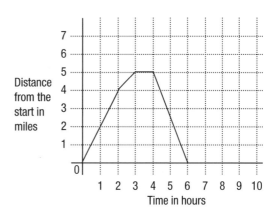

The walker's initial speed was 2 mph; but when the ground became steep and uneven, it dropped to 1 mph. The period when resting (and the speed was 0) is shown by the horizontal part of the graph. The return has a negative gradient as the walker was returning so the distance from the starting point was decreasing.

A common misapprehension is to interpret the *y*-axis as height above rather than distance from the starting point. The story then becomes a walk over a hill, which was steep to start with, then levelled out to a flat top. The descent was very steep indeed. Interpreting line graphs is not easy. As explained in Chapter 19, they should only be used to illustrate data where the interpolation between points makes sense.

Drawing graphs by the traditional method of making a table showing a relationship between *x* and *y*, then plotting these points on a grid and finally drawing a line through the points, is not included in primary school work. However, by Year 6 children are expected to be able to interpret Cartesian coordinates in all 4 quadrants. Before they can cope with this it is necessary for children to have some understanding of negative numbers and how they can be represented on a number line (see Chapter 6). Instead of the origin (0,0) being at the bottom left of the page, it is now in the centre and both axes are marked with positive and negative numbers.

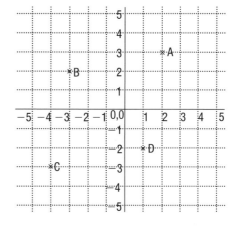

So the coordinates of the point A are (2,3); B is (−3,2); C is (−4,−3) and D is (1,−2). The first number is still the *x*-coordinate and indicates the distance to the right (if it is positive) or to the left (if it is negative) of the origin. Similarly, the second number is the *y*-coordinate and shows the distance above (positive) or below (negative) the origin.

145

Functions

All the line graphs drawn above illustrate a relationship between two sets of numbers. For example, the first graph showed pairs of numbers which added up to 10. If we choose one of the numbers, then we can calculate the other. This type of relationship is called a function and can be expressed in several ways; for example, as a table, as a mapping diagram, as a formula and as a graph. A function is a mathematical relationship between two sets (usually of numbers), where each element of the first set corresponds to one and only one element of the second. The game of 'Guess my rule', introduced in Chapter 8, could equally well be called the function game, as each rule was an example of a function. Rules such as 'add two' or 'square it' are also functions; for each number which is given (input), there is a single answer (output).

As mentioned above, there are several ways of representing functions. Tables, such as the one below, show several numbers and the results from applying a given rule or function.

add up to 10		'add 2'		'square'	
2 ⟶	8	1 ⟶	3	2 ⟶	4
9 ⟶	1	5 ⟶	7	−1 ⟶	1
12 ⟶	−2	11 ⟶	13	1 ⟶	
6 ⟶	4	−13 ⟶	−11	2·5 ⟶	6·25

This is a type of a mapping diagram. Another form of mapping diagram, illustrated below, gives the same information as a relation between two sets of numbers.

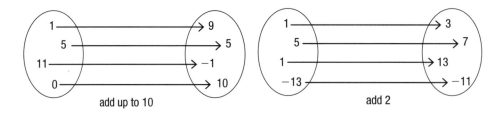

The first set, from which the input numbers can be chosen, is called the domain (or home range) and the second set, made up of all the possible answers, is called the range.

It is also possible to write functions in algebraic form. So 'add up to 10' can be expressed as an equation, for example $x + y = 10$ or $y = 10 - x$ or $f(x) = 10 - x$; 'add 2' becomes $y = x + 2$ or $g(x) = x + 2$; 'square it' becomes $y = x^2$ or $h(x) = x^2$. It is important to understand what these equations mean. 'x' can be any number; it is the input and can take any value in the functions above. As it can vary, it is called a variable. 'y' also takes many values, but its value depends on the value of x, so it is called the dependent variable. For example, if the function is $y = 10 - x$ or $y = x + 2$,

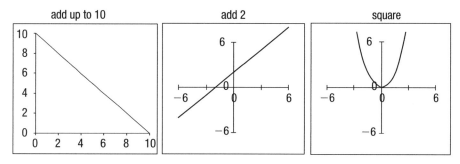

	add up to 10				add 2		
if $x = 2$	then	$y = 10 - 2$	$= 8$	if $x = 4$	then	$y = 4 + 2$	$= 6$
if $x = 5$	then	$y = 10 - 5$	$= 5$	if $x = 7\cdot4$	then	$y = 7\cdot4 + 2$	$= 9\cdot4$
if $x = {}^-2$	then	$y = 10 - {}^-2$	$= 12$	if $x = {}^-2$	then	$y = {}^-2 + 2$	$= 0$
if $x = 3\cdot4$	then	$y = 10 - 3\cdot4$	$= 6\cdot6$	if $x = {}^-14$	then	$y = {}^-14 + 2$	$= {}^-12$

Graphs can be drawn to illustrate these functions.

Every point on the graphs above satisfies the appropriate equation.

Sometimes in maths textbooks 'function machines' are used. These are drawings of a simple 'machine' with the instructions (function) written on the side, the idea being that just as a machine always does the same thing, so a function always applies the same rule. For example:

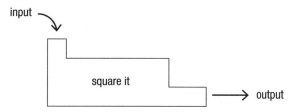

When 1 is put into the machine, then the output will be 1. When 2 is the input, the output will be 4. Notice that when $^-1$ is entered, then 1 is the result, that is two different inputs (1 and $^-1$) have the same output. It will be noted that if a line parallel to the x-axis is drawn on the graph of $y = x^2$ through the point (0,1), then it will cut the graph at two points, namely $^+1$ and $^-1$.

✎ Check 9.1

1 Illustrate the following rules by mapping diagrams:
   a Multiply by –1 and add 2
   b Take away 12
   c Multiply by 2 and add 4

d Divide by 2 and subtract 3

e Square and add 5

f Subtract from 10

g Double then subtract from 50

2 Write the functions in question 1 in algebraic form

3 On graph paper draw X- and Y-axes from -5 to $+5$ with a scale of 1 cm : 1 unit Join the following points in order:

$(0,5), (-3,-4), (4,1), (-4,1), (3,-4), (0,5)$

How many triangles, quadrilaterals, pentagons and other polygons can you find?

Summary

- Cartesian coordinates fix the position of a point by giving its distance from two fixed lines or axes.
- A function is a mathematical relationship between two sets (usually of numbers), where each element of the first set corresponds to one and only one element of the second.
- Functions can be given as verbal instructions, mapping diagrams or in algebraic form.
- Functions can be shown as graphs.

Links with the classroom

1 What games might help children learn how to use Cartesian coordinates in all four quadrants?

2 What classroom activities might help children understand distance–time graphs?

3 Which way of expressing functions is easiest to understand?

4 What sort of investigation might allow Year 6 children to see the relationship between a formula and the corresponding graph?

Challenges!

1 Sketch graphs of the following functions without plotting points.

$y = -2x + \frac{1}{2}$

$y = \frac{1}{2}x - 2$

$y = -x - 1$

$y = \frac{2}{3}x - 3$

$2y = 3x + 1$

2 If you have access to a computer with a graph drawing program investigate linear and quadratic graphs. E.g. the family of graphs of the form $y = 2x + c$, or $y = mx - 4$; the family of graphs of the form $y = ax^2$, $y = x^2 - b$, $y = x^2 + cx$, where c, m, a, b, can take any values.

3

Measurement

Introduction

One of the most common ways in which we use numbers in everyday life is in measurement. Potatoes or apples are bought by weight; to make curtains, the length and width of the windows must be found; petrol for the car is measured in litres; times for lectures (or lessons) are agreed beforehand. Although the units are different, the principles behind these measurements are very similar. Children may have some experience of measuring before they come to school; but it is necessary to discuss the principles and problems explicitly.

General principles of measurement

There are four basic principles underlying all forms of measurement. The simplest is that of comparing magnitudes and ordering objects by a particular attribute. This is usually the starting point in Key Stage 1, together with the appropriate language. This involves establishing the meaning of words implying comparisons, such as shorter, taller, thicker, thinner, heavier, lighter. To start with, children may compare just two objects, but soon they can be expected to arrange three or more objects in a given order. This is a much more complex task, as several objects must be regarded at the same time. The appropriate language needs to be fully explored, so that the children realise that if there are four towers as shown in the diagram, then A is the shortest, D is the tallest, but A, B and C are all shorter than D and B, C and D are all taller than A.

Children have a strong tendency to use 'big' and 'small' for all comparisons connected with size. They sometimes find it quite difficult to use other terms such as 'tall' and 'short' correctly. Also they normally use and understand the 'greater' form before the 'lesser' form. For example they do not say, 'I've got less than him', rather 'He's got more than me!'

The second principle of measurement, used in ordering objects, is the transitivity principle. This says that if it is known that B is greater than A, and C is

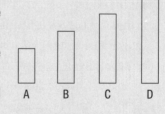

greater than B, then C must be greater than A. For example, if three pencils are considered, and B is longer than A, and C is longer than B, then C must be longer than A.

The third basic principle underlying measurement is that of conservation. This is the realisation that an attribute such as length or weight does not change if the position or orientation of the object is altered. Two aspects of this need to be distinguished. As adults we assume that within normal conditions attributes of an object such as length, area, volume and weight do not vary. This is the nature of matter as we experience it, if it were not so measurement would be impossible. The second aspect is children's understanding of this. Piaget said that young children did not realise that, for example, the length of a piece of wood would be the same whether it was horizontal or vertical. He carried out many investigations into children's understanding of the world around them and regarded conservation as a general principle which only developed slowly. More recent findings such as the work of Donaldson (1978) suggest that the context of the test can make a difference to the children's performance. It is true, however, that young children do not necessarily think as adults. For example, many find it difficult to understand that if a ball of plasticine is divided into smaller balls, the total weight will remain the same. In theory measurement is not much use until conservation is part of the way the children view the world, but in practice actually measuring things is probably the way in which children learn that attributes are conserved in normal circumstances.

Finally most measurement involves stating how many of a given unit match an attribute of an object. For example, in measuring the length of a rod, the number of centimetres that can be fitted along it are counted.

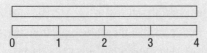

It is worth noting here that there are some conceptual differences between counting and measuring. When counting the number of children in the classroom, the result must be a whole number. It is impossible for there to be 28·5 children! Either there are 28 or there are 29 present. The result must be a whole number, so the quantity is said to be discrete. It is possible for quantities to be discrete and for numbers other than natural numbers to be involved. For example, in English shoe sizes, it is possible to have halves, so 4½ is a valid shoe size. Shoe size is discrete because it is not possible to have a size of 4·2; it is either 4 or 4·5. Only certain values are possible. In contrast, in measuring the length of pencils (or feet not shoes) any number between, say 1 cm and 30 cm may occur. The problem of appropriate degrees of accuracy will be considered later, but in theory any length might occur; for example, 14·2 cm or 14·26 cm or 14·264 cm. Quantities which can take any value between certain limits are called continuous. The number line model referred to in Chapters 3 and 7 is particularly appropriate to illustrate the continuous number scales used in measurement.

Types of scale

Many attributes can be compared, so there are many measurement scales. These can be divided into three main groups or classes.

The ordinal scales only allow objects to be put in order. Examples of ordinal scales are the star ratings of hotels and the grades awarded in GCSE exams. It is possible to say that a B grade is better than a D grade, but it is not possible to say it is twice as good or two degrees better. Such scales can be quite personal and subjective. For example, if children ranked popular TV programs, they would be unlikely to agree completely.

The second group is the interval scales. This includes temperature in degrees Centigrade (or Fahrenheit) and time of day. With these scales it is possible not only to order the objects, but also to compare intervals, though not ratios. So, it is true to say that 4 p.m. is later than 2 p.m., and also that it is 2 hours later than 2 p.m., but it is not true to say 4 p.m. is twice 2 p.m. In these scales the zero is arbitrary. There is no particular reason why midnight should be zero hours, and certainly time does not cease to exist at this moment. Similarly zero on the Centigrade scale may be the freezing point of water, but this does not mean there is no temperature.

The third group is the most common and useful. The ratio scales include measurements of length, area, volume, mass, weight, time interval, angle, electric current and many others. In these scales it is possible to order the objects, to compare intervals (differences) and to compare attributes. Zero means nothing of that attribute. This means that if there are two pieces of wood of lengths 10 cm and 20 cm as shown in the diagram:

then it is true to say that

A is longer than B
A is 10 cm longer than B
A is twice as long as B.

Standard units

It was stated briefly above that measurement usually involves matching a repeated unit against an object. In school, it is usual to introduce informal units first. For example, matches or straws or digits (thumb widths) or hand or feet lengths are used to measure length. The principle of laying them in a straight line and counting them is fundamental. It is soon discovered that feet can be of different sizes, so that different numbers can represent the same length. This gives rise to all sorts of problems, so standard units have been established. In this country two systems are in use, so it is necessary to introduce the children to both. Our traditional imperial system is still used, for example, in cooking (ounces and pounds), whereas the official standards are in metric or SI (Système Internationale d'Unités) units. The great advantage of the latter is that they use a base ten system, with standard prefixes to indicate the size of the units.

The most common prefixes are kilo- (10^3, thousands), milli- (10^{-3} thousandths) and centi- (10^{-2} hundredths). So:

1 kilogram $= 1 \times 10^3 = 1,000$ g	1 m $= 100$ cm	1 m $= 1,000$ mm
1 kilometre $= 1 \times 10^3 = 1,000$ m		so 1 cm $= 10$ mm

This system also makes it very easy to extend the measurement to any degree of accuracy and it is also simple to change from one size of unit to another. So to express 1·35 m in centimetres, it is only necessary to multiply by 100, so 1·35 m = 135 cm. A table of the main SI units can be found on p.153.

Approximate nature of measurement

Although in theory it may be possible to find out exactly how many standard units match a given object, in practice measurement is always approximate. This means it is essential to decide on the required degree of accuracy before the measurement is carried out. The purpose of the measurement will usually dictate the appropriate degree of accuracy. For example, if the length of curtain material is required, then measurement to the nearest centimetre is probably sufficient and it will be safer to over-estimate the length. In contrast, a door that is a centimetre too wide will be useless. Children must be introduced to the problem of appropriate degrees of accuracy and, before they leave the primary school, they should also be aware of the size of possible errors. For example, if a table, measured to the nearest centimetre, is said to be 56 cm long, this means its length is between 55·5 cm and 56·5 cm. The implications of this for area calculations will be explained in Chapter 11.

A further aspect of measurement is learning how to estimate. This grows out of considerable experience of measurement and involves having known points of reference. Examples of such points could be: four apples weigh roughly a pound or half a kilogram; a metre is the distance between my nose and the tips of my fingers when my arm is stretched out or it is a long stride; the width of my thumb is roughly 1 inch or 2·5 cm. People usually build up their own set of reference points which may include: how far they travel to work (or college); how many cups the kettle will hold; how many potatoes they get in 1 kilogram; how far the car will go on a full tank of petrol; the length of their hand span.

In the following six chapters, the main types of measurement used in primary school are examined in more detail. Although some issues arise more than once, each topic has distinct problems so separation seems appropriate. The topics are length (Chapter 10), area (Chapter 11), capacity and volume (Chapter 12), mass and weight (Chapter 13), angle (Chapter 14), and time (Chapter 15).

References

Donaldson, M. (1978) *Children's Minds.* Glasgow: Fontana (Collins).

Haylock, D. (1995) *Mathematics Explained for Primary Teachers.* London: Paul Chapman.

SI units (Système Internationale d'Unités)

Attribute	SI Unit	Abbreviation		Imperial units	Imperial abbreviation	Conversion
Basic units						
length	metre	m		inches, feet, miles	in., ft.	1 in = 2·54 cm 1 ft = 0·3048 m
mass	kilogram	kg		ounces, pound	oz., lb.	1 oz = 28·35 g 1 lb = 0·4536 kg
time	second	s	60 s = 1 min 60 mins = 1 hour			
electric current	ampere	A				
temperature	kelvin	K	degrees Centigrade (°C) K = °C + 273·15	degrees Fahrenheit	°F	$°C = \dfrac{5}{9}(°F - 32)$
angle	radian	rad	1 rad ≈ 57 degrees (°) 1 degree = 60 minutes (') 1 min = 60 seconds (")			
Derived (compound) units						
area	square metres	m^2	1 hectare = 10,000 m^2	square inches, acre		
volume	cubic metres	m^3	cc = cm^3	cubic inches		
*capacity	litre	l	1 ml = 1 cc or cm^3	pints, gallons	1 pint = 0·5683 l	
speed	metres per second	m/s^1 or ms^{-1}		miles per hour feet per second	mph fps	
acceleration	metres per second per second	m/s^2 or ms^{-2}				
force	newtons	N		poundal	pdl	

* capacity is not a SI attribute

Starter

An ant is crawling from one corner to the opposite corner (from A to B) of a cube of side 1 metre.

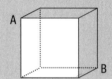

If it only walks along the edges what is the shortest and longest (assuming it must not go over any edge twice) journey? If it can go anywhere on the surface of the cube what is the shortest possible journey?

Definition and units

The definition of length appears simple, but there are several problems in practice. The length of an object is the number of standard units (such as centimetres) which can be laid in a straight line along or beside the object.

The number need not be a whole number, and can be given to any degree of accuracy. The units must be laid end to end so there are no gaps and no overlaps, and they must be in a straight line so that the minimum distance between the two ends of the object is found.

In many practical situations there are conventions about what length or distance means. For example, the height of a person is the length of an imaginary line from the top of their head straight through him to the floor between his feet. This cannot be measured directly, so another line of the same length is taken, perhaps down a wall. The distance between two points on a piece of paper is the shortest possible distance or the length of a straight line between them. Understanding even a simple statement about the height of the table involves knowing that this is the vertical distance from the top of the table to the floor and not necessarily the length of the legs. The distance between two towns is usually measured along roads and so may not be straight. Find out exactly what length is being referred to by airlines in statements such as 'the distance between London and Tokyo is 9562km'.

As mentioned in the general introduction to measurement, young children do not always realise that the length of an object remains the same when the position of the object is changed. For example they may be surprised to discover that their height is the same whether they are standing up or lying down.

Again, if two lines are drawn on a grid as shown in the diagram, children may think they are the same length. This may be the result of concentrating on the position of the ends rather than the distance between the ends. In any case it shows the need for much practical experience and discussion to establish the conservation of length.

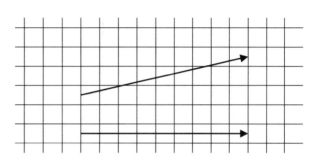

Units

Frequently in school, children use informal units such as matches or straws, before being introduced to the SI units. The metre is the standard unit for length. One difficulty is that the metre is rather long for many situations in the classroom, so the centimetre is the most frequently used unit in primary schools. It is certainly a convenient size for much of the work undertaken by children in school. However, it can lead to difficulties later, for, to quote a DIY (Homebase 48) leaflet, 'The centimetre is not used in the building and allied trades. Measurement is always given in metres or millimetres. Thus 60 centimetres is written as either 0·6 m or 600 mm. 3 m and 42·7 cm is written as either 3·427 m or 3427 mm.' This does not mean metres and millimetres should be used throughout the primary school, for although such units may be appropriate for the building trade, they are not suitable for young children. However, it does mean that children should be aware of the relation of centimetres and metres (100 cm = 1 m) and between centimetres and millimetres (10 mm = 1 cm) by the end of primary school. It is worth stressing that 10 mm = 1 cm as some children expect it to be 100.

Another problem is what to do about the 'bit' left at the end. In fact non-standard units such as matchsticks are usually used to start with, but the problem of inexact matching between a number of units and the object still arises. It is important to discuss this with the children as soon as it arises, even in the reception class. There are several ways of coping.

If the children are happy with the nearest whole number of units, that is fine. But often they will point out that this is not quite right and say something like 'It is four and a bit matches'. This is a valid and accurate observation and they should be allowed to use this if they wish. If they offer 'four and a half', again this might be accepted at Key Stage 1. It might be useful to suggest 'It is more than four but less than five matches long', as this leads to the idea of bounds and can be linked to error analysis later. At Key Stage 2 some ideas of appropriate degrees of accuracy and error limits should be introduced.

So the measurement might be to the nearest centimetre (or half centimetre), with discussion of the rules as to which way to move. So the box above is 5 cm (to the nearest cm) and 4·5 (to the nearest half cm). If it were measured to the nearest ¹⁄₁₀ cm (mm) then it would be 4·6 cm.

In fact the rules of approximation are quite complicated. It might help to introduce these by way of a practical situation, rather than just giving the rules. For example, if there is a street with houses numbered consecutively (i.e. odd and even numbers on the same side) and there is a bus stop outside every tenth house (i.e. outside 10, 20, 30, 40 . . .), which way should a person from a given house go to keep as dry as possible if it is raining? The question of what to do if you live at 5 or 15 must be discussed. Later this can be extended to smaller units, but the general principle remains the same.

At some point in Key Stage 2 it might be suitable to mention the imperial measures of length – the foot, the inch and the yard. The basic unit is the foot, with obvious links to practical ways of measuring, and it provides a good reason for discussing the need for standard units. The fact that the system has a variable base makes it more difficult to use and to change from one unit to another. The inch is defined as ¹⁄₁₂ of a foot and the yard is 3 feet. It is also useful to have a rough idea of equivalences, for example, 1 foot $\approx$ 30 cm and 1 yard is a few inches shorter that 1 metre.

When discussing longer distance, such as that between towns, miles are generally used in this country, but kilometres are the most suitable SI unit. It is probably useful to explain how to convert from miles to kilometres sometime in Key Stage 2. This could be linked to ratios or equations or graphs. As 1 kilometre is less than 1 mile, then for a given distance the number of kilometres will be larger than the number of miles. In fact there are several informal ways of doing this. For example, a rough estimate can be made by thinking of a kilometre as just over half a mile. So 6 miles would be less than 12 km. A more precise method might use 5 miles = 8 km as a starting point. If a calculator were available, then 1 mile = 1·609 km might be used.

 Check 10.1

1 Give the following to the nearest centimetre

> 12·67 cm   1·7328 m   154 mm

2 Give these to the nearest half metre

> 56·496 m   1,542 cm   1,472·186 m

3 Convert the following distances into kilometres, using different methods and degrees of accuracy:

> 11 miles   56 miles   130 miles

Issues arising

Even when making direct comparisons of two bars, children do not always realise the importance of putting two ends carefully at the same level. So they may say that B is longer than A because it sticks out further.

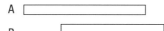

When using standard measuring instruments such as rulers, it is essential to place them correctly, with the 0 at one end of the object to be measured. There are two common mistakes made by children. First, it is easy to place the end of the ruler, not the 0 mark beside the end of the object. Some rulers have no extra piece at the end in order to prevent this particular source of error. Second, the 1 mark is placed beside the end of the object.

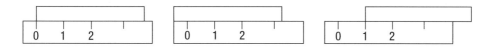

This shows a misunderstanding of how the standard units are arranged and where the numbers are placed. A strip of paper with each centimetre coloured a different colour might be used and the number of centimetres counted, instead of reading off the number from a standard ruler.

In a ruler the units are already placed end to end and in a straight line, but when placing informal units, such as outlines of hands or feet, it is also important to put them in a straight line with no spaces between and no overlaps. This demands considerable manual dexterity as well as an understanding of the need for such care. Children do not necessarily realise that a crooked line is longer than a straight one between the same two points.

If the distance to be measured is longer than the ruler, then some way of marking the position of a convenient length (such as 30 cm) and moving the zero to that point must be used. Also some record of the number of units covered must be kept.

In school, metre sticks, rulers in centimetres, and tape measures (of various types) are usually available, so that a variety of measuring devices can be used. For long distances outside (e.g. the size of the playing field) a trundle wheel could be used. This is a wheel whose circumference is 1 metre, and which has a stick which produces a click each time there is a complete revolution. So by pushing the wheel along and counting the clicks, the distance it has travelled can be obtained. It is important to start with the wheel in the correct position, namely just after it has 'clicked', and to push it in a straight line. This may be a useful way to measure distances of, say, between 10 m and 100 m, but it is not suitable for shorter distances.

If there are difficulties in measuring straight lines, there are even more when curves are considered. If the circumference of a wheel or tin is required, it is possible to make a mark on the wheel and place this against a corresponding mark on a piece of paper. Then the wheel is rolled carefully around exactly once and another mark made on the paper where the mark on the wheel falls; then the straight line distance between the two marks on the paper is the length of the circumference of the wheel. If the distance along a curve is wanted, then a flexible tape measure or a piece of string can be used.

It is important that children not only measure accurately but are also able to make reasonable estimates of length. First they need considerable experience of measuring to build up an idea of the size of standard units. Then one way to encourage estimation of length is to play a game or have a competition. For example, an idea presented by Phil Robbins at an ATM session in Durham involved dividing the class into groups (of 4 to 8). One object in the room is selected (say the width of the blackboard) and each group is asked to discuss and decide on an estimate of the distance. All the estimates are collected (e.g. write them on the board), then the width of the board is measured (to an appropriate degree of accuracy) and the group with the nearest estimate gains a point. Another object is chosen and a further round of estimation takes place. This activity has several advantages. It is impossible for the children to measure the object first, and then deliberately put down an 'estimate' which is a few centimetres out; real discussion can occur within the group; if several lengths are taken, then visual comparison can be made and estimation should improve (to encourage visual comparison a metre rule could be put in an obvious place).

At the end of Key Stage 2 some children may be ready to undertake more difficult tasks, for example to find the average thickness of a piece of paper. This is so small that any of the instruments commonly available in school would be quite useless to measure it directly. However a reasonable measurement of, say, 100 sheets placed on top of each other could be made and the appropriate division carried out. Various practical problems arise, such as the closeness of the packing. Would a new packet of paper be a fairer measure? Do you believe the number of sheets stated on the packet, or must they be counted? How is paper graded? (Actually it is not by thickness but by weight per unit of area, which is not exactly the same thing.)

Calculating lengths

Although measurement is essentially a practical activity, sometimes lengths can be calculated. For example it is possible to calculate the perimeter of a square after the length of one side has been measured.

Perimeter

The perimeter is the distance around the edge of a shape. So the perimeter of a square is four times the length of one of its sides. If the lengths of the sides of any polygon are known, then the perimeter is the sum of all those lengths.

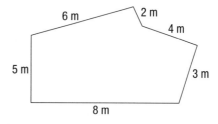

The perimeter of this polygon (or field) is 28 metres. It is not uncommon for children to confuse area and perimeter. Presumably this is because in a rectangle the same numbers are used but the operation is different. It should be pointed out that perimeter is a length (the length of the fence around a field) and this will be measured in length units (metres) so the distances must be added (if two lengths are added the result is a length). In contrast (as will be explained in Chapter 11), area (the amount of grass in a field), is measured in square units (m²) and so the lengths must be multiplied.

The lengths of curves are difficult to find and only the special case of the circle should be covered in primary school. An investigation into the relation between the diameter and the circumference of circles can be an interesting task for children in Year 5 or Year 6. Of course there are practical difficulties, for example how to measure the curve. However, the children may find that the circumference was always just over three times the diameter. This idea of a constant relation is important, for it shows that all circles are similar (see Chapter 16). Some children might be interested in the formula $C = \pi d$ or $C = 2\pi r$ (where C = circumference, d = diameter, r = radius) and the nature of the number π (an irrational i.e. an infinite non-repeating decimal). Once this relation is established, then the length of any circular arc can be found by proportion.

In the diagram the angle at the centre of the circle on which the arc stands is θ and the radius of the circle is r. The circumference of the circle is therefore $2\pi r$. But there are $360°$ at the centre of a complete circle, so one degree would subtend an arc of $\frac{2\pi r}{360}$, and θ will subtend an arc of length $\frac{2\pi r}{360} \times \theta$

For example, if $\theta = 60°$ then $\qquad \frac{60}{360} = \frac{1}{6}$

So the length of the arc $\qquad = \frac{1}{6}$ of the circumference of the circle

$\qquad\qquad\qquad\qquad\qquad = \frac{1}{6} \times 2\pi r$

$\qquad\qquad\qquad\qquad\qquad = \frac{\pi r}{3}$

Or if $\theta = 117°$, then the arc will be $^{117}\!/_{360}$ of the circumference.

Scale diagrams

In the upper primary school scale drawings or plans are usually introduced. Before this can be done, the children should be able to measure lengths to an appropriate degree of accuracy and to understand ratios (see Chapter 5). At first simple scales such as 1 cm on the plan representing 1 m on the ground should be used. After drawing the plan, say of part of the classroom, it should be used to find distances on the ground, then the actual measurement checked. Once the principle has been established, then maps with large scales can be used. The popular 1:50,000 Ordnance Survey series can be used to find distances between places. This may involve the problems associated with measuring curves, appropriate degrees of accuracy (both in the initial measuring and in giving the answer) and the calculation of the ratio with a possible change in units, so it is a complex and worthwhile challenge bringing together several principles.

Pythagoras' theorem

Although Pythagoras' theorem is, in origin, one concerning the area of squares, it is frequently used to calculate lengths. The theorem states that in a right-angled triangle, the square on the hypotenuse is equal to the sum of the squares on the other two sides. Proofs of the theorem are left until Chapter 11, but an example of its use is included here.

40 m

30 m

If a radio transmitting mast is 40 m high and one of the supporting wires is tethered to the ground at a point 30 m away from its base, how long is the wire?

Using Pythagoras' theorem, if w is the length

$$w^2 = 40^2 + 30^2$$

$$w^2 = 1600 + 900 = 2500$$

so $w = 50$ m

✎ Check 10.2

1 Find the perimeter of the polygons shown below:

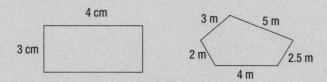

2 Calculate the circumference of the circles shown:

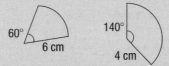

3 Find the lengths of the arcs in the following diagrams:

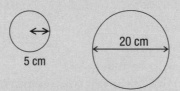

4 If the scale of a plan is 1:100, how far on the ground is a distance of 26 cm on the plan? How long would a fence of 1·34 m look on the plan?

5 In the following right-angled triangles find the unknown side.

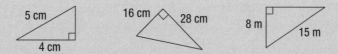

Some questions from National Tests

6 This ring is made of regular pentagons, with sides of 5 centimetres. What is the length of the outer edge of the ring?

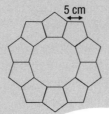

7 Strips of paper are each 30 centimetres long. Steve joins strips of paper together to make a streamer. The strips overlap each other by 5 cm.

How long is a streamer made from only 2 strips? Sunita makes a streamer that is 280 cm long. How many strips does she use?

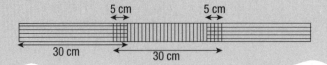

Summary

- The standard unit of length is the metre.
- Methods of approximation should be taught.
- Some children have difficulty in using a ruler accurately.
- Children should be encouraged to estimate lengths before measuring.
- The perimeter is the distance around the sides of a shape.
- The circumference of a circle is about $3 \times$ diameter or πd or $2\pi r$.
- Pythagoras' theorem states that in a right-angled triangle, the square on the hypotenuse is equal to the sum of the squares on the other two sides.

Links with the classroom

1 Suggest ways of helping young children to use a ruler correctly.
2 How would you develop children's ideas about appropriate degrees of accuracy?
3 A pupil said that the perimeter of a rectangle was length times breadth. What confusions does this show? How would you try to help him/her sort them out?
4 Look at various measuring sticks and rulers found in the classroom. Why are there so many types? What problems may children encounter in using them?

Challenges!

1 From a maths copy book of 1812 (private papers)

> As I was walking out one day
> Which happened on the first of May
> As luck would have it I did spy
> A Maypole fixèd up on high
> The which at first me much surprised
> Not being beforehand advertised.
> Of such strange uncommon sight
> I said I would not stir that night

Nor rest content until I'd found
Its height exact from off the ground.
But when these words I just had spoke
A blast of wind the Maypole broke
Whose broken piece I found to be
Exact in length yards sixty three
Which by its fall broke up a hole
Twice fifteen yards from off the pole.
But this being all that I can do
The Maypole now being broke in two
Unequal parts to aid a friend
Ye youths pray then an answer send.

2 The dispatch rider (after a problem by Henry Ernest Dudeney, born 1857)
A dispatch rider rides his horse from the back of an army to the commander at the front, then returns to his position at the rear of the army. The army is 4 miles long, and moves forward 1 mile while the rider gallops from the rear to the front. If the rider returns to the rear at the same speed (and the army is till marching forward), how far has he travelled?

3 If a line of touching pence stretched for 1 kilometre, how many would there be? Discuss different ways of working this out, including what would be a suitable degree of accuracy (or look at a mile of pennies).

11

Area

Starter

TANGRAMS – A TRADITIONAL Chinese puzzle

The seven pieces, shown forming a square, can be rearranged to form many shapes. Can you form those shown?

Which shape has the greatest area? Which has the greatest and which the least perimeter?

Definition and units

One of the definitions of 'area' given in the Oxford dictionary is 'superficial extent'. Perhaps a simpler form is 'amount of surface'. It is actually quite a difficult concept to define, but one which many children meet quite early. These early experiences may include covering a piece of paper with paint, or wrapping up a parcel, or covering the table with newspaper to protect it from paint. However, the concept of the area of a surface (or inside a closed shape) is more idealised and abstract. As in measuring length, the measurement of area involves placing standard units so that they completely cover a surface, but do not overlap.

The conservation of area means that if a 2-D shape is cut up and rearranged, its area is unchanged.

However, it has been shown that not all children grasp this. In an investigation reported in Dickson, Brown and Gibson (1984), it was found that one third of 11 year olds did not conserve area consistently. Two sets of shapes were used. Set A consisted of a square and two right-angled triangles. Set B was a semi-circle and two quarter-circles. Two copies of each set were used, one blue and the other green.

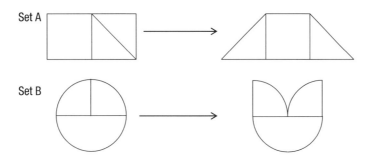

The children were interviewed individually. Both the blue and green versions of set A (see diagram) were shown side by side and arranged in the same way as illustrated on the left of the diagram. The equality of the area of the two sets was established. Then one set (say the green) was rearranged as in the right hand diagram. The children were then asked whether the area of the blue and green cards were the same. The same procedure was followed for the set B. Over one third of them said that one or both sets of shapes were not the same when rearranged.

It is interesting to note that in these examples, although the areas remain the same (i.e. they are conserved), the perimeters are increased by moving the parts (i.e. perimeter is not conserved).

Units

The standard SI units are square metres or square centimetres and are written as m^2 or cm^2. These refer to squares of side 1 m or 1 cm respectively. It should be pointed out that because there are 100 cm in 1 m, there are $100 \times 100 = 10,000$ cm^2 in 1 m^2. In school the square metre is really too big to be of much use; in fact square centimetres are much easier to handle.

In the measurement of large areas (such as fields) the SI unit is a hectare, a square of side 100 m and area of 10,000 m^2, whereas in the imperial system the equivalent unit is an acre (= 4,840 square yards). Which is bigger, a hectare or an acre? Find a rough comparison between the two.

The relation between linear (length) and square (area) units must be discussed with children. As explained above, because there are 100 cm in 1 m, then there must be 10,000 cm^2 in 1 m^2. To illustrate the same principle with a simpler example, consider the square shown with side of length 1 yard (= 3 feet).

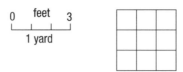

There are 3×3 squares of side 1 foot in the large square of side 1 yard. So $9 \text{ ft}^2 = 1 \text{ yd}^2$.

This relationship between the linear and the area scales applies in many situations. For example, if the linear scale of a plan is 1:100 (1 cm:1 m), then 1 square centimetre on the plan will represent an area of 1 square metre on the ground. This means that 1 cm^2 on the plan will represent $100 \times 100 = 10{,}000 \text{ cm}^2$ on the ground. If a model is made to a scale of 1:12, then the surface area of the model will be in the ratio of $1^2{:}12^2 = 1{:}144$ to that of the object. There is a minor language problem which sometimes arises. What is meant by a '9 cm square'? Does it mean a square with sides of length 9 cm, or does it mean a square with area 9 cm^2, in which case its sides would be 3 cm long? The best solution is to avoid such statements and refer either to a square with sides of 9 cm or a square whose area is 9 cm^2 (read as 9 square centimetres). It might help to suggest that the children write 9 sq cm instead of 9 cm^2 at first.

Issues arising

Children are usually first given regular shapes, often drawn on squared paper, as illustrated, and asked to find the area.

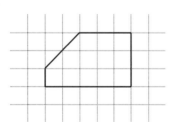

This can be found by counting all the squares inside the polygon. It soon becomes apparent that for rectangles the area can be found by multiplying the length by the breadth. This is sometimes generalised too early into 'Area equals length times breadth' and is then misapplied to other shapes.

It is perhaps useful to find the areas of many irregular shapes before introducing methods of calculation. Shapes cut out of the same wrapping paper can be compared by counting how many repeating patterns appear on each. More formally the shape can be placed under a grid on transparent film and the number of squares inside the shape counted. As with linear measurement, there is the problem of what to do with the 'bits'; but in finding areas there seem to be many more of them. One solution is visually to 'balance' the bits together, so two or more parts are judged to be equivalent to one whole square and counted as such. This is a highly sophisticated way of coping. Another way is first to count all the squares which are entirely inside the shape (this gives a lower bound for the area) and then to count all those which are partly in and partly outside the shape. When these are added to those entirely inside it gives an upper bound for the area. Either the area can be stated to lie between these two figures, or the average of the two can be used as an estimate of the area. For example, consider the accompanying diagram.

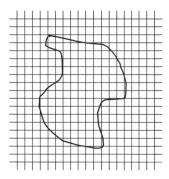

The number of squares entirely inside the shape is 82. The number partly in and partly out is 40. So the area is more than 82 square units and less than 122 square units. A good estimate might be 100 square units. Discuss with others the strategies which might be used to cope with part squares.

Although we talk of square units, it is possible to compare areas by covering them with other shapes such as circles (counters). Some children find it easier to count dots, rather than squares; so 'dotty' paper may be used and on average the estimate of the area will be reasonably accurate.

Check 11.1

1 Find the area of these regular shapes

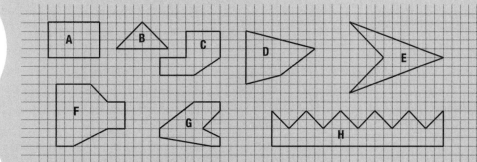

2 Find the area of these irregular shapes using different strategies

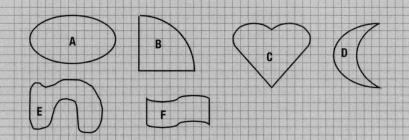

Calculating areas

It is possible to calculate the areas of several regular shapes.

Rectangles

The basic shape is the rectangle, for which, as explained above, the area is length times breadth (as long as the lengths are in the same units).

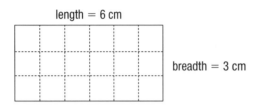

length = 6 cm

breadth = 3 cm

From the diagram the area of the rectangle can be seen as 3 rows of 6 squares or 6 columns of 3 squares. This means the number of squares is 18. As each square has a side of 1 cm, then the area is 18 cm^2. The formula works not only for whole numbers of centimetres but also for decimal parts. Consider the next rectangle.

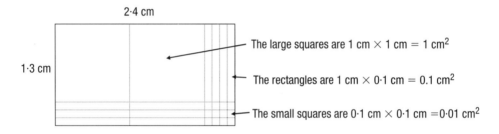

2·4 cm

1·3 cm

The large squares are 1 cm $\times$ 1 cm = 1 cm^2

The rectangles are 1 cm $\times$ 0·1 cm = 0.1 cm^2

The small squares are 0·1 cm $\times$ 0·1 cm = 0·01 cm^2

	large squares = 1 cm^2	rectangles = 0·1 cm^2	small squares = 0·01 cm^2
There are:	2 × 1 = 2	2 × 3 + 1 × 4 = 6 + 4 = 10	3 × 4 = 12
Total in cm^2	2	10 × 0·1 = 1·0	12 × 0·01 = 0·12

So total area is 2 + 1·0 + 0·12 = 3·12 cm^2 (Using a calculator 1·3 × 2·4 = 3·12)

But when this formula is used, it is important to be aware of appropriate degrees of accuracy. Some examples will illustrate this. Consider the next rectangle. Its sides are measured to the nearest millimetre and given as 3·6 cm and 5·4 cm. If these two numbers are multiplied together then the result is 19·44 cm^2. However, the fact that the lengths are measured to the nearest millimetre means that the minimum possible lengths are 3·55 cm and 5·35 cm. By using these measurements the smallest possible area of the rectangle can be found, so 3·55 × 5·35 = 18·9925 cm^2. This smallest possible area is called the lower bound of the area. If the measurements are reliable the area must be larger than this.

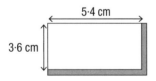

5·4 cm

3·6 cm

Similarly the largest possible area can be calculated by using the maximum lengths and is $3.65 \times 5.45 = 19.8925$ cm^2. This is called the upper bound of the area, for the actual area must be less than this. So in theory the area lies between 18·9925 and 19·8925 cm^2, but using all these decimal places is quite misleading. It would be more appropriate to say that the area lies between 19 cm^2 and 20 cm^2, or the area is 19·5 cm^2 to the nearest half cm^2. It is certainly not appropriate to give the answer to hundredths of a square centimetre. The shaded area in the diagram shows the possible error.

As a further example, some children measured a desk top and found the length was 56 cm and its width was 42 cm (to the nearest centimetre). When multiplied together the figures obtained give 2352 cm^2. To find the possible error, the minimum and maximum areas are found.

Lower bound of the area	= 55·5 × 41·5	Upper bound of area	= 56·5 × 42·5
	= 2303·25 cm^2		= 2401·25 cm^2

In other words the area lies between 2,300 and 2,400 cm^2. So it might be appropriate to say the area was 2,350 cm^2 ± 50 cm^2. Again spurious accuracy is implied if it is stated to be 2,352 cm^2. Children may find it difficult to accept the size of the possible error. If a strip of paper 1 cm wide is laid along one length and one width of the table, this will represent the possible error (like the shaded area in the diagram above). Discussion will reveal that this is almost 100 cm^2 (a 56 + 42 cm strip). Hence the need for a sensible estimate to be to the nearest 50 cm^2.

Parallelograms

If a parallelogram is cut out of paper it can be changed into a rectangle by cutting off a triangle from one end and moving it to the other end.

The area has only been rearranged not altered. Now the area of the rectangle is the length times the height so the area of the parallelogram is the same, i.e. the length of one side times the perpendicular distance to the other side parallel to it.

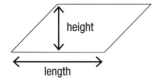

From the diagram the area of the parallelogram = length × perpendicular height.

Triangles

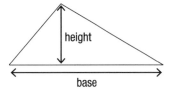

The area of a triangle is ½ × base × perpendicular height.

This formula can be proved in several ways. First it is always possible to draw a parallelogram with a given triangle as half of it. Then the area of the triangle is half that of the parallelogram i.e. half the base times the perpendicular height.

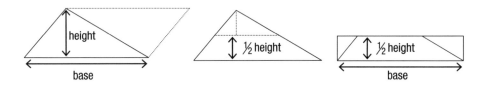

A triangle can always be cut into three pieces as shown and reassembled to make a rectangle. The area has not been changed and is the base times half the height. It is interesting that the first model (parallelogram) gives the area as ½ × (base × height) whereas the second gives base × ½ height. Why are these forms equivalent?

Trapezium

Any trapezium can be divided into a parallelogram and a triangle.

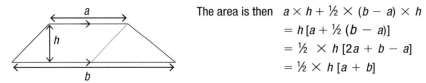

The area is then $a \times h + \frac{1}{2} \times (b - a) \times h$
$$= h\,[a + \tfrac{1}{2}\,(b - a)]$$
$$= \tfrac{1}{2} \times h\,[2a + b - a]$$
$$= \tfrac{1}{2} \times h\,[a + b]$$

This can be thought of as the average length of the parallel sides times the perpendicular distance between them.

Irregular shapes

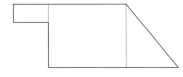

If the shape is semi-regular it may be possible to divide it into shapes whose areas can be calculated. The diagram shows an example.

In theory any polygon can be divided into rectangles and/or triangles and so the area can be calculated if sufficient lengths are known.

Circle

The formula for the area of a circle is πr^2. Again this can be illustrated in several ways. First, if a circle is cut into many equal sectors (say with angle 15°) and arranged as shown, the area is unchanged. If the sectors are made smaller then the shape will become close to a rectangle.

The height of the rectangle will be r, the radius of the circle; and the length will be half the circumference, $c/2$.

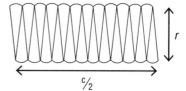

Then area $= \dfrac{c}{2} \times r$

$\qquad\quad = \dfrac{2\pi r}{2} \times r$

$\qquad\quad = \pi r^2$

Another way to think of the area of a circle is to imagine it covered with a rope wound into a spiral. If the rope is cut along a radius and the pieces straightened out, they will form a rough triangle. The height of the triangle is r and the base is $2\pi r$; so the area is $\tfrac{1}{2} \times 2\pi r \times r = \pi r^2$.

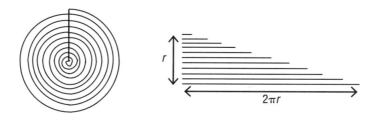

Sectors of a circle

Once the formula for the area of a circle is established, then the area of any sector can be found by proportion.
The area of the sector $= \pi r^2 \times \theta/360$. This principle of proportion or ratio was also used to find the length of any arc (see Chapter 10).

Surface area of 3-D solids

To find the surface area of simple 3-D shapes, it is necessary to calculate the areas of each face and then add them together.

For example, for a cube it is sufficient to know the length of one side; then the area of the surface is 6 times the square of that length. The surface area of the 3 cm cube shown is $6 \times 3 \times 3 = 54$ cm^2.

A cuboid has three pairs of equal faces.

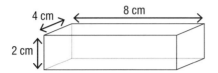

The surface area of the cuboid is

$$2 \times 4 \times 8 + 2 \times 2 \times 8 + 2 \times 2 \times 4$$
$$= 64 + 32 + 16$$
$$= 112 \text{ cm}^2$$

A similar method is used for a triangular prism or a cylinder.

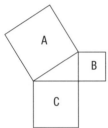

The surface area of the cylinder is

$$2 \times \pi \times 5^2 + 15 \times 2 \times \pi \times 5$$
$$= 50\pi + 150\pi$$
$$= 200\pi$$
$$\approx 628 \text{ cm}^2$$

(See Chapter 18 for further discussion of the nets of solids.)

Pythagoras' theorem

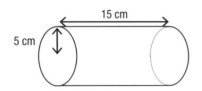

Although the theorem is often used to calculate lengths (see Chapter 10), it is really concerned with the areas of squares. The theorem states that in a right-angled triangle, the square on the hypotenuse is equal to the sum of the squares on the other two sides. In the diagram, this means that the area of square A is equal to the area of B plus the area of C.

It is said that Pythagoras first thought about this when studying patterns in the tiles of the floor. There are various ways of proving the theorem. One of the simplest is given below.

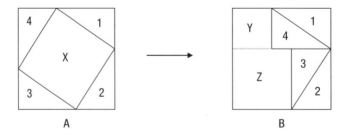

Diagram A shows four identical right-angled triangles (1, 2, 3, 4) arranged to make a large square. The area of this large square can be thought of as the area of the four triangles plus the area of the square X. The square X is the 'square on the hypotenuse' of the four triangles. In diagram B, two of the triangles (3 and 4) have been moved. The area of the large square can now be thought of as the area of the four triangles plus the area of square Y plus the area of square Z. This means that the area of square X = area of square Y + area of square Z.

Squares Y and Z are the squares on the other two sides (not the hypotenuse) of the right-angled triangles. The only principle necessary to follow this proof is the conservation of area, that is, the fact that the areas of the triangles remain the same even when they are moved to different places.

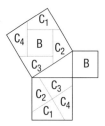

Another way of looking at this is through Perigal's dissection which shows how the squares can be cut and rearranged. Other proofs involve more complicated constructions.

✎ Check 11.2

1 Find the areas of the shapes shown below

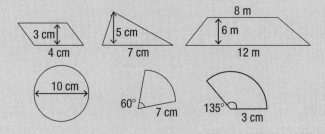

2 Divide the following shapes into simpler shapes and find their areas

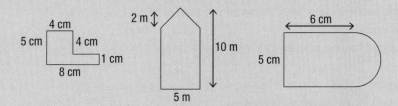

3 Find the surface areas of the following 3-D solids

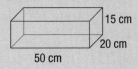

The tetrahedron is regular

Some questions from National Tests

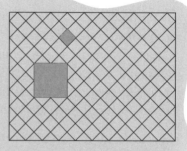

4 The area of the small shaded square is 1 square centimetre.
What is the area of the larger shaded square? On the grid draw 3 squares: one with an area of 4 cm², one with an area of 9 cm² and one with an area of 2 cm².

5 Here is a flag.

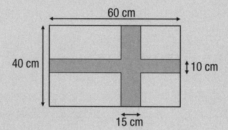

Calculate the area of the shaded cross.

Summary

- Area is the amount of surface of an object.
- The standard units are square metres (m²) and square centimetres (cm²).
- If the ratio of lengths of two similar figures is 1:a then the ratio of their areas is 1:a^2.
- Irregular areas are found by 'counting squares'.
- Area of rectangle = length × breadth.
- Area of a triangle = ½ × base × perpendicular height.
- Area of a circle = πr^2.
- Areas should be given to appropriate degrees of accuracy.

Links with the classroom

1 What aspect of area might be introduced at Key Stage 1?

2 What practical activities might be used to introduce area concepts to Y4s?

3 What apparatus might be useful to children when finding areas of irregular shapes?

4 'I measured the table to the nearest half centimetre, so I can find the area to the nearest quarter square centimetre.' Why might a child think this and how could you help them to a deeper understanding of appropriate degrees of accuracy?

Challenges!

1 The extra square.

An 8 × 8 square is cut into four pieces and rearranged as shown.

A has 8 × 8 = 64 squares, but B has 13 × 5 = 65 squares. Where has the extra square come from?

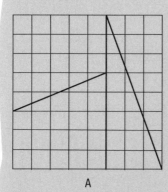

A

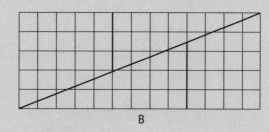

B

2 Investigate the areas of shapes with a fixed perimeter, e.g. 36 cm. Which shape gives the maximum area? Is there a minimum area?

References

Dickson, L., Brown, M. and Gibson, O. (1984) *Children Learning Mathematics*. Eastbourne: Holt, Rinehart and Winston, for Schools Council.

Capacity and volume

Starter – after Tartaglia (16th century)

THREE ROBBERS STOLE a jar containing 240 millilitres of valuable balsam. When they reached their hiding place, they found they only had three empty jars, holding 50, 110, and 130 millilitres respectively. How could they divide the valuable liquid equally between themselves using only the four jars they had? What is the fewest number of pourings necessary?

Definition and units

The capacity of a container is the amount of liquid it can hold. This is measured in litres or millilitres. In the National Numeracy Strategy it is suggested that the standard unit (litre) be introduced in year 2 or 3 and the relationship to millilitres be considered in year 4. It is notable that there is nothing about the volume of an object in the Numeracy Strategy despite its close connection to capacity and area. It seems somewhat arbitrary to include the concept of the amount of 3-D space occupied by liquids whilst ignoring that occupied by solids, especially as capacity is not an SI attribute, whereas volume is a derived SI unit.

The volume of a solid is given in cubic units such as cubic metres (m^3) or cubic centimetres (cc or cm^3). This can be thought of as the number of centimetre (or metre) cubes which can be fitted into the space occupied by the solid (e.g. a brick). So there are two different sets of units for measuring the amount of 3-D space; one for liquids (litres) and one for solids (cubic metres). Fortunately there is a simple relation between these two units, for $1\ cm^3$ or $1\ cc = 1\ ml$. This means, to quote from a DIY (Homebase 48) leaflet, '1 litre is 1,000 cubic centimetres (1,000 cc). To understand this more fully think of a litre as a box with sides $10\ cm \times 10\ cm \times 10\ cm$. You would need 1,000 boxes to fill a space $100\ cm \times 100\ cm \times 100\ cm = 1\ m \times 1\ m \times 1\ m = 1\ m^3$. 1,000 litres $= 1\ m^3$.'

In the same way as there is a problem with the size of the standard unit in length (metre), so there is a corresponding problem with the units for capacity and volume. A litre is too large for most practical purposes in year 2 or 3, so millilitres might be used, but this means the numbers become larger than some children can handle with confidence. The Numeracy Strategy suggests using a scale marked in hundreds of millilitres, but this can be quite difficult to read. Similarly the cubic metre is much too large, so the cubic centimetre (cc or cm^3) might be more appropriate. By Year 6 children should have been introduced to the imperial units of capacity, namely pints and gallons and their rough equivalents in SI units. As with all imperial units children need to be alerted to the irregular base, so there are 8 not 10 pints in a gallon.

Issues arising

The capacity of a container refers to the amount of liquid which it is capable of holding when it is full. So a litre jug is a jug which will hold 1 litre of water when it is full (usually nearly to the top). However, if the jug is half full, how should this be referred to? We could say the amount of water was half a litre or, more precisely, that the volume of water was half a litre. It would be incorrect to say the capacity of water.

Informally, making different shapes with Multilink and counting the number of cubes in each is a good way to compare their volumes. Any cubes can be used, for example the units cubes in MAB. Centicubes can be used to introduce standard units, although they are quite difficult to pack closely (the little pegs always stick out in the wrong direction!). Marbles (of the same size) pack more easily into containers and provide another possible way of comparing capacities.

Calculating volumes

Although the calculation of volumes is not covered in primary school, some strategies for finding the volumes of the more common shapes are considered as the principles are very similar to those used in calculating areas.

Cuboid

The general formula for the volume of a cuboid is often remembered as 'length $\times$ breadth $\times$ height'. This can be demonstrated by building a cuboid with cubes such as Multilink and counting the number used. The practical actions may be simple, but it is difficult to record this with diagrams. For example, the two diagrams below both represent a 4 by 3 by 2 cuboid.

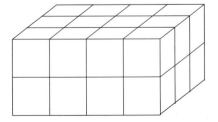 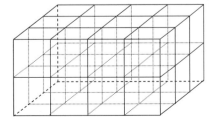

The first one seems simpler, but it does not show all the cubes and some children cannot 'see' it as a 3-D shape. The second has so many lines that it can be confusing. When calculating volumes (as with areas) it is essential that all the measurements are in the same units; then the volume will be in those units cubed. So for example, if the above cuboid were made with centimetre cubes, then the volume would be in cubic centimetres, i.e. $4 \times 3 \times 2 = 24$ cm³.

Just as there was a relationship between the ratios of lengths of similar objects and their surface area, so there is one between their lengths and their volumes. Consider two similar cubes, one of which has twice the linear dimensions of the other, then the volumes are in the ratio of $1^3:2^3 = 1:8$.

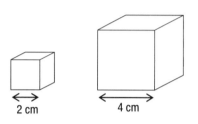

The volume of the smaller cube is $2 \times 2 \times 2$ cm³ = 8 cm³.

The volume of the larger cube is $4 \times 4 \times 4$ cm³ = 64 cm³.

So the ratio of the volume of smaller cube : volume of the larger cube = 8:64 or 1:8. This relation between the linear and volumetric size is true for all similarly shaped objects. So if there are two similar cuboids whose lengths are in the ratio of 1:3, then their volumes will be in the ratio of $1^3:3^3$, that is 1:27.

Prism

A prism is a solid shape which has a uniform cross-section and whose ends are parallel (see Chapter 18). So a cuboid is a special prism with a rectangular cross-section. The cross-section may be other shapes such as triangles and circles. The volume can be considered to be made up of a series of slices of one unit thickness and parallel to the ends.

So the area of the triangular end of the prism is $\frac{1}{2} \times b \times h$, where b is the length of the base and h is the perpendicular height (see Chapter 11). The volume will then be $\frac{1}{2} \times b \times h \times l$, where l is the length of the prism.

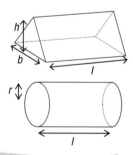

For a cylinder, which is a circular prism, the volume is $\pi r^2 l$, where l is the length. In fact for any prism, the volume is the area of the cross-section times the length.

 Check 12.1

1 Find the volume of the following 3-D shapes:

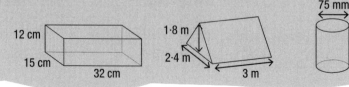

2 'Bradley's Soup' is canned by a small family business. Each morning they make 200 litres of soup.

This is put in cylindrical tins, each of which is 8·4 cm high and has a diameter of 7·0 cm. How many of these tins can be filled from the 200 litres of soup?

On one day per week they make the same amount of soup, but fill 'catering size' tins, which are twice the linear dimensions of the normal tins, i.e. they are 16·8 cm high and have a diameter of 14 cm. What is the ratio of the volume of the normal tins : volume of catering size tins?
How many catering size tins will they be able to fill?

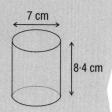

(Note: 1 ml = 1 cm³)

Summary

- The capacity of a container is the amount of liquid it can hold.
- The volume of an object is the amount of 3-D space it occupies.
- The standard units of capacity are litres (l) and of volume are cubic metres (m³).
- If the linear ratio between two similar objects is 1:3 then the ratio of their volumes is 1:27.
- The volume of a cuboid is length × breadth × height.
- The volume of a prism is cross-sectional area × length.

Links with the classroom

1 What practical activities (including games) and what language would be appropriate to introduce children to ideas about capacity and volume in Years 1 and 2?
2 How would you introduce standard measures (litres) in Year 2 or 3? In particular, what context might make the exercise meaningful to children? Would you use measuring cylinders or standard cups?
3 When introducing millilitres, what sort of scale on the measuring jar would be easiest?

Challenges!

1 An A4 sheet of card can be made into two different cylinders: one by joining their shorter sides, the other by joining their longer sides. Investigate their capacities.
2 An open box is made by cutting out squares (of side x cm) from each of the four corners of a 15 cm square card and folding the sides upwards.
Could you create a container from the original 15 cm square of card in a different way? If so, what would the largest volume be?

What value of *x* will give the box with the largest volume?

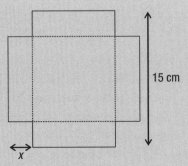

15 cm

x

3 When applications for building extensions to houses are being considered, it is necessary to work out the volume of the proposed extension. In one application it was proposed to change a 'hip roof' to a roof with a gable end. From the measurements given to the left work out the volume of this extension.

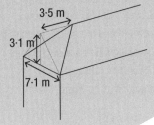

3·5 m

3·1 m

7·1 m

CHAPTER

Mass and weight

Starter – after Tartaglia

WHAT IS THE fewest number of weights needed to weigh any number of whole pounds between 1 and 40? What are the values of the weights? First try it with the weights allowed on only one side of the balance. Does it make any difference if you can put the weights on either side?

Definition and units

There is a problem about the most suitable language to use for mass and weight in the primary school. The source of the problem is that the scientific and (mathematical) meanings of the words are not the same as those used by many people in everyday conversation. In scientific terms the mass of an object is the amount of matter in the object. It is measured in kilograms and does not vary according to its position. The weight of an object is the force exerted on that object by gravity (the attraction towards the centre of the Earth). This can vary for several reasons, including its position, for example whether the object is high on a mountain or at (or below) sea level. This is measured in newtons and is equal to the mass times the acceleration due to gravity. 1 newton is the force necessary to give a mass of 1 kilogram an acceleration of 1 metre per second per second. The acceleration due to gravity near the Earth's surface is approximately 9·8 metres per second per second towards the centre of the Earth. So the gravitational force on an adult female will be between 500 and 600 newtons.

The difference between mass and weight is clearly shown if a 1 kilogram bag of sugar is considered first on the Earth and then on the Moon. The mass of the sugar is 1 kilogram. In scientific terms, on Earth it weighs $1 \times 9·8 = 9·8$ newtons. This is the force which causes it to fall on the ground if it is lifted up and then left unsupported. On the Moon the mass of the bag of sugar is still 1 kilogram. But the force attracting it towards the Moon's surface is much less, being about ⅙ of the gravitational force on earth, because the Moon has a much smaller mass than the Earth. So its weight is

⅙ × 9·8 ≈ 1·6 newtons. So if it were lifted up and dropped on the Moon it would fall less rapidly than on the Earth (ignoring the frictional effects of air on Earth). Pictures of astronauts bouncing about on the Moon's surface show that they are subject to a gravitational force, albeit much less powerful than on Earth. In space away from any planet, there is so small a gravitational force that objects appear to be 'weightless', they float about.

The main source of difficulty is that in general when people talk of the 'weight' of an object they expect it to be measured in kilograms not newtons. It seems that the ideas of weight and mass are often confused, so that when the 'weight' of an object is mentioned, it is the amount of matter in it rather than the force attracting it towards the Earth that is foremost in many people's minds. If one is asked to buy 1 kilogram of potatoes, one thinks of the number of potatoes involved, not the force attracting them to the ground. In practical situations on Earth, as mass and weight vary together, there is no real problem.

Another concept related to mass is that of density. The density of a substance is the mass per unit volume. This is measured in kilograms per cubic metre (kg/m^3) or grams per cubic centimetre (g/cm^3). So, for instance, the density of gold is 19 g/cm^3. This means that every cubic centimetre of gold has a mass of 19 grams.

As children may well come across them at home, pounds (lb) and ounces (oz), which are the imperial units for mass, should be mentioned in school. It is also worth noting the relation between the mass and volume of water in SI units. Under normal conditions 1 litre of water weighs 1 kilogram and 1 ml or 1 cc or 1 cm^3 weighs 1 gram.

Issues arising

First ideas of weight are often introduced in the early years of the primary school. These usually involve the comparative language of weight, for example, heavier, lighter, heaviest, lightest. Practical demonstrations with a simple balance are introduced as a way of testing for differences in weight. Informal units, such as acorns, Multilink and marbles, are again used before standard units are introduced. It seems quite appropriate for a five year old to say, for example, that the weight of a ball is the same as the weight of 6 marbles. In fact if a simple balance is used, it is strictly the masses that are compared. But as the force of gravity is the same on both sides of the balance, the weights are proportional to the masses and so the ratio of the weights is the same as that of the masses.

There is a problem about which standard unit to introduce first. The kilogram is the basic SI unit, but this is really too heavy for children to handle safely. If grams are used the numbers tend to be large and may well be out of the range which Key Stage 1 children can handle with confidence. Usually 10, 20 and 50 gram masses (or weights) are used in the classroom. The question arises as to what they should be called. Some teachers feel they must be accurate and so refer to them as 'a 50 gram mass', others wish to relate the classroom to the children's experience out of school and so call it 'a 50 gram weight'. It does seem strange that the verb 'to weigh' means finding the mass and not the weight of an object. It is probably important for teachers to be consistent in their language and to allow the children some latitude in theirs, especially in the lower part of the primary school. By the time they are 11 years old, children should be aware that there is a difference between mass and weight.

By the end of primary school children should also be aware of the different principle behind the balance beam and the spring weighing machine. In a traditional balance, the beam remains horizontal when the forces which tend to cause it to rotate are equal. It is important that children are shown how to adjust the balance, so that the arm is horizontal when there is nothing on either side before they start using it. This means that a 1 kilogram mass (weight) will balance a 1 kilogram bag of sugar both on the Earth and on the Moon.

Beam balance

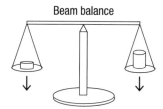

The spring weighing machine works on a different principle. In this case, the force (weight) which compresses (or extends) a spring is measured by the degree of compressions (or extension). This is usually shown by an arrow moving over a calibrated scale or dial. This means that if a 1 kilogram bag of sugar is attached on Earth, the reading will be much higher than it would be on the Moon.

Spring weighing machine

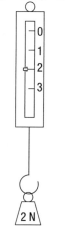

Some children find it difficult to understand and read the gradations on the dials of kitchen scales. The task is complex as illustrated below by the diagrams of parts of common dials overleaf. Only the first part of each dial is shown as children are most likely to be concerned with weighing masses between 20 and 500 grams. A and B are both from scales used in primary school. A weighs objects up to 1 kilogram with marks at 5 gram intervals. B is from some general purpose scales using a 25 gram interval and can weigh objects up to 5 kilograms.

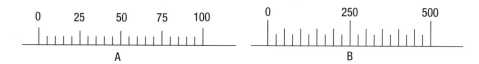

The latter can be a challenging task for children in Year 3, who need to distinguish between the shorter marks which are at 25 gram intervals and the longer ones which are at 50 gram intervals. The numbers are quite large and may be outside the range with which they feel confident. The situation with scales which might be found in the home is no simpler. Both the scales shown as C and D were on kitchen scales which weighed up to 5 or 6 kilograms.

To use such scales involves understanding ratio or fractional parts. For example it is quite a complicated procedure to find the value indicated by the smaller marks in scale C. First the size of the labelled interval must be found (100 g), then the number of subintervals or spaces (but not marks) within this established (5). Finally the size of the subintervals is found by dividing the first by the second, i.e. $100 \div 5 = 20$. So the smaller marks indicate 20, 40, 60, 80 grams. This means that estimation must be used if 50 grams were required. To use D with confidence it is necessary to be able to count in 25s and interpolate if necessary. Explicit discussion not only in the early stages but throughout the primary school should help children gain confidence.

Calculations

There are few occasions when it is necessary to calculate a weight; it is usually a matter of measuring it directly, with an appropriate device. However, if density is introduced, then suitable methods of calculation must be indicated. To find the density of an object, it is necessary to find both its volume and its mass. The mass can be measured on a balance beam or a spring weighing machine, to the required degree of accuracy. If the object is a regular shape, then its volume can be calculated. If it is irregular, then the volume of water it displaces when completely submerged can be found. Both the principle behind this correspondence and the practical method of using it must be discussed before the children begin. Since density is mass per unit volume, it is found by dividing the mass by the volume, making sure both are in appropriate units.

✎ Check 13.1

1 The density of gold is approximately 19 g/cm³. Find the mass of the ingot.

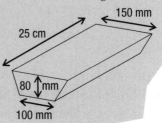

Summary

- Mass is the amount of matter in an object and is measured in kilograms.
- Weight is the force tending to pull an object towards the Earth and is measured in newtons.
- A beam balance compares masses.
- A spring weighing machine measures force.
- Density is mass per unit volume.

Links with the classroom

1 Which standard units would you use in a Year 2 classroom? What would you call them?
2 How would you present the distinction between mass and weight to Year 6s?

Challenge!

Put in order of density: tomato soup, fresh tomatoes, baked beans, spaghetti, butter, bread, porridge oats. How would you calculate the density of each?

14

Angles and compass directions

Starter

A WOMAN WALKS due south for 1 km then due east for 1 km and then due north for 1 km, ending up at her starting point. How is that possible?

Definitions

The concepts of compass directions and angles are closely connected. In the National Curriculum right angles are first introduced in Year 2 and compass directions in Year 3. The four primary compass directions (North, South, East, West) are at right angles to each other. In some ways the concept of angle is much more complicated than that of compass directions because angles are experienced in two ways. The dynamic view is of an amount of turning whilst the static view looks at the way two straight lines meet each other. The dynamic view has the advantage that it can include any angle, even ones greater that 360°, whereas the static view really only includes angles up to 360°. Consider the two statements:

> from the palm tree on a bearing of 315° take 20 paces then dig
> the corners of the door should be right angles

In the first case there is an implicit instruction to stand under the palm tree, face north, then turn 315° in a clockwise direction before walking 20 strides. In the second it is the relative directions of the sides of the door that are being described. Clearly these are related and the units used to measure them are the same. Children often find the dynamic form the easier to understand at first.

Compass directions

In primary school children should be introduced to the eight compass points (N, S, E, W, NE, NW, SE, SW).

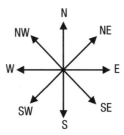

Initially north should be the direction in which a compass needle points and the direction towards the north pole (and the pole star, if a child mentions it). South is the direction of the sun at midday. The east–west line is at right angles to the north–south line. This may sound simple, but various misconceptions can arise. Most children understand that north and south are in opposite directions, but some have difficulty remembering which is east and which is west.

This may be linked with a confusion with left and right. If facing north, then east is on the right and west on the left, but if facing south, east is to the left and west on the right. When reading a map to direct a car, it is clearly most important to understand this. Another possible source of confusion is the way we refer to winds. The direction north is that direction we face if we look towards the north pole. However, a north wind comes from the north and so would be blowing in our face.

As they get older, children realise that the magnetic north pole (the point towards which compass needles point) is not the same as the geographic north pole. In fact, as noted on Ordnance Survey maps, the magnetic pole moves slowly in relation to historic time.

Of course, the reason for introducing compass directions to primary children is to enable them to describe positions and directions accurately and clearly for everyday use. For example, in geography they need to be able to describe a journey on a map or grid, or give relative positions of places on a map.

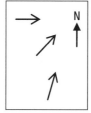 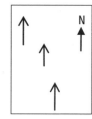

Because the north and south poles are so far away from England, on maps such as the Ordnance Survey 1:50,000 the lines of longitude (lines pointing north–south) are considered parallel. Having learnt that the north pole is a specific place, some children imagine that on a map north is the direction towards the letter N, whereas it should be parallel to the arrow shown.

Units of angle

The standard unit for measuring angles is the degree. A complete turn is 360°. The Babylonians used a number system with a 60-base and appeared to use

the approximation of 360 days in a year. They were particularly interested in astronomy, using angles in their observations.

In the early stages of learning about angles children should be introduced to terms such as half-turn, quarter-turn and full-turn. It should be noted that to describe a turn fully it is necessary to give both the amount and the direction. So a complete command might be 'make a quarter-turn in a clockwise direction'. It would be perfectly possible to achieve the same result by making a three-quarters-turn in an anti-clockwise direction; but the actual turn would be different.

Because it is very common in the man-made world around us, the first static angle to be used is the right angle (or square-angle). Children can be given or make their own 'right angle' by folding a piece of paper in half, then carefully folding the fold to the fold, so getting a right angle. They can then look for and test angles between lines or edges around the classroom.

By the end of primary school children should have been introduced to the names for different types of angles as they are in the National Curriculum. In practice, knowing the names but having no feel for the size of angles is useless. Children need plenty of practical experience of working with angles in a range of situations, such as using LOGO, or orienteering.

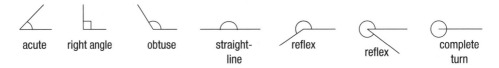

It should be noted that if two lines meet at a point, two angles are made. If one is acute or obtuse, then the other is reflex. From the definition of a degree a complete turn is 360°. Then it is clear from the diagrams that a right angle is equal to a quarter-turn and so is 90°, and the straight line is a half-turn and so 180°.

Issues arising

There is often some confusion over the meaning of the words 'perpendicular', 'vertical', and 'horizontal'. If two lines are perpendicular it means that they meet or cross at right angles. So all the pairs of lines shown here are perpendicular.

Horizontal really means parallel to the Earth's surface, in other words level with the ground. So the level of water in a jar is horizontal. Many surfaces such as a tabletop are roughly horizontal, as things will stay on a level surface. Vertical means directly upwards (or downwards) away from (or towards) the centre of the Earth. It is perpendicular to the horizontal. The walls of a house should be vertical for safety.

By convention, a line across the page is often regarded as horizontal and a line perpendicular to it as vertical. Strictly if the page is lying on, say, a desk or table then all lines are horizontal. It is only when the drawing is an elevation that the lines across the page represent horizontal lines on the ground and those up and down the page represent vertical distances. It is better only to use the words horizontal and vertical in the 3-dimensional world and not with reference to drawings.

Children should be encouraged to relate the dynamic and static ideas of angle. If they understand this connection, they should not make the mistake of thinking that the size of angle is affected by the length of lines defining it. So for instance, the two angles shown here are equal, despite the unequal length of the lines.

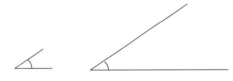

Angles are usually measured with a protractor, but many children find this a difficult instrument to use. Circular protractors or angle measures are much easier to use and reinforce the connection between the dynamic and static aspect of angle.

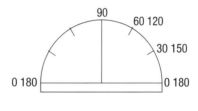

In the circular protractor, there are two plastic circles joined at the centre. The inner circle has an arrow on it and can be rotated. This action links the dynamic and static aspect of angle. It is also more obvious that the centre of the protractor must be placed on the point of the angle. Many children find the traditional semi-circular protractor difficult to use. If there is no alternative, it is a very good idea to ask pupils to estimate the angle first and only then decide which scale to read from. The protractor is not always placed correctly. One common mistake is to put the lower edge of the protractor over one of the lines defining the angle to be measured.

Calculations

It is often possible to calculate the size of angles by using various standard facts.

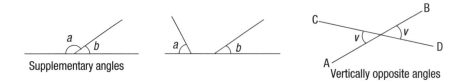

Supplementary angles

Vertically opposite angles

In the first diagram the two angles (called supplementary angles) add up to 180°, as they are on a straight line. Note that the two angles in the second diagram do not add up to 180°. In the third diagram two straight lines AB and CD cross each other. The angles opposite each other (such as the two marked 'v') are equal.

If two parallel lines are crossed by another straight line, then there are several useful relationships.

The basic relation is between two angles, such as those marked 'c', which are equal and are called corresponding angles. From this other equal angles can be deduced.

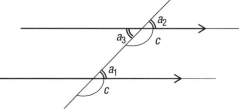

For example, $a_1 = a_2$ (corresponding angles)

$a_2 = a_3$ (vertically opposite angles)

so $a_1 = a_3$

Angles in the relation of a_1 and a_3 are called alternate angles.

Angles in a triangle

The interior angles of any triangle add up to 180°. This can be demonstrated or proved in several ways.

If an arrow (or pencil) is laid on the base of a triangle (1), moved to the vertex (point) then rotated through the first angle (a) it will lie along the second side (2). If it is moved to the next vertex and rotated through the second angle (b), it will lie on the third side (3). Finally if it is moved to the third vertex and rotated through the third angle (c) it will lie along the base as shown (4). For arrow 1 to lie over arrow 4 it is necessary to rotate it through 180°. This means that by moving through $a + b + c$ the arrow has moved through 180°, so the angles of the triangle add up to 180°.

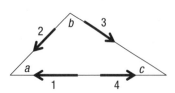

There is a program showing such an arrow moving around a triangle on the CD. Another demonstration is what Papert calls the 'total turtle trip theorem'.

Imagine turtle (or a person) starting at point A and looking towards B then walking around the triangle keeping account of the angles through which he turns. To get back to his original position he will turn through $(180 - b) + (180 - c) + (180 - a)$. But he has made one complete turn, which is 360°.

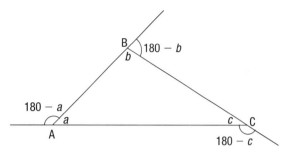

So
$$(180 - b) + (180 - c) + (180 - a) = 360$$
$$180 - b + 180 - c + 180 - a = 360$$
$$540 - b - c - a = 360$$
$$540 - 360 = a + b + c$$
$$a + b + c = 180$$

The same fact can also be proved through a simple construction.

Through one vertex draw a line parallel to the opposite side of the triangle.

From the diagram

$a^1 = a^2$ (corresponding angles)
$b^1 = b^2$ (alternate angles)

but the angles
$c^1 + b^2 + a^2 = 180°$ (supplementary angles on a straight line)
so $a^1 + b^1 + c^1 = 180°$
that is the angles in a triangle add up to 180°.

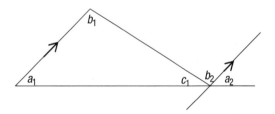

Angles in quadrilaterals

The same sort of demonstration can be used to show that the angles in a convex quadrilateral add up to 360°.

Check 14.1

A question from National Tests

1 Find the angles marked in the diagram

2 In this diagram AB is parallel to CD

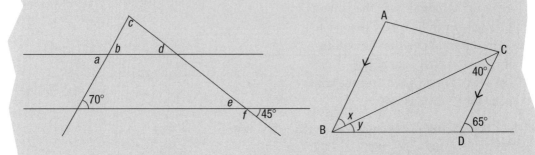

Calculate the value of the angles x and y. (Do not use an angle measurer.)

Summary

- Angles are measures of turning.
- Standard units are degrees, where $360° = 1$ full turn.
- Supplementary angles add up to $180°$.
- Vertically opposite angles are equal.
- Alternate and corresponding angles are equal.
- Interior angles of a triangle add up to $180°$.
- Interior angles of a convex quadrilateral add up to $360°$.

Links with the classroom

1 How would you introduce compass directions to children in Year 3?

2 Which units of angle and what names for them are suitable for use at Key Stage 1?

3 How would you teach children to use a protractor or an angle measurer?

4 What practical activities might help children relate the dynamic and static aspects of angles?

5 What activities might help children understand the meaning of the term 'perpendicular'?

Challenges!

Investigate the dissection of regular polygons with even numbers of sides into rhombi. How many rhombi are needed? How many different rhombi are there? What about their angles? (From an article by Melrose 1998.)

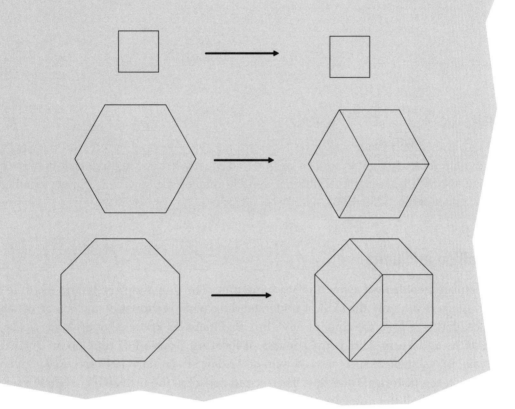

References

Melrose, J. (1998) 'But, it's like . . .', *Mathematics Teaching*, **162**, 31–5.

Papert, S. (1980) *Mindstorms: Children, Computers and Powerful Ideas*. Brighton: Harvester Press.

Time

Starter

I AM A brazen lion (fountain); my spouts are my two eyes, my mouth and the flat of my right foot. My right eye fills a jar in two days, my left eye in three and my foot in four. My mouth is capable of filling it in six hours; tell me how long all four together will take to fill it? (Greek 50AD)

Definition and units

There are two distinct aspects in studying time. The first aspect is 'telling the time'. This covers not only the skill of understanding what is shown on a clock or watch face, that is telling 'the time of day', but also includes knowledge of days, weeks, months and years. This is the process of locating a period of time on an ordinal scale. So a statement such as 11.30 a.m. on Friday, 9th January 1998 specifies a given time on the historical time line. The second aspect is the measuring of time intervals. Although the units are the same, this is measured on a ratio scale. The 35th minute of a football game is the minute that starts exactly 34 minutes after the initial whistle and lasts 1 minute. The time when the initial whistle is blown is zero time (for that game).

In the early stages of primary school children are usually introduced to the way to name a given day, that is, give its date. This involves knowing the names and order of the days of the week; the names and order of the ordinal numbers (first, second . . .); the names and order of the months and possibly the name (number) of the year. Our system for locating time in this way is quite irregular. There are seven days in a week (and the school routine emphasises this), but the months have a variable number of days in them and are not whole weeks. There are 12 months in the year, but the number of days is either 365 or 366.

The year and the day are the only 'natural' units of time. The day is the time the Earth takes to make one complete revolution on its own axis in relation to the Sun (i.e. the average time between one midday and the next). The year is the time the Earth takes to make one complete circuit around the Sun. This takes roughly 365 ¼ days. To allow for this the Julian calendar (introduced by Julius Caesar) decreed that every fourth year (a leap year) should have 366 days, while the others should have 365 days. Unfortunately the Earth only takes 365 days, 5 hours and 49 minutes to complete its circuit, so there is a slight migration of dates, so January 1st will drift towards spring. To correct this, the Gregorian calendar (introduced by Pope Gregory XIII) says that a year is a leap year if its number is divisible by four unless it is a century, when it is a leap year only if it is divisible by 400. So 1900 was not a leap year, but 2000 was. The naming of the centuries (and millennia) can be confusing, for example the twelfth century includes the years from 1100 to 1199AD. At some point children must be told about BC (before Christ) and AD (anno domini, Latin for 'in the year of the Lord', i.e. after Christ).

The subdivision of the day into hours, minutes and seconds is arbitrary, but a convention that must be learnt. We choose to take midnight as the time when we start counting the time of day, so it is called 0 hours. There are 24 hours in one day, and each hour is divided into 60 minutes and each minute can be subdivided into 60 seconds. As with angular measurement, the 60-base originally came from Babylonia. The variability of the base alone makes telling the time quite difficult, but it is complicated further by the several ways of stating the time. For example, the following all refer to the same time:

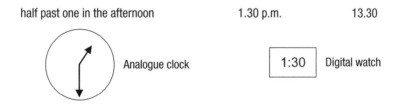

half past one in the afternoon   1.30 p.m.   13.30

Analogue clock   1:30 Digital watch

In the early stages of measuring time intervals, it is usual to concentrate on intervals such as 1 minute. As stopwatches are complicated, a simple device such as a sand timer is often used. Later, when more accurate measurements of time are required, seconds must be used and the 60-base introduced.

The concept of speed is closely related to time. Speed is a measure of the rate of travel. It is expressed in metres per second or kilometres per hour. As the units show, it is a measure of the distance travelled in unit time (see Chapter 5). The units are abbreviated to m/s ($\frac{m}{s}$) or ms^{-1} using the index notation (see Chapter 3) and km/h or kmh^{-1}. The imperial units are feet per second (fps) or miles per hour (mph). This idea of a rate involving two different units is quite difficult for some children, especially if average rates (speeds) are included.

Issues arising

Most children learn how to record the date without too many problems. There may be some confusion (for example in some computer software) between the American form of month, day, year and the English day, month, year. Other forms are possible, for example, year, month, day (as in Japan). In primary school the convention of day, month, year should be used, so 6/1/98 means 6th January 1998 and 12/12/00 means 12th December 2000.

Children's ages are usually given in years and months. There are one or two problems which may arise in this connection. If birthdays are entered into a database and an attempt is made to calculate the children's age by subtracting their birth date from the current date, the answer may be given in a number of days. There is no simple way to convert this into years and months. There are several ways to write children's ages. In a table it is clearest if the years are in one column and the months in another. If any calculations are carried out it must be remembered that there are 12 months in a year. Sometimes the ages are written with a dot between the years and months, but this form can cause problems. If 6·8 means 6 years and 8 months, difficulties arise if the ages are ordered as if they were decimals, for 6·11 (6 years and 11 months) would be put between 6·1 and 6·2., i.e. it would be considered as more than 6 years and 1 month but less than 6 years and 2 months. Other ways may be used, so that it is very important to be aware of the particular convention.

There are many more problems in recording the time within the day. There are several different ways, and children need to understand them all and be able to move from one to another. The first challenge is to understand the analogue clock face. By convention, the clock face only shows 12 hours and has 12 at the top with the other numbers spaced equally around. Most clocks have two hands, so in effect there are two different scales around the clock, even if only one is shown. It may help young children to have a clock face with both the numbers for the hours (say in black for the hour hand) and those for the minutes (say in red for the minute hand). Traditionally, children are taught to tell the whole hours, the o'clock times, such as 2 o'clock first. The next stage is to subdivide the hours into quarters and learn the conventions used when giving the time to the nearest quarter hour (quarter past, half past, quarter to).

The move to using minutes as well as hours needs practice. It is probably best to concentrate on telling the time to the nearest 5 minutes at first, but there are some difficulties, especially as there are basically two ways of stating the time. The traditional way associated with the analogue clock face is, for example, 25 past 4 (i.e. 25 minutes after 4 o'clock) or 25 to 10 (i.e. 25 minutes before 10 o'clock). The digital notation is entirely numbers. The number before the dot (looking like a decimal point) or colon (:) refers to the hours and the number after the dot to the minutes, so 4.25 (read as four twenty five) is the same as 25 past 4. However, 25 to 10 would be

9.35 (i.e. 35 minutes after 9). To understand this equivalence, children need to know that there are 60 minutes in an hour.

It may not be necessary for children to know the origin of a.m. and p.m., but it is an interesting sidelight on how measurements of time developed. The morning was 'ante meridiem' that is before the time the sun passed the meridian (was highest in the sky) or noon, and the afternoon was post meridiem (after the sun had been at its highest). In fact p.m. is just an abbreviation of the Latin for afternoon. It was possible, on a sunny day, to find the time the sun was at its highest by observation (for example by the length of the shadow of a stick) and then hours could be measured by other means, for example candle or water clocks or, later, mechanical time keepers.

The National Numeracy Strategy suggests that children should be introduced to the 24-hour clock in Year 5. This is related to the digital form of telling the time and is used, for example, in railway timetables. Problems can occur with the 24-hour clock times. Midnight is taken as the starting point and is written as 00.00. The times in the morning are just like the digital form, so 10.40 means 10 hours and 40 minutes, or in traditional form 20 to 11 (20 minutes before 11 o'clock). In the 24-hour clock midday has no special status and the hours are counted from midnight, so 1.00 p.m. is 13.00, 2.00 p.m. is 14.00 and so on. It is very easy to make mistakes and read, say, 16.00 as 6 o'clock and not 4.00 p.m. Children will need much practice in giving times in several forms and moving from one to another.

Because of the 60-base, it is quite difficult to find the time interval between two times of day, especially as the standard way of writing the time appears to suggest it might be treated as numbers in the decimal system. For example, if the train leaves one station at 9.46 and arrives at the next at 10.12, how long does the journey between the two take? Probably the best way to find the time taken is to use a counting-on method.

So, from 9.46 to 10.00 is	14 minutes
from 10.00 to 10.12 is	12 minutes
then the total time taken is	$14 + 12 = 26$ minutes

The same method can be used even if the time goes over midnight. For example, how long does it take to travel from Edinburgh to London, if the train leaves Edinburgh at 19.30 and arrives at London at 00.45?

19.30 to 20.00 is	30 minutes
20.00 to 00.00 (= 24.00 midnight) is	4 hours
00.00 to 00.45 is	45 minutes
So the total time taken is	30 minutes + 4 hours + 45 minutes
	= 4 hours + 75 minutes
	= 4 hours + 1 hour + 15 minutes
	= 5 hours 15 minutes.

If foreign travel is included then some discussion of time zones is necessary. These are related to the rotation of the Earth and the fact that the Sun is 'overhead' at places on the same meridian at the same time. Because the Earth rotates through 360° in 24 hours, then it will move 15° in 1 hour. This means that the time zones are roughly 15° (of longitude) wide. The International Date Line roughly follows the 180° meridian through the Pacific Ocean. So for example, if you travel from Japan (140°E) to Samoa (170°W) leaving Japan on Sunday evening, you would arrive in Samoa on Sunday morning. However, if you left Samoa late on Sunday evening and travelled to Japan, you would arrive on Tuesday morning.

These days the measurement of time can be very accurate. The Earth is not an entirely regular timekeeper, so the scientists use the vibrations of crystals as their standard. As with other forms of measurement, it is useful to discuss appropriate degrees of accuracy. In the Olympic games, times are given to the nearest hundredth of a second, but in school sports, the nearest tenth of a second is probably sufficient. Lectures (or lessons) may be timetabled to the nearest minute, but in practice, they are more likely to be to the nearest five (or even ten) minutes.

One of the problems with measuring time interval is that the scientists insist that time passes at a constant rate, yet it does not feel like that in direct experience. Five minutes in the dentist's waiting room can feel longer than an hour at the cinema (if the film is good). Time interval can be measured informally by sand timers, or pendulums, but in the upper primary school stopwatches might be used.

 # Check 15.1

1 Complete the following table

Analogue	Digital	24-hour
Quarter to 9 in the morning		
	10.50 a.m.	
		00.20
	4.35 p.m.	
		20.15
20 to 3 in the afternoon		

2 Find the time intervals between the following times. Discuss your methods with friends.

Half past nine and quarter past ten

3.46 p.m. and 5.23 p.m.

twenty to nine and ten to twelve

11.35 a.m. to 2.15 p.m.

14.50 to 15.26

3 A support teacher assessed the reading ages of 10 pupils at the beginning of Year 5

Pupil	Actual age		Reading	
	Years	Months	Years	Months
A	9	07	7	11
B	9	01	8	06
C	9	03	6	10
D	9	08	9	02
E	9	01	10	04
F	9	11	9	00
G	9	05	8	10
H	9	07	7	09
I	9	06	8	01
J	9	00	7	08

What percentage of the 10 pupils had a reading age more than 1 year 6 months below their actual ages?

Rates

As they are closely related to the measurement of time, speeds and other rates must be considered briefly, despite the fact that they have already been touched on in Chapter 5. Speed is a measure of how far has been travelled in unit time (usually seconds or hours). The children probably first come across it in speed limits for car travel, for example, the 30 mph limit in built-up areas. This is in fact quite a complicated measure. It does not mean that the car goes 30 miles in an hour, but rather that if it continued at the same speed for an hour it would cover 30 miles. It is probably simpler to think of it as 44 feet per second, or, changing it into SI units, about 13·41 m per second. In fact at the primary level it is more common to compare times over the same distance rather than speeds. So, on sports day it is the times taken to run, say, 100 m that are recorded and discussed, not the speeds of the runners. Even in practical science investigations, for example running little cars down a slope covered by different materials to study friction, it is the time taken to cover a fixed distance that is measured. This can be measured directly (with a stopwatch) and is a simpler concept.

Other rates may be more useful in primary school. For example, the investigation of pulse rates (or heartbeats) after different amounts of exercise. In this situation, the number of beats per minute is counted directly, and as the unit time is used there is no calculation necessary to obtain the rate. Similarly, when studying the effect of varying the length of pendulums, it is usual to count the number of swings per minute.

However, there are a few common difficulties in rate problems some of which are illustrated with the two following examples.

1 Two people go on a day's hike. They leave at 9.00 am and walk 7½ miles before stopping for lunch at midday. In the afternoon they walk at 1½ mph for 1 hour (it was very steep). What was their average speed in the morning? How far did they walk altogether? What was their average speed for the whole day?

To find an average rate, it is usually necessary to find the total distance (or whatever is being measured) and the total time, then divide the total distance by the total time.

	Distance (miles)	Time (hours)	Average speed (mph)
In the morning	7·5	3	($7.5/3 = 2.5$)
In the afternoon	($1 \times 1.5 = 1.5$)	1	1·5
Total distance	$7.5 + 1.5 = 9$		
Total time		$3 + 1 = 4$	
Average speed			$\frac{9}{4} = 2.25$

In this case, the correct average speed is 2·25 mph. However, if the two speeds given (2·5 and 1·5) are simply averaged the result appears to be 2 mph.

2 If a car is travelling at 60 mph on a motorway, how long will it take go in 10 miles, 5 miles? If there is heavy traffic and the average speed drops to 30 mph, how long will it take to go 10 miles?

As speed is distance divided by time, then distance is speed multiplied by time, and time is distance divided by speed. A table can be used to set out the calculations.

Average speed (in mph)	Distance (in miles)	Time (in hours)
60	10	$10 \div 60 = \frac{1}{6}$
60	5	$5 \div 60 = \frac{1}{12}$
30	10	$10 \div 30 = \frac{1}{3}$

In the first two parts of the question (time taken to go 10 miles and 5 miles) the proportion between the distance and the time is direct. When the speed is the same, it will take half the time to cover half the distance. That is, the time varies directly with the distance (they increase or decrease together). However, in the third part of the question when the speed is halved, then the time taken to cover a given distance is doubled. This is a case of indirect proportion. If the distance considered is the same, then the speed varies indirectly with the time. So as the speed increases the time decreases and vice versa.

Check 15.2

1 Ann walks at 2 metres per second and runs at 5 metres per second. How long does she take to go 50 metres at each pace? If she walks 50 metres and then runs 75 metres, what is her average speed over the 125 metres?

2 1 tap full on fills a bath in 10 minutes. If 2 taps are turned full on, how long will they take to fill the bath?

3 Arthur can build a house in 10 days. Bert takes 12 days, while Charlie needs 15 days. If the three men cooperate, how long will they take to build the house?

Summary

- There are two aspects in the study of time: 'telling the time' and measuring time interval.
- The standard units have an irregular base (60 minutes = 1 hour).
- There are several ways of stating and recording the time of day.
- Children often find problems involving rates difficult.

Links with the classroom

1 How would you introduce the 24-hour clock to a Year 5 class?

2 In finding the period of time between 9.40 and 12.15 a pupil wrote:

```
  12.15
−  9.40
   2.75     Answer 2 hours 75 mins
```

What misunderstandings does this reveal? How would you try to correct them?

3 How could you use a calendar as a source of mathematical investigations?

Challenges!

1 Find out more about time zones. If it is 3 p.m. in June in London, what time is it in Paris, Lagos, Perth, Rio de Janeiro, Karachi, Tokyo, San Francisco, Moscow?

2 If 1st January 1998 was on Thursday, which day of the week would 1st March be? What about the 31st December? What day was 1st January 1950? What will 1st June 2012 be?

PART

Shape

There is no obviously logical sequence in which to present material about 2-D and 3-D shape, any more than there is a self-evident order in which to teach these topics. They form a complex and untidy network. Learners need to move around within this network, following a range of paths in order to acquire a reasonably rich grasp of the key ideas. To describe shapes we need symmetry and angle concepts, and yet these concepts themselves cannot be understood without reference to other shape properties. Again, 3-D shapes cannot properly be characterised without 2-D shape terminology. However, as we shall see, 2-D shapes are strictly speaking the surfaces of 3-D objects. So just where should this section start? A decision had to be made. Chapter 16 deals directly with the properties of 2-D shape. Chapter 17 extends the treatment by examining 2-D shape applications and investigations, while Chapter 18 goes on to discuss 3-D shape. You are strongly encouraged to tackle this material from various starting points within the three chapters.

Questions of whether one shape is the 'same' as or 'different' from another demand our attention several times in what follows. We will see that criteria for sameness and difference are the results of human decisions, and that these are not always crystal clear. Since language issues are of such significance in the elementary mathematics of shape, Chapter 16 opens with some brief general observations about how mathematical language seems to work.

(Note: in the next three chapters diagrams have been numbered (e.g. Figure 16.1, 16.2, etc.). This is necessary as an aid for readers, whereas numbering is not required in other chapters.)

CHAPTER

16

2-D shape

ONE FRIEND INSTRUCTS another to draw a rectangle. The person following the instructions takes them literally and deliberately ignores what her instructor 'really means'.

'Draw a straight line.'

'OK.'

'Now draw another line at right angles to the first.'

'No, no! The lines must meet!'

'Oh, come on! I meant that the ends of the lines should meet!'

Evidently it is going to be a little while before the rectangle is successfully completed.

The 'game' is only possible because most uses of ordinary language require contexts both for the speaker to mean something reasonably precise, and for the hearer to grasp it. The context actually serves to help and support effective communication. When I say 'You are standing on my foot', what I actually intend to convey differs from the meaning of my words considered apart from a context. I am unlikely to be providing information, and am probably asking you to get off my foot as soon as possible. If I say 'You are standing on my foot' to a perversely literal-minded person, she might simply thank me for the information. The friend who is taking the drawing instructions in the above game is responding to language in a similar way. She knows what her partner 'really means', but disregards the contextual clues, working solely with the literal meaning of the words.

Now much mathematical language *should* carry a precise meaning in itself, a meaning which must be extractable from it without regard to any possible context. Thus the process of understanding this meaning can differ significantly from the process of understanding what is communicated through uses of ordinary language. The demands for mathematical precision present a substantial intellectual challenge for children and adults alike. Moreover there is no simple route to a competence in extracting these precise meanings from mathematical language. The acquisition of such a competence is likely to involve much negotiation between teachers and learners. Questions of linguistic precision will occupy a central place in our discussion about 2-D and 3-D shape.

Classifying 2-D shapes

You may think this is easy. However, there is a little more to it than meets the eye. Consider just three of the reasons for some surprising complexities here.

a Many children come to associate a shape term such as 'triangle' with a typical image. Images of triangles tend to be equilateral (all sides equal) and neatly sitting on their bases.

Figure 16.1

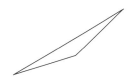

Figure 16.2

To classify a shape, they compare it with their mental image. If it resembles their image, they decide that it is a triangle. Otherwise (e.g. Figure 16.2) it is something different.

A few adults still think like this about some 2-D shapes, if not about triangles! Unfortunately using mental images to classify shapes is not mathematically satisfactory. Children have to learn that Figures 16.1 and 16.2 both represent triangles despite their very different shapes. They have to appreciate that this is so because they are both closed shapes with three straight sides, or even because they are both ways of joining three points by straight lines. They need to move away from thinking of shapes only as wholes, and to learn to consider the properties or parts of shapes.

b We are not always clear whether shape definitions are inclusive, or exclusive. For instance, most of us remember that isosceles triangles have two equal sides (Figure 16.3).

Figure 16.3

We may be much less clear about whether to call equilateral triangles special kinds of isosceles triangles. Do isosceles triangles have *two and only two* equal sides? Or do they have *not less than* two equal sides? The former definition is 'exclusive' while the latter is 'inclusive'. To add to the difficulty mathematical dictionaries or other sources of 'official' definitions do not always agree with each other about the inclusive/exclusive issue, or indeed about other matters. We will note examples shortly. Ultimately none of this is of any particular mathematical significance. What is important is that teachers work with a clear definition, which is reasonably close to normal mathematical usage, and that they help children to understand that definition. It is a matter of convention, and convention is occasionally not as clear as it might be.

c Shape terms vary enormously in specificity. A shape may belong to a number of families. For instance, 'square' is a highly specific term for a shape with four equal sides and four right angles, whereas 'quadrilateral' is a very general term covering any polygon with four straight sides. Hence all squares are quadrilaterals, but not all quadrilaterals are squares.

'Side', 'edge', 'face', 'corner' and 'vertex'

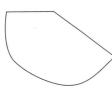

Figure 16.4

I want to suggest a consistent usage of 'side', 'edge', 'face' (surface), 'corner' and 'vertex' ('vertices' plural). There is nothing absolute about the suggestion, and it is not enshrined in 'official' mathematics. Here it is. Let us use the term 'side' only in describing 2-D shapes. Thus triangles have three sides, rectangles four sides, and so forth.

Sides can be curved. Figure 16.4 has two straight sides and one curved side.

'Corner' can be employed quite happily in 2-D contexts too, so triangles have three corners. Let us agree **not** to use the word 'side' in connection with 3-D shapes. The cuboid illustrated in Figure 16.5 shows the use of 'vertex', 'edge' and 'face'. 'Surface' would do just as well as 'face'. Arguably we could still talk about 'corners' on 3-D shapes. But we would be speaking of the corners of the 2-D shapes which form the surfaces of 3-D shapes.

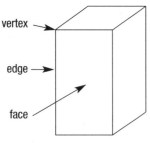

Figure 16.5

Thus just 7 vertices are visible in the cuboid as shown in Figure 16.5, but presumably it could be said that there are 12 corners showing, 4 on each of the visible faces. My preference is not to speak of corners on 3-D shapes.

For younger children the term 'point' seems harmless if used of either 2-D or 3-D shapes. If used of the latter, it would mean 'vertex' rather than corner.

Surfaces may be curved rather than 'flat'. Thus Figure 16.6 has a curved surface and two flat surfaces. It is worthwhile to maintain this consistency and clarity of language when teaching primary pupils. If allowed, they will readily conflate 2-D and 3-D language and shape terms.

Figure 16.6

Polygons are closed shapes with three or more straight sides. 'Polygon' is one of the most general terms for shapes that primary pupils learn. However, it still does not cover all the 2-D shapes they encounter. 'Circle' is an obvious example here.

'Triangle' again is a very general term. It may be defined as a polygon with three straight sides. Triangles can be *scalene*, meaning that they have no equal sides. They can be *isosceles*, in which case at least (?) two sides are equal, or *equilateral*, meaning that they have three equal sides. All *equilateral* triangles are also *equiangular*, that is they all have equal angles also. Triangles can be *right-angled*, but cannot have more than one right angle. (Why?) A triangle could have one obtuse angle (an angle greater than 90°), but could not have more than one angle like this. The reason is obvious. What is it?

Quadrilaterals are polygons with four straight sides. It is odd that the term 'quadrilateral' is not more widely used in primary schools. It does precisely the same job for four sided polygons which 'triangle' achieves for three sided polygons. Primary age children tend to be taught about special kinds of quadrilaterals, such as squares, rectangles, kites, trapezia (plural of trapezium), and rhombi (plural of rhombus).

Rectangles are quadrilaterals with four right angles. Each side is equal in length to the side opposite to it, hence squares are special rectangles. Incidentally, rectangles are themselves special kinds of parallelograms (see the account of parallelograms below). Undoubtedly in ordinary speech the term 'rectangle' means a quadrilateral with four right angles, whose sides are *not* all equal. So the mathematical version of the term conflicts with ordinary usage.

Squares are quadrilaterals with four right angles and equal sides. Hence squares are special kinds of parallelograms, of rectangles, and, depending on the precise definition of 'rhombus', special kinds of rhombi. 'Square' denotes a highly specific class of shapes.

'Oblong' has no very precise mathematical meaning, but in common speech it refers to rectangles which are not squares.

Parallelograms are quadrilaterals where each side is equal in length to the side opposite to it and each side is parallel to the side opposite to it. The characteristic 'image' of a parallelogram does not contain right angles. However, rectangles are special kinds of parallelograms. In this respect, the term 'parallelogram' is used inclusively, and fortunately the dictionaries seem to concur.

Kites are quadrilaterals with two pairs of adjacent equal sides, as in Figure 16.7. On this definition, squares and rhombi

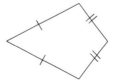

Figure 16.7

more generally turn out to be special kinds of kites. As before, if we summon up a mental image of a 'typical' kite we might want to reject this point. Our rejection is based on faulty 'shape image' thinking.

The diagonals of any kite are perpendicular to each other. Examples are shown in Figure 16.8. Can you prove this?

According to the definition of kite, Figure 16.9 is also a kite. How could you show that its 'diagonals' intersect at right angles? How exactly is the term 'diagonal' being used?

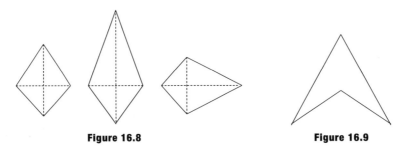

Figure 16.8   **Figure 16.9**

Rhombus. This is an equal-sided quadrilateral with opposite sides parallel. (According to this definition, squares belong to this category, though normal usage rarely allows this, and some dictionary definitions of 'rhombus' suggest the absence of right angles, e.g. the exclusive definition of 'rhombus' as 'parallelogram with sides of equal length but no right angles, diamond-shaped' features in the *Collins GEM English Dictionary*.) Since any rhombus is a kite, the diagonals of any rhombus are perpendicular to each other, as shown in Figure 16.10. The rhombus on the left is in fact a square.

Trapezium. This is often defined as a quadrilateral with two unequal parallel sides, an example of which is illustrated in Figure 16.11.

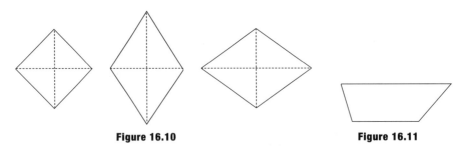

Figure 16.10   **Figure 16.11**

However, we again have to be clear whether we are working with a definition which is exclusive or inclusive. If we say that the quadrilateral must have only ONE pair of parallel sides, then parallelograms cannot be trapezia. This *exclusive* definition is probably the commonest one, but you may be able to find other accounts. One of our team in fact prefers the inclusive definition.

'Sorting trees' may be used to think about the properties of shapes: Chapter 19 discusses 'sorting trees' as one kind of device for classifying and displaying data.

In Figure 16.12, shapes are being sorted according to whether they are parallelograms or not. The shape starts at the bottom of the tree. It moves up to the junction of the two branches. Since it is clearly not a parallelogram, it is directed up the 'no' branch.

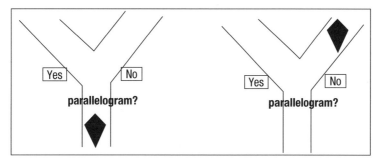

Figure 16.12

Figure 16.13 shows a more complex tree where the quadrilaterals have already been fed into the tree from the bottom, and allocated to the appropriate branches according to their properties. Is the inclusive or exclusive notion of trapezium being used here?

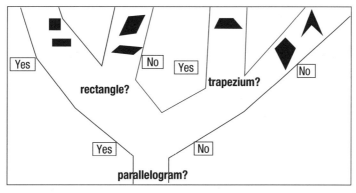

Figure 16.13

You may care to devise decision trees of your own and test out your own shape definitions.

Other polygons

Pentagon, hexagon, heptagon and octagon. These are respectively 5, 6, 7 and 8 sided shapes. Their sides need not be equal, as Figure 16.14 illustrates.

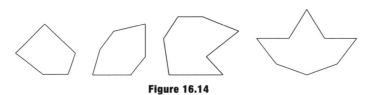

Figure 16.14

Regular pentagon, hexagon, heptagon and octagon. These are respectively 5, 6, 7 and 8 sided shapes with both equal sides *and* equal angles, as shown in Figure 16.15.

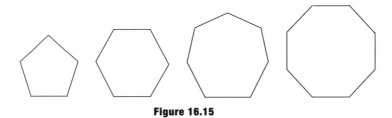

Figure 16.15

It is essential to specify that the angles and the sides are equal for regular polygons. After all, the hexagons in Figure 16.16 have equal sides, but not equal angles.

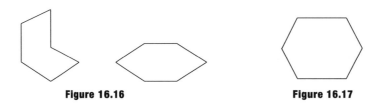

Figure 16.16   **Figure 16.17**

And the hexagon in Figure 16.17 has equal angles but not equal sides!

Circle

It is interesting to think of a circle as the limiting case in a series of polygons with increasing numbers of sides. Children producing circles using the computer language LOGO will become familiar with this fact. They may well draw polygons with 90 or even 360 sides to simulate circles. They are likely to try out their thinking on their friends, who act as robots taking directions. To steer the robot round in a circle, he must be told to go forward a little way, to turn a little, to go forward a little way, to turn a little way and so on. In this fashion he will begin to pace out a curve, at least after a fashion. He probably won't quite close his 'circle', since he will not be very good at 'perfect' steps. Figure 16.18 shows part of a series of polygons which gradually look more and more like circles.

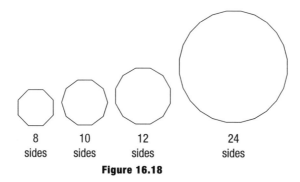

Figure 16.18

Using a pair of compasses to draw circles gives us a useful clue as to how to define 'circle'. Take two points, A and B, and begin to move B while keeping A still. If B moves in such a way that it keeps the same distance from A all the time, then B will move in a circle around A. This is known as the locus of B moving at a fixed distance from A. The pair of compasses models this idea. Assuming the point and the pencil are kept rigidly at the setting with which you begin, the pencil can only move in a circle round A.

Introduction to 2-D symmetry

Line symmetry

A shape has 'line symmetry' if the shape on one side of the line 'mirrors' the shape on the other. A paper shape could be folded along a line of symmetry, and the edges would match precisely. Alternatively, a mirror could be placed along the line, and the part visible, plus its reflection in the mirror, would look just the same as the original shape. The line may sometimes be called the *axis* of symmetry. Each 'half' may be said to be a reflection of the other. Each of the shapes in Figure 16.19 has just one of its lines of symmetry marked. Where are the others?

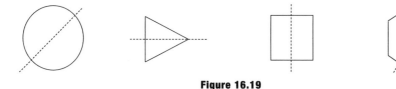

Figure 16.19

Rotational symmetry

Suppose I draw round a square tile, as in Figure 16.20.

I can then turn the tile clockwise through 90° around its centre, and it will fit back onto its original outline, as in Figure 16.21.

Figure 16.20   Figure 16.21

If I continue to turn the square about its centre, it will again fit onto its original outline after another 90°, and once more after another 90°. As we rotate a square about its centre through one complete turn, or 360°, we find four positions in which the square fits its original outline. We say the square has rotational symmetry of order 4.

An equilateral triangle when rotated about its centre has three positions in which it will fit its original outline; it possesses rotational symmetry of order 3. Suppose we want to calculate the angle the triangle must be turned before it fits back onto its outline. There are three positions in which it fits on the outline during a total turn of 360° about its centre. Hence the required rotation for it to fit once again will be 360° ÷ 3 or 120°.

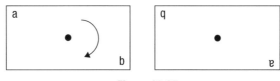

Figure 16.22

A rectangle which is not a square has two positions during a turn of 360° about its centre in which it will fit a starting outline, shown in Figure 16.22. Hence it has rotational symmetry of order 2. The turn required for it to fit its outline again is 360° ÷ 2 or 180°.

Relationship between rotational symmetry and line symmetry

a   If a shape has two lines of symmetry then necessarily it has a rotational symmetry of order 2. If a shape has three lines of symmetry, it will have rotational symmetry of order 3. If it has n lines of symmetry and n is greater than 1, it will have rotational symmetry of order n.

You might like to think through why this is so. We will discuss a couple of cases. Consider the shape illustrated in Figure 16.23. It has two lines of symmetry, a 'vertical' (up the page) line and a 'horizontal' (across the page) line. Figure 16.24 represents the left hand 'half' of Figure 16.23. If Figure 16.24 is reflected in a vertical mirror placed immediately to its right, we obtain Figure 16.25.

The interesting point to note is this. We reflected Figure 16.24 to produce Figure 16.25. Suppose instead we rotate it clockwise through 180° about P, as shown in Figure 16.26.

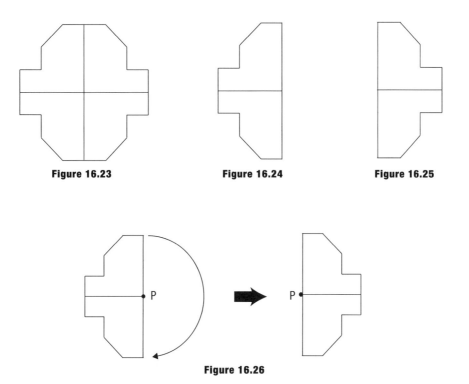

Figure 16.23 | Figure 16.24 | Figure 16.25

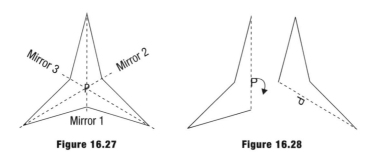

Figure 16.26

The result, as we can see, is identical to the result of reflecting Figure 16.24. The reason for this is the horizontal line of symmetry.

Now let us consider a shape with three lines of symmetry. According to the rule, this shape ought also to possess rotational symmetry of order 3. Why is this? 'P' in Figure 16.27 marks the point where the 'mirrors' intersect.

Figure 16.27   Figure 16.28

Take one 'half' of the shape in Figure 16.27, namely the 'half' which is reflected by vertical mirror 1. You can see this in Figure 16.28.

Rotate this 120° in a clockwise direction about point P. This is how far we would expect to turn a shape with rotational symmetry of order 3 before it fits back onto its original outline. What happens is that it becomes exactly like the top 'half' which is reflected by mirror 3. You can see how it looks after the 120° turn by checking Figure 16.29.

Now rotate this 'half' once again about point P by 120° in a clockwise direction. Figure 16.30 shows the result.

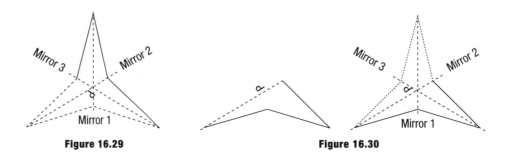

Figure 16.29   **Figure 16.30**

It becomes the bottom 'half ' which is reflected by mirror 2. The 120° rotations map onto the reflections produced by the three mirrors.

Carry out some experiments yourself, either with scissors and paper, or on the computer. Create a shape (not a square!) with four lines of symmetry, and experiment with rotations so that you can see why it must have rotational symmetry of order 4.

b If a shape has only *one* line of symmetry, this implies nothing about its rotational symmetry. If we like, we can say that the shape has rotational symmetry of order 1. However, this is a vacuous statement, since *all* shapes have rotational symmetry of order 1! There is bound to be one position in which the shape fits onto itself. And in any case, shapes which have *no* lines of symmetry also have this 'empty' property of rotational symmetry of order 1.

c The converse of (a) above does not necessarily hold. A shape can have rotational symmetry *without* having line symmetry.

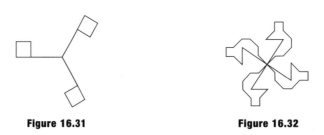

Figure 16.31   **Figure 16.32**

Figure 16.31 has rotational symmetry of order 3 but no line symmetry.
Figure 16.32 has rotational symmetry of order 4 but no line symmetry.

'Similar' and 'congruent'

One 2-D shape is said to be similar to another if the angles are the same, even if the size is different. Thus in Figure 16.33, triangle A is similar to triangle B, the angles being the same and hence the second triangle having similar proportions to the first. Again, in Figure 16.34, quadrilateral D is similar to quadrilateral C, having the same angles and being proportionately smaller.

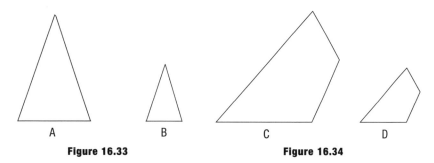

Figure 16.33   **Figure 16.34**

Intuitively, shapes are 'congruent' if they are identical in shape and size. But, as they say, it depends what you mean by 'identical in shape'. Consider the shapes in Figure 16.35.

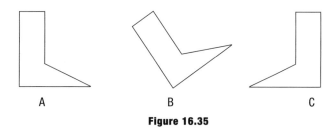

Figure 16.35

Is shape B 'identical' to A? It is, but you need to rotate it in order to make it fit exactly on A. Is C 'identical' to A? In one sense it is not, since it is a *reflection* of it. However, in deciding whether shapes are congruent, we are allowed to rotate them or reflect them. If as a result of some combination of these processes one shape may be fitted exactly on another, we say that they are congruent.

Check 16.1

1 Decide which of the following are true, and which are false.
   a All squares are similar to each other.
   b All hexagons are similar to each other.
   c All regular pentagons are similar to each other.
   d All circles are similar to each other.

e No kites are parallelograms.

f No rectangle and square can be congruent.

g All isosceles triangles are similar to each other.

h In a right-angled triangle, the opposite side (the hypotenuse) need not be the longest side of the triangle.

2 What type of triangle has one line of symmetry?

3 What type of triangle has three lines of symmetry?

4 Is there a triangle which possesses rotational symmetry but no line symmetry?

5 Sketch how the shape illustrated in Figure 16.36 would look when reflected in a 45° mirror (shown by the dotted line).

6 Trace the shape shown in Figure 16.37. In the simplest way you can think of sketch in some additions to the shape so that it acquires rotational symmetry of order 5.

7 Figure 16.38 (Adapted from Key Stage 2 SAT for Level 6.) 'Shape B is a clockwise rotation of shape A about the point P. What is the angle of rotation in degrees? You may use an angle measurer.' (The original wording has been retained.)

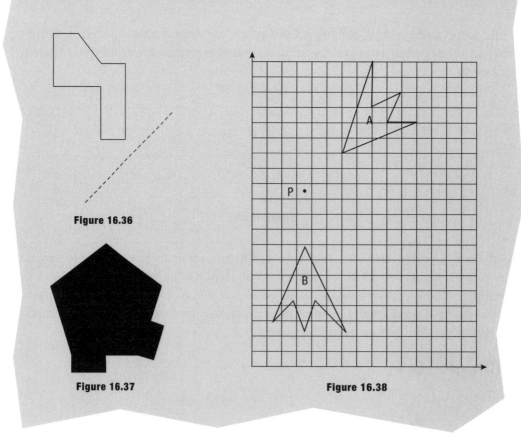

Figure 16.36

Figure 16.37

Figure 16.38

Summary

- Much of the complexity of shape concepts is tied to the language used.
- Some shape definitions are inclusive while others are exclusive.
- Mathematicians can mean some very precise things by 'same' and 'different' when they are talking about 2-D shape. These terms depart from ordinary usage and are sometimes linked to ideas of congruency.
- More than one line of symmetry has implications for rotational symmetry but not vice versa.

Links with the classroom

1 How would you discuss with a child what was the same and what was different about two equilateral triangles, one of which was bigger than the other?

2 How would you convince a six year old that a 'square' might be the 'same' as a 'diamond'?

3 Does it matter that Key Stage 1 children are often given sorting activities in which 'square' shapes are put into one set, while 'rectangle' shapes are put into a different set?

2-D shape applications and investigations

Tessellations

'TESSELLATION' SIMPLY MEANS 'tiling'. The word comes from the Latin 'tessella', the small square stones used for making mosaic pavements. Shapes 'tessellate' if they can be used to cover a surface without gaps between them. Equilateral triangles, squares and regular hexagons tessellate, as shown in Figures 17.1, 17.2 and 17.3.

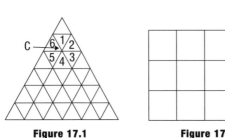

Figure 17.1   **Figure 17.2**   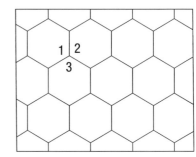 **Figure 17.3**

To understand why, we need to think about the angles in the shapes. In the triangle tessellation (Figure 17.1), each internal angle is 60°, and 6 triangles can be thought of as 'sharing a corner' (C in Figure 17.1). 6 × 60 makes 360°, the complete turn constituted by the point where the corners are 'shared'. The internal angles of a regular hexagon are 120°, and three of them share a corner in Figure 17.3. 120° × 3 = 360°. Four squares share a corner, and hence we have 4 × 90° = 360° (see Figure 17.2).

A tessellation of regular polygons, all of one kind and with their corners meeting at a point, is known as a regular tessellation. It is possible to show that only certain polygons can be used to form regular tessellations. To do this, we need a way of calculating the internal angles of regular polygons.

Figure 17.4 illustrates an equilateral triangle. In the course of drawing this shape, three equal turns must be made. One of them is shown as α. When the triangle is complete, we have turned through 360°. Hence 3α is 360°, α is 120° and β is 180° − α which is 60°. Generalising from this example, the internal angle of a regular polygon may be found using the formula $180 - \frac{360}{n}$, where n represents how many sides the polygon has. Thus we have $180 - \frac{360}{3}$, giving 60° for triangles. The same formula results in 90° for squares, 108° for regular pentagons, 120° for regular hexagons, about 128.6° for regular septagons, and 135° for regular octagons.

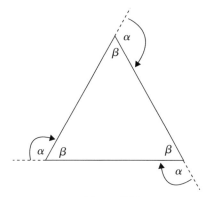

Figure 17.4

In regular tessellations, regular polygons meet at a point. As we have just seen, a complete turn round this point is 360°. We can consider how the complete rotation might be made up by examining the possible factors of 360°. Figure 17.5 rehearses the possibilities.

1	360	This pair of factors does not cover any possible shape.
2	180	This pair of factors does not cover any possible shape.
3	120	This covers the tessellation of regular hexagons. Three meet at a point, as in Figure 17.3.
4	90	This covers the conventional tessellation of squares. Four meet at a point, as in Figure 17.2.
5	72	This pair of factors does not help. 72° is not the internal angle of any regular polygon.
6	60	This covers the regular tessellation of equilateral triangles. Six triangles meet at a point, as in Figure 17.1.
8	45	45° is not the internal angle of any regular polygon. The smallest angle in a regular polygon is 60°. No more cases need to be considered.

Figure 17.5

This method of demonstrating the possible regular tessellations is an informal 'proof by exhaustion' (see Chapter 2).

Regular pentagons do not tessellate, but some pentagons do (see Figure 17.6). Why don't regular pentagons tessellate?

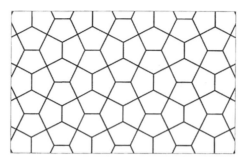

Figure 17.6

Some polygons lend themselves to a variety of tessellations even when we restrict ourselves to tiling with that particular shape only, as shown in Figures 17.7, 17.8 and 17.9.

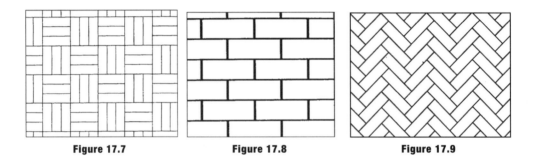

Figure 17.7   **Figure 17.8**   **Figure 17.9**

Some shapes may be tessellated to form a larger shape which is mathematically similar to the units which make it up. Such shapes have been dubbed *reptiles*. An obvious example is the square, since all squares are similar in any case. Can you find other examples of *reptiles*?

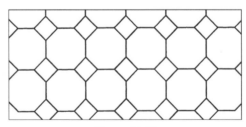

Figure 17.10

We can of course have tessellations of more than one shape, as in Figure 17.10. Why is it possible to create a tessellation of regular octagons and squares as shown here?

Semi-regular tessellations

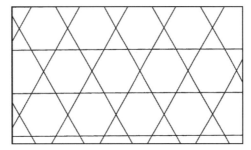

Figure 17.11

These are made up from regular polygons of two or more kinds in such a way that the arrangement of corners is the same at each vertex. The tessellating pattern can be defined by writing in order the number of sides of the polygons which surround each vertex. Thus in Figure 17.11 we have a 3636 pattern (triangle, hexagon, triangle, hexagon), and in Figure 17.12 we have a 3464 pattern (triangle, square, hexagon, square). There are eight semi-regular tessellations. Can you find any of the six which are not shown here?

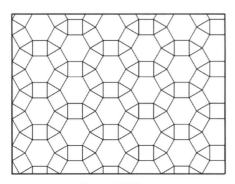

Figure 17.12

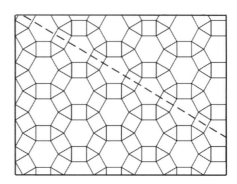

Figure 17.13

It is helpful to think about *transformations* in the context of tessellating patterns. A transformation of a given shape is a new shape where each point in the new shape is related in a particular way to a corresponding point in the original shape. The National Curriculum includes four types of transformations. These are translation, enlargement, reflection and rotation. In Figure 17.12 the 'same' regular hexagon could be thought of as being moved to different places in the pattern. This is translation. The 'same' square is seen translated, and also subjected to a whole series of rotations of 60°. The 'same' triangle is seen translated, and also rotated 180°. The notion of 'same' employed here is at once conventional and sophisticated. It means of course that the shapes are *congruent* in the sense outlined above.

We can also see reflections in Figure 17.12. Where might a mirror be placed so that the visible part of the pattern together with its 'reflection' in the mirror would look just the same locally as the original pattern (i.e. ignore the rectangular boundaries)? Figure 17.13 illustrates one possibility. Moreover the pattern contains equilateral triangles and their reflections. Can you find any composite shapes which are reflected across the tessellation?

Scalene triangle tessellations

Figure 17.14

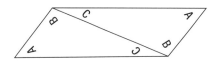

Figure 17.15

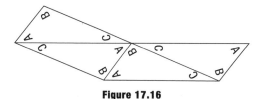

Figure 17.16

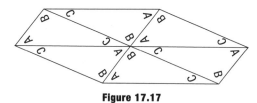

Figure 17.17

Figure 17.18

Any triangle will tessellate. First, draw round a scalene triangle, and label its angles, as shown in Figure 17.14.

Now move the triangle into a new position by turning it 180° and fitting it against the original outline, as shown in Figure 17.15. Draw round it once more.

Keep turning your triangle through 180°, fitting it against triangle outlines already present, and drawing round it in its new positions. You will gradually create a tessellation of scalene triangles, as shown in Figure 17.16 and Figure 17.17. You can think of your triangle as being subjected to a specific transformation to produce this tessellation. Each time you move it you rotate it 180° about the midpoint of one side of your triangle.

Labelling the angles enables us to see why such a tessellation is possible. Where six triangles meet there are two angle As, two Bs and two Cs, that is, two straight angles, 2 × 180° or 360°. This thought may be used as an informal proof that the angles of a triangle add up to 180° (see Chapter 14).

Tessellating your triangle in this way enables you to see that any scalene triangle is in fact a *reptile*, as shown in Figure 17.18. The larger triangle may also be seen as a particular transformation of the original, namely an *enlargement*.

How to tessellate quadrilaterals which are not rectangles

This process is very similar to that described above with scalene triangles. Once the initial quadrilateral is drawn round a template, turn this through 180° and fit it back against one of the original sides. Draw round the template once more. Extend this in all directions and continue until the paper is covered, as shown in Figure 17.19. If the angles are labelled, and the place where four quadrilaterals meet is examined, it can be seen that there is one of each angle. If it has already been shown that the angles of any quadrilateral add up to 360°, then we now have an explanation of why any quadrilateral can tessellate. As with the tessellation of triangles, the transformation involved is a rotation of 180° about the midpoint of one of the sides of the quadrilateral.

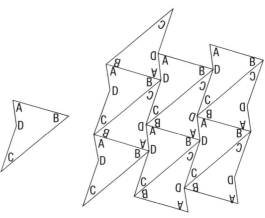

Figure 17.19

Transformations and Cartesian geometry

We have already mentioned transformations. They may also be usefully understood as relationships between sets of coordinates on graphs, and this is how they are discussed here. They can be thought of as mappings between one set of points and another (see Chapters 8 and 9).

In Figure 17.20 shape C is a *translation* of shape A. This means, crudely, that we have the same shape in a new place. If we show it on a graph, we can see that the coordinates of the corners of the new shape may be derived from that of the original shape by adding 6 to the value of x in each of the original coordinates. (0,0) becomes (6,0) and so on.

Shape B consists of a simple *reflection* of A about the X-axis. Its coordinates could be derived from A by multiplying A's Y coordinates by ⁻1. Shape D is said to be an *enlargement* of shape A. It is enlarged by a factor of 2. Shape D could be produced from shape A by extending lines from its 'centre of enlargement' (in this case, the origin of the graph) through shape A's corners, so that for example the distance from the origin to **n** is twice the distance from the origin to **m**. For a shape to be an enlargement of A by a factor of 3, the lines from the centre of enlargement to the corners of

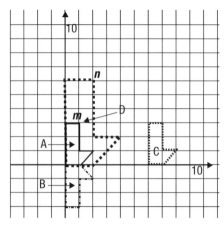

Figure 17.20

the new shape would have to be three times as long as those from the centre of enlargement to the corners of the original shape, and so on. Alternatively, we can think of shape D in relation to shape A as the shape resulting from multiplying A's coordinates by 2. So point **m** is (1,3) while the corresponding point **n** in the enlarged shape D is (2,6).

Some constructions

How to construct an equilateral triangle

Draw a straight line of any length. Now set your compass so that the pencil is the same distance from the compass point as the length of your line. Put the point of your compass on one end of the line and draw an arc. Without changing your compass setting, place the point of your compass on the other end of the line, and draw an arc which crosses over the first, as in Figure 17.21. Finally, join the intersection of the arcs to each end of your line, as in Figure 17.22.

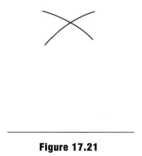

Figure 17.21

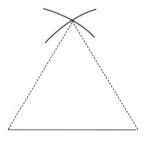

Figure 17.22

How to bisect a line

Bisecting a line means drawing a line which is vertical to a given line which passes through the middle of that line.

The first stage resembles that for constructing an equilateral triangle. But it does not matter whether you set the compass at the length of the line you wish to bisect. Draw arcs from **a** and **b** both above and below the line **ab** as shown in Figure 17.23. Then simply join the two intersections of the arcs. The dotted line shown in Figure 17.23 bisects line **ab**.

How does this work? Figure 17.24 is a development of Figure 17.23 by adding some extra lines and letters. We have joined **a** to **m** and to **n**, and also joined **b** to **m** and to **n**.

(If you think you managed to prove that the diagonals of a kite must intersect at right angles in your study of Chapter 16, you may like to refer back to it at this point.)

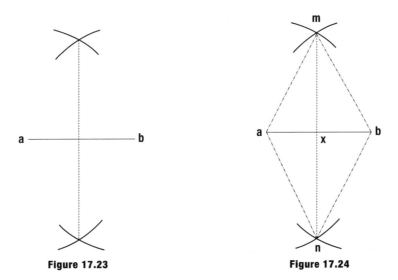

Figure 17.23   Figure 17.24

The method of construction implies that **am** = **bm** and **an** = **bn**.

So triangle **man** is congruent to triangle **mbn**, since the sides of the first triangle are equal to the sides of the second.

(A section in Chapter 2 discusses conditions for congruency in some detail)

Hence ∠ (angle) **amx** = ∠ **bmx**

So triangle **amx** ≡ triangle **bmx** (most readers will remember that ≡ stands for 'is congruent' in this kind of context). The triangles are congruent because two of their sides are equal and we know the 'included' angles (the angles between the pairs of sides known to be equal) are equal.

So **ax** = **xb**

Also ∠ **axm** = ∠ **bxm**

But as ∠ **axm** + ∠ **bxm** = 180° each angle must be 90°.

Constructing triangles with sides of given lengths

Suppose you are asked to draw a triangle with sides of 10 cm, 5 cm, and 6 cm. First draw one of the lines, say that to be 10 cm long. Then set your compasses at a distance of 5 cm. In Figure 17.25, the compass point is placed on **A** and an arc drawn. The compass is then set to 6 cm, and an arc drawn from **B**. Finally, **A** and **B** are joined to the intersection of the arcs, and the triangle is completed, as shown in Figure 17.25.

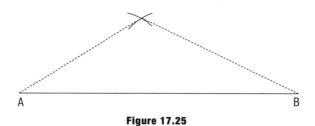

A   B

Figure 17.25

 # Check 17.1

1 Draw a quadrilateral with two lines of symmetry and no right angles. To what other shape families does this quadrilateral belong?
2 Some kites are rectangles, according to the definitions given above. Which? Why?
3 Draw a quadrilateral with rotational symmetry and no line symmetry. Can a quadrilateral with these properties ever be a kite? Why?
4 Which is the only 2-D shape with an infinite number of lines of symmetry?
5 Which shape fits back on its original outline after it has been turned 72° about its centre?
6 What angle must a regular octagon be turned about its centre before it fits back in to its original outline? Why?
7 Study Figure 17.26. Sketch at least six shapes which are translated across this pattern. In a process similar to that used with Figure 17.13, find some lines on this pattern on which a mirror could be placed so that the visible pattern plus its reflection is identical to the original pattern. Sketch as many single shapes and composite shapes within the pattern as you can which have rotational symmetry of order 6. Find some composite shapes which have rotational symmetry of order 3 (only).

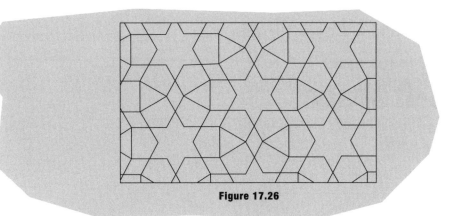

Figure 17.26

Summary

- Tessellating shapes cover surfaces without leaving gaps.
- Tessellations may be made up from one type of shape, or from more than one.
- Regular tessellations comprise patterns of regular polygons, all of one kind and with their corners meeting at a point.
- Equilateral triangles, squares and regular hexagons can each be used to form regular tessellations.
- Many tessellations contain examples of transformations, i.e. translations, rotations and reflections.
- Any triangle may be used to form a tessellation, as may any quadrilateral.

Links with the classroom

1 How might we explain to lower juniors why squares tessellate?
2 Imagine a discussion with juniors about the functioning of a pair of compasses. What points would you want to emerge about the nature of circles?
3 Would you teach children how to form tessellations with scalene triangles, or would you want them to try to make the patterns themselves first? What reasons would you give for your answer?
4 Make up some questions which Year 2s might tackle by studying Figure 17.26. Create some investigations which Year 6s might attempt using the same pattern.

3-D shape

2-D and 3-D

STRICTLY SPEAKING, WE can only encounter 2-D shapes as the surfaces of 3-D objects. 'Flat' shapes purporting to represent 2-D items are in fact very 'thin' 3-D shapes. A 'net' of a 3-D shape may be obtained by, so to speak, spreading it flat, but this way of thinking represents a mathematical abstraction. It may be modelled by the physical cutting up of a cardboard box, and the spreading of the result flat to form a net, but we must remember that this is only a model.

Some important 3-D shape families

Prisms

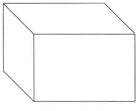

Figure 18.1

These have two 'ends' which are parallel equal polygons, and normally all the other faces are rectangles. Figure 18.1 shows a square prism.

The term 'cuboid' covers a particular class of prisms where the polygonal cross-section is a rectangle. According to this account, cubes are themselves special types of cuboids, though this kind of inclusive usage is not normally encountered. The prism in Figure 18.1 may be seen in two ways. It may be regarded both as a square prism, and as an ordinary rectangular prism. Figure 18.2 shows a triangular prism, the shape commonly associated with Toblerone chocolate.

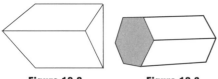

Figure 18.2   Figure 18.3

Figure 18.3 shows a hexagonal prism.

If you took a piece of cardboard in the shape of a triangle, and then piled up many identical pieces exactly on top of the first, you would create a triangular prism, as in Figure 18.4. (Strictly speaking, of course, even the first piece of cardboard is itself a triangular prism.)

A cylinder does not quite fit the prism definition given above, but could be seen as a limiting case in a series of prisms involving polygon faces with increasing numbers of sides. Cylinders could be made by piling up circular shapes as in Figure 18.5. Another way of looking at Figures 18.4 and 18.5 is to see a prism as a 3-D shape which can be sliced *in a certain way* to produce 'thinner' examples of the same kind of prism with which you begin.

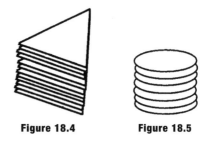

Figure 18.4   **Figure 18.5**

Some definitions of prisms allow for the possibility that the surfaces other than the polygons at each 'end' might be parallelograms which are not rectangles. Thus the top surface in Figure 18.6 is a rectangle, as is the bottom. However, the other faces are parallelograms which are *not* rectangles.

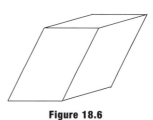

Figure 18.6

The 'slice' test still applies, in that the prism shown in Figure 18.6 could be sliced up into thinner instances of the same prism. The slices can be made to be similar to the prism from which they have been sliced.

Pyramids

These are solids with straight edged bases and sloping triangular faces meeting at a point. They are named after their bases. For instance, a square pyramid is shown in Figure 18.7, while a pentagonal pyramid is illustrated in Figure 18.8.

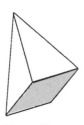

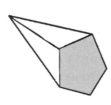

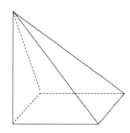

Figure 18.7   **Figure 18.8**   **Figure 18.9**

The pyramids which primary children normally encounter are 'right' pyramids – that is, their points are vertically in line with the centres of their polygon bases. Pyramids need not be like this. A rectangular pyramid is shown in Figure 18.9. It is not a 'right' pyramid.

Regular solids or regular polyhedra

There are five regular solids, or regular polyhedra. In each case, the faces are all equal regular polygons, and whichever face the solid is stood upon, it looks the same. For example, the regular tetrahedron is shown in Figure 18.10. Each of its four faces is an equilateral triangle. Two nets for this solid are illustrated in Figure 18.11.

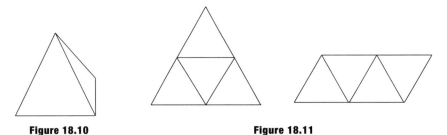

Figure 18.10   **Figure 18.11**

The familiar cube is the second regular solid. Each of its six faces is a square.

The regular octahedron is shown in Figure 18.12. Each of its eight faces is an equilateral triangle. Figure 18.13 shows one possible net. Can you find any other nets for the regular octahedron?

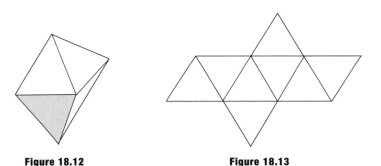

Figure 18.12   **Figure 18.13**

A regular dodecahedron is shown in Figure 18.14. Each of the 12 faces is a regular pentagon. The net is also illustrated in Figure 18.15.

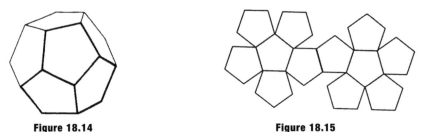

Figure 18.14   **Figure 18.15**

Figure 18.16 shows a regular icosahedron. Each of its 20 faces is in equilateral triangle. Its net is shown in Figure 18.17.

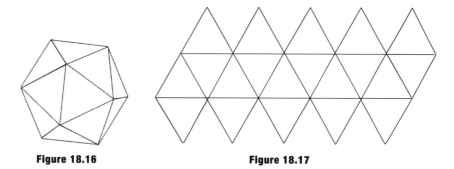

Figure 18.16   **Figure 18.17**

It is worth trying to obtain a set of polydrons, or other materials for creating 3-D shapes. Having made some basic 3-D shapes as described above, it can be fun to try to imagine more complex possibilities and then to build them. For instance, each face of a cube could be replaced by four equilateral triangles joined as they are for one 'half' of an octahedron.

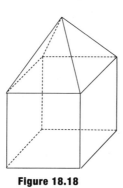

Figure 18.18

Figure 18.18 shows the top face of a cube replaced in this way. When the 'replacements' are complete you will have used 24 triangles, and made a complex shape with plenty of symmetries. Or each face of a regular dodecahedron could be replaced by an 'umbrella' of five equilateral triangles, making a complex 'stellated' 3-D solid. This is satisfying to make, but it needs a good many triangles. (How many?)

Euler's rule

The 3-D shapes which are likely to be encountered by primary children exhibit a particular rule between the number of vertices, edges and faces. If you add the number of faces and the number of vertices together it totals two more than the number of edges. Examples are shown in Figure 18.19.

3-D shape	number of edges	number of vertices	number of faces
cube	12	8	6
triangular prism	9	6	5
tetrahedron	6	4	4
octahedron	12	6	8
square pyramid	8	5	5

Figure 18.19

There are 3-D shapes which do not obey this rule. Some mathematicians in the nineteenth century were not pleased about this, and referred to such cases as 'monstrosities'. This only goes to show that mathematicians are as irrational at times as the rest of the human race. Can you find any exceptions to Euler's rule? Later theories were able to locate Euler's rule within a wider framework or field of study called topology. The 'monstrosities' within this more comprehensive theory turn out to have different but predictable relationships between edges, vertices, and faces (or their topological equivalents).

Exploring nets

B is one of 35 different possible hexominoes (arrangements of 6 congruent squares joined together by common sides). It could also be folded up to make a cube, i.e it is one of the nets for a cube. Can you find the others? In your explorations you will have to decide when one hexomino is the 'same' or 'different' from another. The figure of 35 assumes that only congruent hexominoes are the 'same'. See Chapters 16 for more about 'same', 'different' and 'congruent'. Equipment such as polydrons provides an easy and enjoyable resource to use in this enquiry, and the results can be recorded on squared paper. A variation of this very familiar investigation is to look for the nets of 'cubes without lids', which of course will be arrangements of 5 congruent squares or pentominoes.

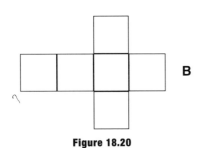

B

Figure 18.20

Some 3-D shapes with curved surfaces

The familiar cone in Figure 18.21 is in fact a right circular cone. That is, a straight line could be drawn from the centre of its circular base, at right angles to the plane of that base and it would extend to meet the point of the cone.

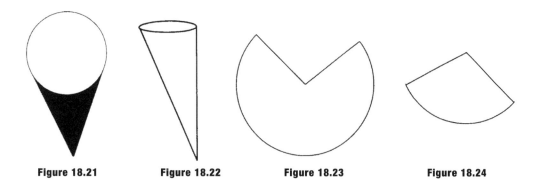

| Figure 18.21 | Figure 18.22 | Figure 18.23 | Figure 18.24 |

But a cone need not have its point in line with the centre of its circular base. See Figure 18.22. Each of the pieces of paper shown in Figures 18.23 and 18.24 could be formed into right cones. What would the most obvious mathematical difference be between these two cones?

If you make a cone out of play dough or something similar, you can try slicing it up in various ways. In how many different ways can you slice a right cone (starting from the whole cone each time) so that triangular faces are revealed? What other shaped surfaces can be produced by 'sectioning' your whole right cone in different ways?

Children should also learn the terms *sphere* and *hemisphere*. Attempting to make a net for a sphere and failing is a useful background for beginning to look with top juniors at the challenges of map projections.

Planes of symmetry in 3-D shapes

Intuitively, planes of symmetry may be thought of as ways in which 3-D objects may be sliced to leave two identical 'halves', such that one half is the reflection of the other. It is easy to see that in the case of prisms with rectangular surfaces and polygonal bases some of the planes of symmetry are extensions of the lines of symmetry possessed by the bases. Pyramids need not possess any planes of symmetry, although the examples encountered by primary children normally do.

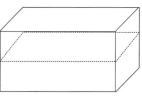

Figure 18.25

 Check 18.1

1 How many planes of symmetry does a cube possess?
2 Decide which of the following statements are true:
  a 'Right' cones have an infinite number of planes of symmetry.
  b No pyramids are prisms.
  c A pyramid can never have less than four triangular surfaces.

3 How many planes of symmetry does a regular pentagonal prism possess?

4 Which regular polyhedron could be passed through a square hole of an appropriate size in such a way that at one point it would fit exactly into the hole?

5 What 3-D shape could be made up from a net which comprised two congruent hexagons and six congruent rectangles?

6 Which 3-D shapes would you say had just one edge? Two edges?

7 Any cube is *similar* to any other cube. Find six other 3-D shapes of which this is also true.

Summary

■ Prisms and pyramids gain their names from their polygon 'bases'.

■ The five regular polyhedra are the regular tetrahedron, the cube, the regular octahedron, the regular dodecahedron and the regular icosahedron.

■ Nets are 'flat' shape patterns which could be folded into 3-D shapes.

■ Euler's rule for 3-D shapes: $V + F = E + 2$

Links with the classroom

1 How would you explain to lower junior children the difference between 2-D and 3-D shape?

2 How would you explain the difference between a prism and a pyramid?

3 What kinds of 3-D properties might be readily identified by Key Stage 1 children, and used by them to sort 3-D shapes?

5

Data handling

Introduction

Data handling is now part of the National Curriculum in mathematics throughout the primary school. This may be a comparatively recent introduction but there is good reason for its inclusion. We are continually presented in the media with facts and figures about the world, sometimes with the intention of misleading. Children should be introduced to the way data is collected, how it should be analysed and methods of presentation. They should be encouraged to develop a healthy scepticism towards claims from advertisers, politicians and pressure groups, all of whom use statistics to present their arguments. It might be argued that the ability to understand quantitative data presented in a variety of forms is the cornerstone of present day numeracy.

Data handling

Chapter 19 includes some consideration of common methods of collecting, recording, analysing, presenting and interpreting data together with some of the problems and shortcomings encountered. Children usually enjoy this type of work and it can provide a context for developing other aspects of their mathematics. Although only fairly simple methods are covered, these should lay the foundations for children's developing understanding. Some simple statistical measures are included although they would only be introduced to older primary pupils.

Probability

The National Curriculum also includes ideas about simple probability. These concepts can be difficult, but if introduced carefully will help children understand a little more about such diverse things as insurance, risk, games and betting. In Chapter 20 some basic ideas are covered, and these should provide a sound foundation. Again children usually enjoy such investigations and they can provide a context for developing further their understanding of some basic number concepts, such as fractions.

CHAPTER

19

Data handling

Introduction

IN THIS CHAPTER, the five stages of data handling are described and some of the problems and possible sources of error are discussed. The five main stages are: posing the questions, collecting the data, analysing the data, presenting the results and interpreting the results. The stages are not necessarily separated in time; for example, the analysis, presentation and interpretation are often interwoven. But for the purposes of discussion it will be simpler to take them separately.

Posing questions

Before collecting any data, it is necessary to decide on the point of the enquiry, that is to formulate the questions. In school, ideally the questions would arise from the work the children were doing. Probably the best data handling activities arise from questions the children themselves pose. If at all possible the children should have some part in deciding what questions to investigate. The questions themselves can sometimes be framed in more challenging ways. For example, instead of 'Find how many children in this class are born in each month of the year', try several shorter questions such as 'Which is the most common month for birthdays in this class?' 'Is it the same for boys and girls?' 'Do birthdays of brothers and sisters tend to fall in the same month?' The nature and number of questions affect how the data should be collected and the way it is analysed. For the first question above, it would be sufficient to ask each child in the class the date of his or her birthday and simply record the month. For the second group of questions it is also necessary to record the child's sex and the birthdays of his or her brothers and sisters.

There should be an established progression of the types of questions tackled throughout the school. In Key Stage 1 they will be fairly simple factual questions, such as the number of brothers and sisters. Later some relation between two measurements might be considered, such as the length of a person's hand-span and his height. Although the relation between height and weight is well established it is probably not wise to study this, as some children may be very sensitive about their weight (or height). A less sensitive comparison might be between the volume and weight of pupils' bags. More complicated questions about opinions and values might be suitable in Year 6. For example, the problem of whether a by-pass for a city should be built, destroying farmland and woodland, could be studied using a questionnaire.

Collecting data

Children will almost certainly need some guidance on designing a good record sheet, but they should be allowed to develop their own ideas even if this means they run into difficulties. In Key Stage 1 it is probably best if a simple form is used on which the children have to put a tick or cross in a given column. Various issues must be discussed even at this stage. How will they know when they have asked everyone and how will they avoid asking anyone twice? Are they quite clear about the meaning of the categories used? The question above is simple because one person can only have a birthday in one month and the months are a well-defined set. But with other questions it may be more complicated. For example, if the question is 'What pets do the children in this class have?' several problems might arise. Does this mean any pet owned by the child's family or only those which the child regards as their own? If a child has several pets how are these recorded? For example if they have one dog, two cats and five fish, how are these recorded? What about, for example, a horse which is shared between two children? Is this question fair to those children who have no pets?

Other questions are complicated and sensitive. For instance, questions about brothers, sisters and size of family are not straightforward since some children may not live with both their natural parents and may live with step siblings. Teachers may either wish to avoid these issues or use the data handling as an opportunity to share the diversity of all forms of family structure.

There is a general problem with questions concerning favourite things (for example, food or colours or TV programmes). Is it better to ask 'What is your favourite food?' (which runs the risk of having 20 different choices), or 'Which of these foods (showing a list of about 6 or 8) is your favourite?'? The latter is much easier to handle, but does not find out about children's favourite foods, because their choice is constrained. Later, questions about correlations may be asked. For example, 'Is there a relation between the height of a person and the distance they can jump from a standing start?' A table must be used to ensure that the pairs of measurements are kept together. In Year 5 and Year 6 the children may want to use short questionnaires, but they are difficult to construct. The meaning of the question must be unequivocal. Again, the problem arises whether to constrain the answers or allow them to be free. In market research, one technique is to provide statements and ask the extent of agreement or disagreement (on a 5 or even 9 point scale). These may allow statistical analysis, but the statements are necessarily out of any context. If children are going to use a questionnaire, they should do a small pilot first.

There is the issue of accuracy and consistency. Copy the data as little as possible, as each time provides opportunities for errors to creep in. It may be advisable for the children to work in pairs with one child asking the questions and the other recording the answers (with the first one acting as a check). The problem of consistency arises when more than one person is involved. The meaning of terms and categories must be fully discussed before recording starts and some procedure established for dubious cases.

The problem of fair sampling might arise. For example, if each pair of children is asked to interview ten people, the question arises how these ten are to be selected. If they are allowed to choose ten friends, then it is likely that each sample will have a sex bias, for most children have more friends of the same than of the opposite sex. If a list of possible people is used, then it can either be divided into groups of ten, or each person can be given a number and groups selected by using random numbers. The point is not to make a perfect sample, but to make the children aware of some of the difficulties of constructing an unbiased sample.

Analysing data

Types of data

There are three main types of data covered in primary schools. The most suitable type of analysis and presentation depends on the type of data. Categorical data are grouped into categories or classes and the number in each class counted. For example, the colour of the children's hair, the way they come to school (walking, by car, bus, train), their favourite food are all categorical data. The categories or classes used are distinct and cannot be ordered.

In the second type of data the classes are defined by numbers but these are discrete, that is only certain values can be obtained. For example, shoe size, house numbers, test marks and the number of people in the family all provide data in discrete classes. In the case of the number of people in a family, this must be a whole number. It would be impossible for there to be 4·5 or 3·8 people living in a house. Similarly the number of the house, if it has one, will be a whole number or possibly something like 32a or even 32½. With English shoe sizes it is possible to have classes such as 1½ or 2 but not 1·7 or 1·9. In a test the results are usually given as a number out of 10 or 50 or 100 and only certain marks can be gained. The classes are discrete if the measure can only have certain values and there can never be a value intermediate between them. To make the data easier to handle, the numbers are sometimes divided into classes. This would probably be unnecessary for the number of people in the family, for the number of different values is usually small (only about 6). In shoe sizes or house numbers there may be a much greater range so some grouping is useful. So for example, the classes of shoe size might be under 1, 1 and 1½, 2 and 2½, 3 and 3½, 4 and 4½ and over 4½.

In the third type of data, the classes are defined by continuous variables. This most commonly involves some form of measurement. For example the length of children's feet, the weight of apples, the time taken to run 100 metres all provide continuous data. The children's feet may be any length between, say, 10 cm and 30 cm. In theory it is possible to have any value, for example 12·5 or 12·9 or 12·75 cm might occur. To make such measurements easier to handle they are divided into classes. As any value is theoretically possible, the definition of the classes must be quite clear. It is ambiguous to define the classes as under 15, 15–20, 20–25, and so on since it is not clear to which class a measurement of exactly 20 cm would belong. Instead it should be stated as, say, less than 15, 15 and more than 15 but less than 20, 20 and up to but not including 25 and so on. This can be abbreviated in several ways, for example, <15, 15 to <20, 20 to <25 or under 15, 15−, 20−, 25−, and so on. In the primary school, class intervals should always be equal.

Preliminary analysis

Depending on the nature of the data and the organisation of the data collection sheet, it may be advisable to reorganise the data. For example, if the lengths of the children's feet have been measured, then it is necessary to decide on suitable class intervals and to count how many fall in each class. This is often done by constructing a frequency table, as illustrated.

length in cm	tallies	number
<15	II	2
15–	III	3
20–	IHI I	6
25–	IHI I	7

Some children have problems with tallies. This usually concerns the cross stroke. Traditionally the fifth count is drawn as a stroke across the previous four so making a bundle of 5 altogether. Some children make five upright strokes first, then draw a line across them. It is not clear whether this then makes a bundle of 5 or 6. If this is a problem, then a long line of ticks or crosses can be used. Depending on the data, an ordered list or a dot graph may be useful. Examples are shown below.

An ordered list of length of children's feet (in cm):

12·5, 13·8, 16·2, 17·5, 17·5, and so on

A dot graph:

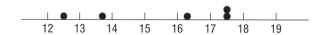

✎ Check 19.1

1 State whether the following data are categorical, discrete or continuous.
  a baby's weight over its first year
  b colour of hair
  c temperature of a person who is ill
  d batting scores of a cricket team
  e amount of rainfall
  f goals scored by a football team
  g make of cars

2 The following were the results of 10 football matches (involving 20 teams) one Saturday:

  3 − 0   2 − 1
  0 − 1   0 − 0
  1 − 5   0 − 1
  2 − 0   1 − 1
  0 − 2   2 − 2

Make a frequency table of goals scored by each team.

3 The following marks (out of 10) were scored by 20 children in a Maths test:

  7   10   4   6   6   4   7   6   2   4
  9   7   5   3   7   8   7   5   6   8

Make an ordered list and a dot graph of the data.

Presenting results

The data collected can be shown as diagrams or tables or summarised by statistical measures. In this section, different types of diagrams are discussed first, then some of the simpler statistical measures are described.

Graphs and diagrams

The main types of diagrams mentioned in the National Numeracy Strategy (1999) and the QTS Numeracy Skills Test (1999) are shown in the tables below.

National Numeracy Strategy (1999)

Year	Tables/statistics	Graphs/diagrams
1	lists simple tables	real objects or pictures
2		pictograms (1 symbol : 1 unit) block graphs (1 block : 1 unit)
3	simple frequency tables	pictograms (1 symbol : 2 units) bar chart (intervals labelled in 1s or 2s) Venn & Carroll diagrams (1 criterion)
4	tally charts frequency tables	pictogram (symbol representing 2, 5, 10 or 20 units) bar chart (intervals labelled in 2s, 5s, 10s, or 20s) Venn & Carroll diagrams (2 criterion)
5	mode	bar line charts (vertical axis labelled in 2s, 5s, 10s, 20s or 100s)
6	frequency tables with grouped discrete data range median mean (average)	line graphs bar charts with grouped discrete data pie charts (interpretation)

QTS Numeracy Skills Test

Tables/statistics	Graphs/diagrams

tables of various types
mean
median
mode
quartile
range
inter-quartile range
	bar charts (vertical and horizontal)
	    composite or stacked bar charts
	    percentage bar charts
	box and whisker diagrams
	cumulative frequency graphs
	line graphs
	pie charts
	scatter graphs

At Key Stage 1 there should be a simple correlation between the representation and the objects. Sometimes the actual objects can be placed on a 'graph', for example, if the question is about the colour of 'Smarties', then the actual sweets can be stuck onto paper to make a graph. Instead of the actual objects, drawings or pictures can be used, as long as they are all the same size. For example, if the question is about pets, then drawings can be used as shown.

Pictogram of children's pets

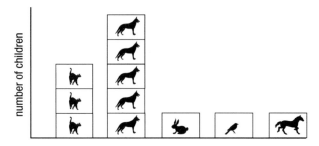

It is important for each drawing or at least the box in which it lies to be the same size. Classification into distinct categories, such as pets, is fairly straightforward. A given pet can only belong to one category; it cannot be both a dog and a cat.

In representing data, the move from pictograms to block graphs is quite small. In the latter case a simple block is used rather than a picture. An example of a simple block graph illustrating eye colour is given.

Block graph of eye colour

At Key Stage 2 more complicated diagrams and graphs should be introduced. Pictograms in which a single drawing represents a group of units can be effective. For example, in the diagram below, one represents 10 hours of sunshine.

Pictogram of sunshine recorded in January

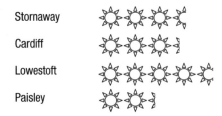

Stornaway

Cardiff

Lowestoft

Paisley

Bar charts are widely used. They may be drawn either horizontally or vertically. The lengths of the bars are proportional to the value they represent. A scale should be provided at the side. If the quantities are categorical or discrete, the bars should not touch each other; if the variables are continuous, then they should. The examples below show diagrams to illustrate data about the way some children came to school (categorical) and their heights (continuous).

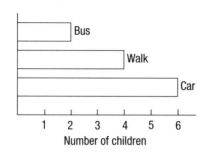

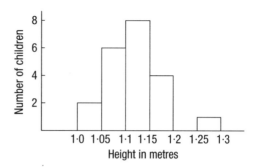

The QTS Numeracy Skills test also includes other types of bar chart. In the composite (or stacked) bar chart, each bar is subdivided into parts. For example, suppose 5 children took three maths tests, each marked out of 10 and scored as shown:

	Test 1	Test 2	Test 3
A	5	4	8
B	6	3	7
C	7	8	9
D	8	6	7
E	4	2	6

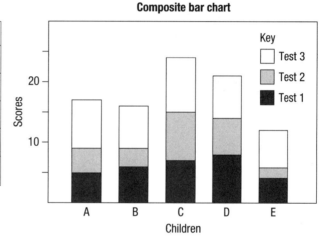

Composite bar chart

Their results could be illustrated by a composite bar chart, as shown. This is useful when the sum of the three tests is important, e.g. if they provide the term's grade. It is easy to compare the totals, but more difficult to compare parts, e.g. which child did best in the third test? Both A and C did well, but it is necessary to look carefully at the scale to find out which section is longest.

Another aspect of data handling, which is usually introduced in Key Stage 1, is categorisation and sorting. For example, when discussing shapes (using coloured plastic shapes), children may be asked to sort them and explain the reason behind their action. They might think of colour and put all the red ones together and all the blue ones in a different place. Or they might look at the shape so that the groups might be circles and triangles and rectangles. Or again they might think about rolling, so it would be shapes which will roll and those which do not.

However if two or more attributes are taken into account, the task becomes much more difficult, for example, if both the colour and shape of some classroom shapes are considered. There are several ways of representing this type of task.

First a decision tree can be used. If possible each question should be phrased so that the answer is either 'Yes' or 'No'.

So we have four sets at the end: black triangles; black shapes which are not triangles; triangles which are not black; shapes which are not black and are not triangles. These four sets can also be represented as a Venn diagram or a Carroll diagram.

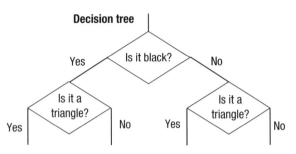

Decision tree

Venn diagram

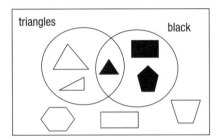

Carroll diagram

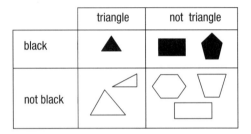

In the Venn diagram children often find the idea of the intersection of two sets difficult. This is the area where the two sets overlap and where objects with both attributes are placed. In the above Venn diagram this is the central area in which black triangles are placed. Another difficulty children have concerns the space outside the two sets, i.e. the space outside both circles but inside the rectangle. In the above case, this is for shapes which are not triangles and are not black. The Carroll diagram is a simple correlation or contingency table, but children sometimes find this difficult. The use of the negative, for example 'not black' and 'not triangle' adds to the difficulty. If the shapes were only red and blue and were only triangles or rectangles, it would be tempting to think of a simplified sorting tree. The first question might be 'What colour?' with the possibilities of 'red' and 'blue' and the second question might be 'What shape?' with the two possibilities of 'square and 'rectangle'. Children would probably find this easier to manage, but it is not satisfactory mathematically. It is no longer a binary tree, as it is possible for there to be colours other than red and blue and shapes other than triangles and rectangles.

Although the skills necessary for the construction of pie charts are complicated, children usually find them quite easy to interpret. They are a particularly clear way of comparing proportions, for example in

Pie chart showing eye colour

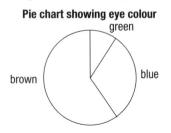

data from two different groups. However, they should only be used when the total represented by the whole circle (or pie) has meaning. So, in the example of eye colour, the whole circle represents the total number of children in the sample.

If the data were about pets, then it would be less clear what the complete circle represented. It would not be the number of children who had pets, unless they all had just one. It would not necessarily be the total number of pets, unless each pet had been recorded, that is if a child had, say, two cats then 2 cats were recorded. The other problem with a pie chart is that categories or classes with no representatives are not shown. So, if a bar chart were used there could be a category of, say, 'horses' or 'tortoises' which no child in the group had as a pet but this would not show on a pie chart.

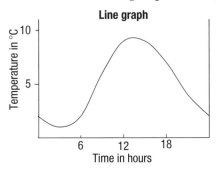

Line graph

Line graphs (*x–y* graphs) are only suitable for continuous data and if the interpolated line makes sense. For example, if the temperature were only recorded at, say, 1-hour intervals, during a day, it is reasonable to suppose that the temperature would pass through all the intermediate values. In fact the drawing of a smooth line between them assumes the temperature change was even.

At the top of the primary school, it might be suitable to introduce contingency tables and scatter diagrams. These are used to show a correlation between two measures. For example, if the marks of ten children in both a Maths and an English test are known, is there any relation between the two?

Maths	84	45	54	48	63	24	71	58	46	59
English	75	62	56	52	58	45	62	68	55	52

A contingency table is similar to a Carroll diagram, but has several classes on each side of the table. The pairs of marks are then entered into the table. For example, the first pair of 84(M) and 75(E) go into the cell >79 (M) and 60–70 (E). All the pairs of marks are put into the appropriate cell and the number in each cell totalled.

Contingency table

Maths

English	20–39	40–59	60–79	>79
20–39				
40–59	1	4		
60–79		3	1	1
>79				

For a scatter diagram, two axes are drawn, in this example, one for Maths marks and one for English marks. Each pair of marks is then plotted as a single point on the graph, so each point represents the marks from a particular person. In the example used there are really too few pairs of marks to give any strong indication of any correlation. There is slight evidence of a weak correlation, for the pupils with higher marks in Maths tended to get higher marks in English as well (or vice versa). This conjecture could be tested by gathering further data.

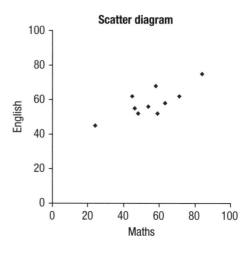

If there are more children in the sample, the marks are sometimes grouped into classes. For example, the following data refer to marks out of 50 in a class of 30 children.

Range of marks	0–9	10–19	20–29	30–39	40–50
Number of children	1	7	12	6	4

A cumulative frequency table shows how many values are less than a given value. It can easily be obtained from a frequency table by adding class frequencies, so in the table below the number of children who had marks less than 20 was 1 + 7 = 8; the number less than 30 was 1 + 7 + 12 = 20.

mark up to-	10	20	30	40	50
number of children	1	8	20	26	30

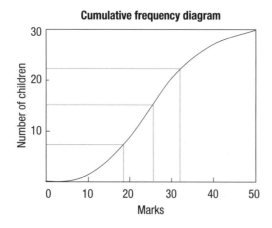

A cumulative frequency curve can be drawn from this table by plotting the points and joining them with a smooth curve, as shown in the diagram. From the cumulative frequency curve, the median and the quartiles can be estimated.

The median is the middle value with 50% of the distribution on either side. This can be found from the cumulative frequency curve by finding the point half way up the Y-axis, drawing a line parallel to the *X*-axis to the curve, then finding the value of *X* at this point (as shown on the diagram). The lower quartile has 25% and the upper quartile has 75% of the distribution below it and can be found in similar ways, as shown in the diagram. In the example shown, the lower quartile ≈ 18, the median ≈ 26 and the upper quartile ≈ 32. This means that 25% of the marks were below 18, 50% were below 26 and 75% were below 32. Other measures such as the tenth or nineteenth percentile are sometimes used in educational statistics and refer to the values below which 10% or 19% of the distribution lie.

If, for example, it is desired to compare several schools' exam results, it is normal to use summary statistics. One common method is to use the lowest mark, the lower quartile, the median, the upper quartile and the highest mark of each school. These can be shown by a box and whisker diagram. For example, the results (as percentages) from five schools were as shown in the table below:

School	lowest mark	lower quartile	median	upper quartile	highest mark
A	25	34	45	53	68
B	12	25	35	45	61
C	20	42	55	68	90
D	32	40	45	50	59
E	15	38	45	53	71

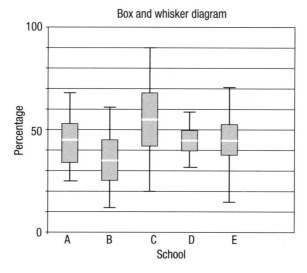

The box and whisker diagram shows the same figures. It is easier to see the differences between the schools. For example, although A, D and E all have the same median, E has a much greater spread and D has a remarkably small difference between the lowest and highest marks. Although school C has the greatest median and by far the greatest top mark, it has a great range, so the lowest mark is lower than both A and D.

Check 19.2

1 Represent the hair colour of 20 children graphically.

Hair colour	Number of children
Blonde	5
Red	1
Light brown	8
Dark brown	4
Black	2

2 A class of 20 children was asked about their pets. Represent the data graphically.

Pet	Number of children
Dog	8
Cat	6
Fish	2
Rabbit	3
Horse	1
None	8

3 The mean monthly temperatures through the year are shown below. Draw a graph to illustrate the data.

Jan	Feb	March	April	May	June	July	Aug	Sept	Oct	Nov	Dec
4	5	6	9	11	14	16	15	14	10	7	5

4 The marks in Maths and French tests are listed below. Draw a contingency table and a scatter diagram to represent these data.

Maths	18	32	44	47	56	71	76	84	86	93
French	40	68	53	35	84	75	58	26	48	77

5 The following is a frequency table for marks in a Maths test. Draw a bar chart and a cumulative frequency curve from the data. Estimate the median and the quartiles.

Score	0	1	2	3	4	5	6	7	8	9	10
Frequency	0	1	0	2	3	6	8	9	7	3	1

Statistics

With numerical data it is possible to calculate descriptive statistics, that is, numbers which describe the data in some way. Those statistics which give an indication of the value of the middle of the data are called averages or measures of central tendency. Such averages are often used to represent the whole data set. There are three of these, which will be illustrated by considering the following 20 figures which are the number of words in consecutive lines of a book.

10, 10, 11, 10, 3, 9, 2, 10, 9, 12, 9, 9, 12, 11, 9, 8, 9, 11, 9, 13

It is often useful to arrange the numbers in ascending order so:

2, 3, 8, 9, 9, 9, 9, 9, 9, 9, 10, 10, 10, 10, 11, 11, 11, 12, 12, 13

The mode is the most frequent value, which, in the illustration above, is 9. The median is the middle value if all the values are arranged in order of magnitude. It divides the distribution into two equal parts. If there is an odd number of values it is the middle value. If there is an even number of values, as in the illustration above, it is the average of the two middle values. As there are 20 values, it will be the average of the 10th and 11th values. These are 9 and 10, so the median is 9·5. The quartiles can also be calculated as the mid values of each half. So the lower quartile is the average of the 5th and 6th values, which is 9, and the upper quartile is the average of the 15th and 16th values, which is 11. The arithmetic mean or average is obtained by adding all the values and dividing by the number of values.

$$\text{Mean} = \frac{\text{sum of all values}}{\text{number of all values}}$$

In the case above this is $\frac{186}{20} = 9\cdot3$. In the illustration used, all three measures of central tendency are quite close together (mode = 9, median = 9·5, mean = 9·3), but this is not always the case. The table below compares some of the advantages and disadvantages of the three measures of central tendency.

	Advantages	Disadvantages	Examples of use
Mode	Simple to understand. Unaffected by extreme values. It is always an actual value.	Cannot be used in further statistical calculations.	In market research for, say, shoe size.
Median	Simple to understand. Unaffected by extreme values.	Cannot be used in further statistical calculations. It may or may not represent an actual value.	Useful in 'normal' distributions.
Mean	Can be calculated exactly. Makes use of all the data. Can be used in further statistical calculations.	Greatly affected by extreme values. May not be an actual value.	Most widely used in statistics.

As well as having a figure for its central tendency, it is useful to have some indication of how 'spread out' a distribution is. The range is the simplest measure. This is the difference between the highest and the lowest value in the data. So in the above example, it is $13 - 2 = 11$. This is greatly affected by any extreme value. The inter-quartile range is the difference between the upper and lower quartiles, in this case $11 - 9 = 2$. The mean deviation is the average deviation from the mean. To find this the differences between the mean and each value is found and their average (ignoring their sign) calculated. This is 1·7 in the example above. Simply ignoring the sign of the difference is not satisfactory mathematically, so the standard deviation is used.

To find this, the difference between each value and mean is found, these are squared, and then the mean or average of all these squared differences is calculated. The standard deviation is the square root of this average. In the illustration above it is approximately 2·6. This is not suitable for use in primary school, but is often provided by calculators or in computer statistical packages. At Key Stage 2 the idea of the spread of a distribution may well be introduced simply by comparing the shape of the graphs and looking to see how 'spread out' or 'bunched' it appears.

 Check 19.3

Find the mode, median and mean of the following data (from questions 19.1)

1 The number of goals scored by 20 football teams on one Saturday:

3 0 0 1 1 5 2 0 0 2 2 1 0 0 0 1 1 1 2 2

2 Marks in a Maths test

7 10 4 6 6 4 7 6 2 4 9 7 5 3 7 8 7 5 6 8

Interpreting results

As the earlier stages may take a considerable time, the final stage of data handling is often omitted. It is however, important for children to discuss the implications of what they have done. At Key Stage 1 the interpretation should be quite simple. For example some questions might be displayed beside a bar chart of pets. These might include: 'Which is the most common pet?' or 'How many children have cats?' or more interesting ones such as 'Why do you think no-one has an elephant?' The first two questions above are simply asking the children to describe what they have found. This is valuable at all stages and involves understanding the diagram or graph produced.

In the upper primary school it is possible to try to find out if there is a correlation between two measures. Care must be taken in presenting the results. Statistical techniques can only indicate that there is co-variation, not that there is a causal link. For example, if the length of hair and favourite sport were entered into a contingency table, it might appear that there was a connection between short hair and football. This does not mean that there is a causal link between them. It merely states that those who like football tend to have short hair (and vice versa).

One important aspect of data handling and statistics outside school is prediction. The work carried out in school is probably not suitable to make real predictions, but it would be useful for children to be aware of some of the problems. In business, trends over time are often plotted in graphs and the line is extrapolated to predict future values. This makes the assumption that the factors affecting production (or whatever) will remain the same. In practice this is unlikely, and the usefulness of the prediction depends on how little change there is. Another type of prediction is illustrated by political opinion polls. In these a number of people are interviewed and their opinions are assumed to be representative of the whole population. The problem of constructing a reliable sample is complicated. It is not sufficient to go out into the street and interview, say, the first 100 people that come along. This would almost certainly be biased. Some groups such as the disabled and elderly, would probably be under-represented, others would be over-represented. In school this might be touched on by discussing whether results from another class or from the whole community (village, town, district) would be similar or different. This problem of fair sampling can arise even in Key Stage 1. For example, if the colours of the sweets in tubes of 'Smarties' are being investigated, it can be interesting to ask the children to predict whether the colours of the next tube will be exactly the same as in one that has already been analysed. In the early years they usually think there will be the same distribution and are very surprised to find out that even the number of sweets can vary.

At some point in the interpretation of results, questions about the reliability and validity of the data should be discussed. What problems in data collection (e.g. classification problems, missing data) might affect the results? With calculators and computers it is very easy to produce professional looking graphs and impressive figures, but the results are only as good as the original data. These days we are bombarded by so-called facts and figures. However, their value depends heavily on the way the original data were collected and the assumptions made during analysis, and these are rarely explained. It is important to enable the children to be critical about what they see and hear. If pupils are allowed to engage in all stages of an enquiry including the setting up of the questions at the outset, the negotiation of categories, the design of data collection sheets and the choice of graphical representation, then they should become aware of the type of problems which might be encountered and the limitations these impose.

Finally in any data handling exercise, there should be a review at the end to find out whether the original questions have been answered and what additional questions have arisen. It is also useful to note any particular problems that occurred and how to avoid them in future.

Use of computers

There are several data handling packages available for schools. There are two different ways in which educational data handling packages can be used. First they can be used simply as a graph-drawing facility. Once the data have been collected, they are entered into the program and professional-looking graphs can be produced. The entering of the data can be a problem. If the children enter the data they may be slow and not particularly accurate, and only a few of them can work at the computer at the same time. An advantage is the ease with which a variety of graphs can be riewed, making it possible to discuss the merits of different representations with the whole class or group.

The second use of the computer is to give the children some experience of handling a simple database. It is probably best to start with extracting information from one that is already entered. The children must be given some sort of model for the database before they start using one. The simplest is that of a card index, with each card having the details of one person or creature on it. The cards can then be sorted by any of the attributes recorded. A progression should be established within the school so that children develop their IT skills as well as their mathematical understanding.

Summary

- There are five main stages in data handling: posing questions, collecting data, analysing data, presenting results, interpreting the results.
- A good record sheet is very useful.
- Categories need to be discussed.
- There are three types of data: categorical, discrete, continuous.
- Frequency tables can be constructed.
- There is a wide variety of graphs and diagrams available.
- The three measures of central tendency are the mode, median and mean.
- Measures of spread include the range, the inter-quartile range and the standard deviation.
- A review of achievements, problems encountered and questions arising should be made at the end of any data handling exercise.
- Computer programs can be useful, for example, data bases and graph-drawing tools.

Links with the classroom

1 Which types of representation are suitable for Key Stage 1?
2 How would you introduce Carroll diagrams with two criteria to children in Year 4?
3 Suggest some questions which might be tackled by Year 4 within a project on 'Sports'.
4 A Year 6 class is doing a project on 'Our Community'. Suggest some possible questions for investigation, including opportunities to look at the correlation between factors. How might work on measures of central tendency be covered?

Challenges!

1 Julia plays in her school netball team. She will be selected to play for the county team next season if her mean score of goals for the school team after the first 7 games is at least 12. After 6 games her mean score of goals is 11·5.

a What is the total number of goals that Julia has scored in these 6 games?

b What is the least number of goals she must score in the next game in order to be chosen for the county team?

c In the seventh game she scores 13 goals. Does her mean score increase or decrease, and by how much?

2 Moving averages (from Searl)

This is a game for 5 or 6 people. The first 4 or 5 each choose a number between say 10 and 100. The last person chooses another number as a 'target average'. The average of the first 4 or 5 numbers is found (with a calculator). Turns are then taken to choose a further number to move the average towards the target. Continue adding further numbers until sufficiently close (decide on this at the beginning).

References

Searl, J. (1998) 'Mathematics, technology and mathematics education: some reflections', *Mathematics Teaching*, **162**, 24–8.

CHAPTER

Probability

We MUST BELIEVE in luck, otherwise how can we explain the success of those we don't like? (Jean Cocteau quoted in Wells)

Introduction

Until the introduction of the National Curriculum, probability was rarely taught in primary schools. However, in recent documents such as the National Numeracy Strategy (1999) it appears in the teaching programmes for Years 5 and 6. In fact there are many aspects of everyday life, as diverse as the National Lottery and insurance premiums, which are linked to probability theory. This is a fairly recent branch of mathematics whose foundations were laid in seventeenth-century France. Chevalier de Méré posed some classic problems around 1650, including one about how the stakes in a game of chance should be divided if the game were interrupted part way through. Brilliant mathematicians like Pascal and Fermat took these up and developed modern theories of probability. It is an area of mathematics in which a clear head is more important than calculating skill.

In the primary school the language of probability and practical examples are more important than calculating procedures. Most children have some relevant experience and enjoy this aspect of mathematics.

Language

As with all branches of mathematics, it is necessary to establish the meaning of the terms used. In the National Curriculum and the National Numeracy Strategy there is a list of some examples of the language used, including 'evens', 'fair', 'unfair', 'certain', 'likely', 'probably' and 'equally likely'. An early activity might be asking the children to make up statements which could be put into boxes labelled 'very unlikely', 'unlikely', 'evens', 'likely' and 'very likely'. This can lead to much discussion as to the meaning of the terms and the statements.

At a later stage (probably Year 5 or Year 6), the probability scale can be introduced. This is a numerical measure for probability ranging from 0 for an impossible event to 1 for a certain event. Again the children can be asked to invent statements and place them on a long probability line with 0 at one end, 0·5 (evens) in the middle and 1 at the other end. Probabilities can be given as fractions or decimals. So the probability of 'evens' is either 0·5 or ½. The process of estimating probabilities is very much a personal matter, and sometimes uncovers superstitious beliefs. For example, people often say that the probability of their passing an exam is low, when they know it is reasonably high, but they want to avoid 'tempting fate'. It is a sensitive area, so care should be taken not to ridicule children's ideas.

The study of probability provides a rich context in which to develop children's ideas about fractions. The statement that the probability of getting a head when tossing a coin is ½ can be interpreted in several ways. It can be seen as saying that there is a chance of 1 in 2, or 1 out of every 2, or that half of the time it should be a head. It is a particularly appropriate form of representation when all possibilities have been listed and the number of acceptable outcomes counted (e.g. getting a head), for then

$$\text{the probability} = \frac{\text{the number of acceptable outcomes}}{\text{the number of possible outcomes}}$$

Working out probabilities

Single events

A distinction is often made between theoretical and empirical probabilities. In cases like throwing a fair die (singular of dice), it is assumed that all the possibilities can be listed and that they will all be equally likely. This means that the ideal or theoretical probability of a single event can be calculated. For example, in tossing a fair coin, it will either be a head or a tail (it is assumed it will never land on its edge). As these are the only two possibilities, their probabilities must add up to 1, and as they are both equally likely, then the probability of the result being a head is ½ and of a tail is also ½.

However, in some cases, such as tossing a matchbox or drawing pin, the possibilities can be listed, but experience tells us that they are not equally likely. This means the only way to attach probabilities to them is to carry out an experiment and count how often each possibility occurs. If a large number of cases are observed, then the frequency of each possibility can be taken as a measure of its probability. For example, if a drawing pin was tossed 100 times and it landed on its point 30 times and on its back 70 times, then the probability of it landing on its point would be 0·3.

Many practical uses of probability involve using frequency of occurrence as a measure of probability. For example, insurance premiums are calculated by looking at the frequency of occurrence of the event in the past. So, if the number of claims for storm damage increases, then the premium for storm insurance will increase eventually. In primary school a record might be kept about whether chips or mashed potatoes were offered for dinner for a month. These figures could then be used to predict the probability of there being chips on a given day in the future. For example if chips were served on 8 out of 20 days, then the probability of having chips would be $\frac{8}{20}$ or 1 in 2½.

It is difficult to prove whether an actual die or coin is fair or biased. For, by the very nature of probability, the theoretical prediction will only be true over 'the long run' and it is to be expected that any given trial will depart from this to some extent. For example, if a fair die is tossed there are six possible results; 1, 2, 3, 4, 5, or 6; these are all equally likely so the probability of getting one of them, say a 6, is ⅙. But in practice if a die is tossed, say, 24 times the frequencies with which the different faces were uppermost might well not be equal. Children might then jump to the conclusion that their die was biased. So it is a question of how great a departure from the theoretical result is counted as significant. Similarly with cards, it is possible to work out theoretical probabilities. For example, what is the probability of drawing a picture card from a pack of 52 cards? There are 12 picture cards in the pack, so the theoretical probability is $\frac{12}{52} = \frac{3}{13}$. However, if a card were drawn 13 times (and replaced after the draw) it would not be surprising if more or less than 3 picture cards occurred. Despite this, it is possible to work out theoretical probabilities for many games of chance and the odds offered are usually linked to these.

Multiple events

It is often necessary to consider more complicated events. Considering first a fairly simple example, if two coins are tossed, what is the probability that the result will be two heads? The possible results are two heads, a head and a tail, and two tails. This might lead to the idea that the probability of two heads would be ⅓. However, these events are not equally likely, as illustrated in the accompanying table, where H represents a head and T a tail.

First coin	Second coin
H	H
H	T
T	H
T	T

So there are four possible outcomes, each of which is equally likely and so the probability of two heads is ¼ or 0·25. This method of listing all possibilities in a table is useful when considering two independent events. Events are said to be independent when the result of the first does not affect the second.

Another example of two independent events is tossing two dice. If the spot values are added together, the possible results range from 2 to 12, but all numbers are not equally likely as shown in the second table.

Score	Numbers on dice						Frequency	Probability
2	1,1						1	$\frac{1}{36}$
3	1,2	2,1					2	$\frac{1}{18}$
4	1,3	2,2	3,1				3	$\frac{1}{12}$
5	1,4	2,3	3,2	4,1			4	$\frac{1}{9}$
6	1,5	2,4	3,3	4,2	5,1		5	$\frac{5}{36}$
7	1,6	2,5	3,4	4,3	5,2	6,1	6	$\frac{1}{6}$
8	2,6	3,5	4,4	5,3	6,2		5	$\frac{5}{36}$
9	3,6	4,5	5,4	6,3			4	$\frac{1}{9}$
10	4,6	5,5	6,4				3	$\frac{1}{12}$
11	5,6	6,5					2	$\frac{1}{18}$
12	6,6						1	$\frac{1}{36}$

The possible outcomes of two independent events like this can also be shown in a table with one outcome along the top and the other down one side. It is a good idea to use two dice of different colours so that it is immediately obvious that events such as (3,4) are different from (4,3). In the case of the two dice (red and black) it would be as shown in the third table.

		Second (black) die					
		1	2	3	4	5	6
First (red) die	1	1,1	1,2	1,3	1,4	1,5	1,6
	2	2,1	2,2	2,3	2,4	2,5	2,6
	3	3,1	3,2	3,3	3,4	3,5	3,6
	4	4,1	4,2	4,3	4,4	4,5	4,6
	5	5,1	5,2	5,3	5,4	5,5	5,6
	6	6,1	6,2	6,3	6,4	6,5	6,6

This actually shows the structure of the situation revealing it as the Cartesian product (see Chapter 5). This means that the total number of possible outcomes (or pairs of outcomes) is the number of possibilities in the first event multiplied by the number of possibilities in the second event, in this case $6 \times 6 = 36$. If we were considering tossing a coin and throwing a die, the number of possible outcomes would be $2 \times 6 = 12$. Tables like this can be used in many investigations, for example, how many types of sandwiches can be made if there are three types of bread and four types of fillings? (See Chapter 5.)

But if there are more than two events or variables, then some other form of recording is necessary. For example, how many different outfits can a person wear if they have two hats, two tee-shirts and two pairs of shorts? To keep it simple, let the hat, tee-shirt and shorts all be either blue (B) or green (G). One way of setting this out is in a tree diagram.

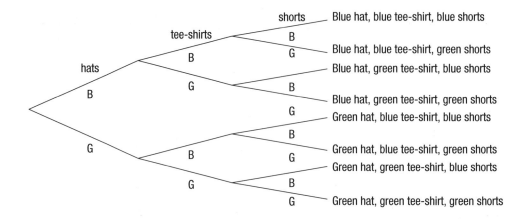

So altogether there are 2 × 2 × 2 = 8 possible outfits. This is quite a complicated example, but simpler cases can also be illustrated with tree diagrams.

For example, the results of tossing two coins can be shown. Tree diagram (a) shows the same four possible outcomes as the table used before.

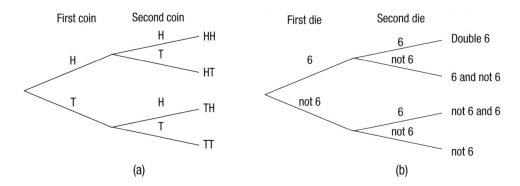

The probability of getting two sixes if two fair dice are thrown can also be illustrated with a tree diagram as shown in (b). If we are only interested in the number of sixes thrown, we can classify the results simply as '6' or 'not 6'.

This diagram appears to indicate that there are only four possibilities. In one sense this is true, but this is somewhat misleading, as the probabilities of the four cases are by no means equal. This will be discussed in more detail later.

Check 20.1

1 If two fair dice are tossed, what would be the probability that:
   a both dice show the same number
   b there is at least one six
   c the sum of the two numbers is even
   d the sum of the two numbers is greater than 9?

2 In a sandwich bar there are three types of bread (wholemeal, brown, white), four fillings (cheese, tuna, ham, egg) and three salads (lettuce, tomato, cucumber). How many types of sandwiches with a filling and a salad can be made? If some sandwiches only have a filling and no salad, how many varieties can be made?

3 When you drop a matchbox onto a table, there are three ways it can land:

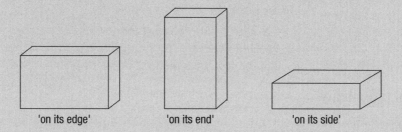

'on its edge'   'on its end'   'on its side'

Jane has found the probability of the matchbox landing 'on its end' is approximately 0·1 and the probability of it landing 'on its side' is approximately 0·6.

a What is the probability that it will land 'on its edge'?

b Jane drops two identical boxes. What is the probability that both will land 'on their edges'?

c Jane and Sarah are playing a game. Jane says 'I will drop two boxes. If they land the same way up, I win. If they don't land the same way up, you win.'

Who is the more likely to win the game? Show all your working.

4 Are these games fair?

a Place a counter on the start. Roll two dice and work out the difference in spot values. If the score is 0, 1 or 2 move 1 space to the left. If the score is 3, 4 or 5 move 1 space to the right. Repeat until you win or lose.

WIN				START				LOSE

b The following is a 'fairground game' which costs 10p a turn. A counter is placed on the 'start' square and the player tosses a coin. If the result is a head, the counter is moved one square to the right, if it is a tail, the counter is moved one square to the left. The player must toss the coin and move the counter exactly four times. The player collects the amount written on the square on which the counter finally lands.

	Tail ←				Head →			
10p	50p	5p	£1	START 2p	£1	5p	50p	10p

Some questions from National Tests

5 In a box of crisps there are cheese, chicken and plain packets. The probability of picking a chicken packet is 7 out of 10. The probability of picking a cheese packet is 1 out of 5. What is the probability of picking a plain packet?

6 A charity raffle sells red tickets, blue tickets and green tickets.

These tickets are sold: Red tickets numbers 1 to 50

Blue ticket numbers 1 to 70

Green ticket numbers 1 to 80

Calculate the probability that the ticket for the first prize has the number 63 on it. Calculate the probability that the ticket for the first prize is blue.

Conditional probability

In many situations, events are not independent. For example, consider the probability of drawing two picture cards from a pack of 52 cards. In this case, when one card has been drawn, this affects the probability of the second card being a picture card. The probability of the first card being a picture card is $^{12}\!/_{52} = ^{3}\!/_{13}$. But to work out the probability of the second card being a picture, it is necessary to know what happened in the first draw. If the first card was a picture card, then there will be only 11 picture cards left in the 51 cards remaining, so the probability of the second card being a picture will be $^{11}\!/_{51}$. In fact the probability of both cards being picture cards can then be calculated as $^{3}\!/_{13} \times {}^{11}\!/_{51} = ^{33}\!/_{663} \approx 0\cdot05$ or 1 in 20.

It may not be obvious why the two probabilities are multiplied together. Consider again tossing two fair coins and the probability of getting two heads. This can be illustrated in several ways.

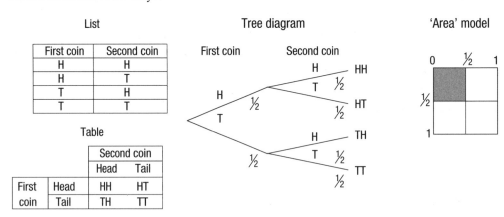

List	
First coin	Second coin
H	H
H	T
T	H
T	T

Table

		Second coin	
		Head	Tail
First coin	Head	HH	HT
	Tail	TH	TT

From the list or the table, if each of the four results are equally likely, then the probability of two heads must be ¼ or 0·25. As explained earlier, this is Cartesian product situation, so the total number of possible pairs of outcomes or final results is $2 \times 2 = 4$ and only one of these is two heads, so the probability is 1 out of 4 or ¼. The 'area' model, which is closely related to the Cartesian product, shows the links with the multiplication of the fractions (see Chapter 7). In the tree diagram, the fractions beside the lines are the probabilities of the events recorded on that line. So for the first coin the probability of a head (H) is $\frac{1}{2}$. The probability for a head (H) with the second coin is also $\frac{1}{2}$. The probability of two heads (HH) is then 'half of a half' or $\frac{1}{2} \times \frac{1}{2} = \frac{1}{4}$.

It is possible to look at the probability of getting two sixes when tossing two dice in a similar way. When throwing the first die the probability of getting a six is $\frac{1}{6}$. Similarly when throwing the second die, the probability of getting a six is $\frac{1}{6}$. So the probability of getting double six is $\frac{1}{6}$ of $\frac{1}{6}$, that is $\frac{1}{36}$. The diagrams below illustrate this in varied ways.

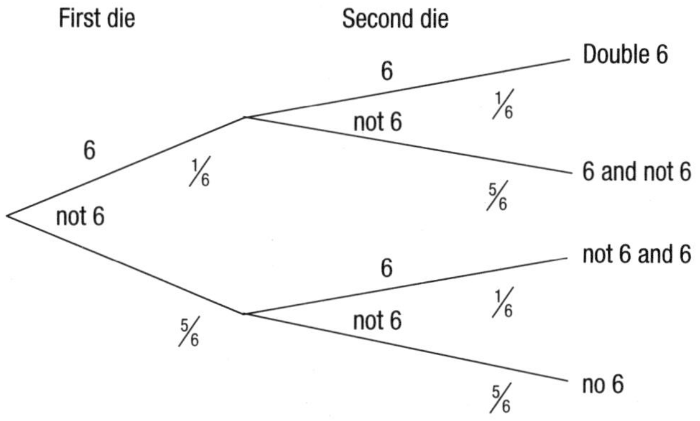

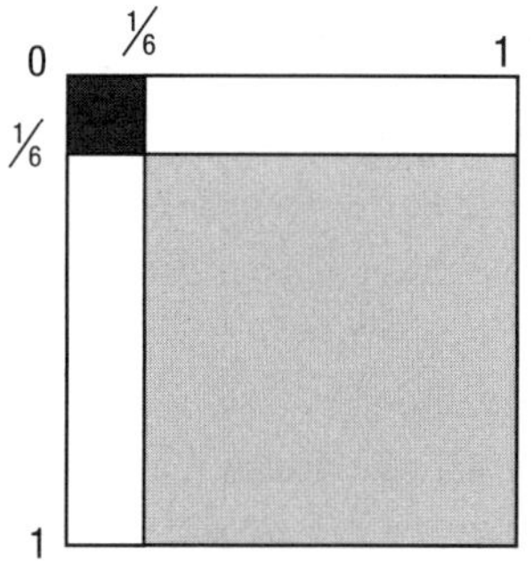

In the tree diagram the probabilities are written as fractions. The probability of getting a 6 in one throw of a die is $\frac{1}{6}$, so the probability of getting 'not 6' is $\frac{5}{6}$. These fractions are recorded by the appropriate branches. So the probability of getting a double 6 is a 'sixth of a sixth' or $\frac{1}{6} \times \frac{1}{6} = \frac{1}{36}$. This is also illustrated in the 'area' or Cartesian product model by the black area.

It is also possible to calculate the probabilities of getting one 6 or no sixes. From the tree diagram, the probability of getting no sixes is $\frac{5}{6} \times \frac{5}{6} = \frac{25}{36}$. In the 'area' model this is shown by the grey shading. The probability of getting one six can be worked out in two different ways. As the total probabilities of double six, one six and no sixes must add up to 1, then the probability of one six is

$$\begin{aligned} 1 - (\tfrac{1}{36} + \tfrac{25}{36}) &= 1 - \tfrac{26}{36} \\ &= \tfrac{10}{36} \\ &= \tfrac{5}{18} \end{aligned}$$

Or by looking at the tree the probability of a six followed by not a six is $\frac{1}{6} \times \frac{5}{6} = \frac{5}{36}$. The probability of not a six then a six is the same. So the probability of getting one six (either first or second) is $\frac{5}{36} + \frac{5}{36} = \frac{10}{36} = \frac{5}{18}$. In this case the probabilities are added because either event fulfils the condition of just one six.

To investigate two events which are not independent, consider taking balls out of a bag which has a few coloured balls in it. This may seem artificial, but the numbers can be kept small and the same principle can be applied to more complicated situations like drawing cards from a pack or the National Lottery. If there are 5 balls in a bag, 3 black and 2 white, and two balls are taken out (without replacement), what is the probability that they will both be black?

In the following diagram there are 3 black balls (B1, B2, B3) and 2 white balls (W1, W2).

First ball	Second ball	Result	
B1	B2	B1, B2	2 blacks
	B3	B1, B3	2 blacks
	W1	B1, W1	1 black, 1 white
	W2	B1, W2	1 black, 1 white
B2	B1	B2, B1	2 blacks
	B3	B2, B3	2 blacks
	W1	B2, W1	1 black, 1 white
	W2	B2, W2	1 black, 1 white
B3	B1	B3, B1	2 blacks
	B2	B3, B2	2 blacks
	W1	B3, W1	1 black, 1 white
	W2	B3, W2	1 black, 1 white
W1	B1	W1, B1	1 black, 1 white
	B2	W1, B2	1 black, 1white
	B3	W1, B3	1 black, 1 white
	W2	W1, W2	2 whites
W2	B1	W2, B1	1 black, 1 white
	B2	W2, B2	1 black, 1white
	B3	W2, B3	1 black, 1 white
	W1	W2, W1	2 whites

There are five possible outcomes when drawing out the first ball (5 balls in the bag). There are only 4 possible outcomes when drawing out the second ball (there are only 4 balls left in the bag), so altogether there are 20 possible different outcomes (5 × 4). Of these 20 outcomes, 6 of them include 2 black balls, so the probability of both balls being black is 6 out of 20 or $\frac{3}{10}$. The following tree diagram shows the same in summary form.

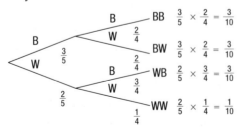

The probability of two black balls is then $\frac{3}{10} = 0.3$. It will be noted that if the probabilities of all possibilities (BB, BW, WB, WW) are added up, then the total comes to 1.

This type of tree diagram can be used to analyse the probabilities in the

National Lottery. As the numbers for the Lottery are large, a simplified example will be worked. So if 2 numbers out of 16 are chosen, rather than 6 numbers out of 49, the following tree diagram can be drawn with ✓ for a selected number and × for a number which was not selected.

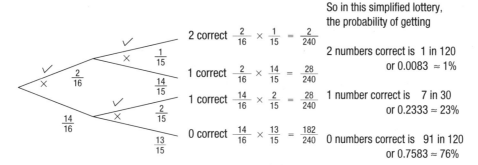

So in this simplified lottery, the probability of getting

2 correct $\frac{2}{16} \times \frac{1}{15} = \frac{2}{240}$

2 numbers correct is 1 in 120 or 0.0083 ≈ 1%

1 correct $\frac{2}{16} \times \frac{14}{15} = \frac{28}{240}$

1 correct $\frac{14}{16} \times \frac{2}{15} = \frac{28}{240}$

1 number correct is 7 in 30 or 0.2333 ≈ 23%

0 correct $\frac{14}{16} \times \frac{13}{15} = \frac{182}{240}$

0 numbers correct is 91 in 120 or 0.7583 ≈ 76%

A larger diagram with six numbers (for the National Lottery) being chosen becomes complicated, but the principle is the same. Needless to say the probability of winning is very much smaller because of the large number of possibilities.

 Check 20.2

1 There are 6 coloured balls in a bag: 3 red, 2 blue and 1 yellow.
   a If I draw out one ball, what is the probability of it being blue?
   b If I draw out two balls (without replacement), what is the probability of there being one red and one blue?
   c If I draw out two balls (without replacement), what is the probability that they are different colours?
2 If three cards are drawn from a pack of 52 cards, what is the probability of getting:
   a three picture cards
   b a king, a queen and a jack (in any order)
   c no picture cards?

Summary

- There are many words which express degrees of uncertainty and probability.
- Probabilities can be placed on a scale between 0 (impossible) and 1 (certain).
- In some cases (such as tossing a coin) it is possible to work out theoretical probabilities; in other cases (such as tossing a match box) it is only possible to obtain an empirical estimate of probability by repeated trials.
- Tables can be used to list all possible outcomes of two independent events.
- Tree diagrams can be used for conditional probabilities and for cases involving more than two events.

Links with the classroom

1 Many children (and adults) feel it is harder to throw a six with a single die than any other number. What activities and questions might challenge this assumption?

2 'I've thrown 5 heads, so it must be a tail next'. How would you challenge this assertion with Year 6 children? (This is the so-called Gambler's fallacy.)

3 What sort of apparatus, equipment and classroom organisation would you use to investigate throwing dice or tossing coins? (If you give 30 children a coin each and suggest they toss it 10 times, the result is likely to be complete chaos!!)

4 Is it useful to use the term 'fair' in discussing probabilities?

Challenges!

1 On each day that I go to work, the probability that I leave home before 0800 is 0·2. The probability that I leave home after 0810 is 0·05.

   a What is the probability that I leave home between 0800 and 0810 inclusive?

   b The probability that I am late for work depends upon the time I leave home. The probabilities are given in the table below.

   I work 230 days each year. Estimate how many times I would expect to be late for work in a year.

time of leaving home	before 0800	between 0800 and 0810	after 0810
probability of being late	0·01	0·1	0·2

2 Explain why the probability of getting three numbers correct in the National Lottery is about 1 in 52.

3 In an American TV game show contestants choose one of three doors. Behind one of the doors there is a major prize, say a car, and behind the other two there are goats. After the contestant has chosen one door, the host (who knows where the prize is) opens one of the other two doors to reveal a goat. The contestant is then given the choice of staying with their first choice or swapping to the other unopened door. Can probability theory give any guidance in this case?

References

Fleet, T. (1991) *Chance Encounters* [Nuffield Maths. Challengers D. Teacher's Handbook]. Harlow: Longman.

Fleet, T. (1991) *Decision Maths* [Nuffield Maths. Challengers E. Teacher's Handbook]. Harlow: Longman.

Wells, D. (1986) *The Penguin Dictionary of Curious and Interesting Numbers*. Harmondsworth: Penguin Books.

Endpiece

IN WRITING THIS book we have been responding to both our own interest in trainee teachers' knowledge of mathematics, and to the more official requirements of the Teacher Training Agency. The danger here is that student teachers are seen as lacking or inadequate in some way. We prefer to see them as needing to reshape what they know so that they are better prepared for the ways pupils see mathematics and better able to help them create more sophisticated and interconnected networks of knowledge.

Our view of understanding is crucial here, encompassing factual, conceptual and strategic knowledge as outlined in the beginning chapters. After reading this book it may also be helpful to think of functional understanding, a construct of Michael de Villiers (1994) which he describes as:

> understanding the role, function or value of specific mathematical content or of a particular process . . .

This is not a narrow sort of understanding which only concerns applications to the real world but also concerns the connections within mathematics itself, which help to unify and fill out our present understandings. It would refer to the way in which the number system had to be expanded in response to problems in algebra, e.g. the solution of the equation $x + 5 = 2$. It would encompass the way in which proof is valued because it is concerned with clear thinking, good working definitions and deductive processes. Importantly, it is also concerned with knowing the limitations of mathematical processes, e.g. the problem of over interpreting poor data in statistics, or giving answers to 6 decimal places when measurements are only accurate to the nearest whole number. To us, this functional understanding refers to the place which mathematics occupies in human culture, an emphasis we have tried to place by giving historical and culturally specific examples throughout the book, but an aspect which invites further exploration.

As well as being competent and knowledgeable, we also prefer to see our trainee teachers as creative and enthusiastic individuals who will help pupils to see the wonder and beauty in mathematics as well as its utility. If there have been moments in reading this book when the reader has experienced delight and curiosity as well as satisfaction at getting to the bottom of something they have never really understood, we will have achieved one of our aims.

One thing which has stimulated us in writing has been the way in which we have all learned from each other. We are three very different individuals with different histories and different perspectives on mathematics. As we met together we started to ask each other questions such as 'Is that always true?' 'How do you do this?' 'What if the lines of symmetry aren't perpendicular?' This was greatly helped by the fact that we knew each other, we were not trying to impress or silence each other, and we were working together on a common goal. Above all we were each prepared to ask the really simple questions like 'I don't understand that; can you explain what you mean?' We sincerely hope that the readers of this book will be similarly helped by working with peers and tutors, and later get into the habit of working on their mathematics with other teachers and in-service providers. This may simply be working through classroom activities[1] but at your own level. It can be a joy.

The teacher's knowledge of mathematics and her knowledge of teaching mathematics are difficult to disentangle, and after the initial training period most subject knowledge will be developed through teaching implications. Even in this book, which is focused on the mathematical knowledge needed for primary teaching, we have found it difficult not to write about teaching. We would expect this distinction to become blurred over time, but at the beginning stages we hope that this book will help the reader to develop connections and alternative models or pictures. Hopefully, these will be useful in the search for another way of explaining something or the need to extend pupils' limited and limiting understandings to encompass more complex models and representations.

The important thing to realise, though, is that this is just a beginning. We hope you continue to extend and develop your own understanding of mathematics by sharing and reflecting upon your own experiences. If mathematics is not going to be your curriculum specialism you could still keep up to date by subscribing to a general primary teaching journal which includes mathematical articles, or reading articles in the *Times Educational Supplement*. If you do intend to be a curriculum leader in mathematics, then you should seriously consider joining one of the two professional associations[2] or persuade a group of local schools to join and enjoy the benefits of cluster membership. These suggestions will supplement the existing professional development provision in your school and locality. The best thing you can bring to all these opportunities is a willingness to learn yourself, to work with colleagues and to ask the really obvious questions which others may not have the confidence to raise.

References

Villiers, Michael de (1994) 'The role and function of a hierarchical classification of quadrilateral', *For the Learning of Mathematics*, **14**(1).

Notes

1 A good example here would be 'Primary Points of Departure' selected from 'Points of Departure 1–4' and rewritten by Jenny Murray for the Association of Teachers of Mathematics (ATM).

2 The Association of Teachers of Mathematics, 7 Shaftesbury Street, Derby DE23 8YB.
Web site: http://www.atm.org.uk/
The Mathematical Association, 259 London Road, Leicester LE2 3BE.
Web site: http://www.m-a.org.uk

QTS skills tests – topics covered in support materials

(Chapters in which topics are covered are given)

Topics	Chapters
Averages (mean, median, mode)	19
Bar charts (vertical and horizontal; including stacked bar charts and percentage bar charts)	19
Box and whisker diagrams (median, range, upper quartile, lower quartile, inter quartile range)	19
Conversions (currency e.g. French francs to pounds sterling; measurements e.g. kilometres to miles; lbs. to kilograms)	5
Cumulative frequency (median, quartiles)	19
Formulae	8
Fractions, decimals and percentages (converting fractions to decimals and to percentages and vice versa; calculating with percentages)	7
Line graphs (including trend lines; median and quartile lines)	19
Pie charts	19
Proportion	5
Range	19
Ratio	5
Scatter graphs (making comparisons; identifying correlation)	19
Tables (including age standardised scores)	15, 19
Time (age in years and months; time in hours and minutes)	15

Further information about the skills test and support materials can be found on the web, at http://www.canteach.gov.uk

APPENDIX

Using the programs on the CD

THE SIX DEMONSTRATION programs provide an opportunity to see some key mathematical ideas presented in a new way. They have been written to exploit the ability of the computer to provide immediate feedback and animation of diagrams.

One of the best ways to learn is to talk and listen to others. This involves negotiating the meanings of terms, exploring new ideas and revising 'known facts' in the light of new insights. So the best way to use the programs is to regard them as scaffolds for discussion with others, especially if one is a 'more experienced practitioner'.

More flexible versions suitable for use in the classroom have been written and it is hoped that these may be published. For details, please contact Jennifer Suggate (email address Jennifer.Suggate@dur.ac.uk).

The programs should run if the disc is inserted into the CD drive. Select the appropriate folder for PC or Mac. When the contents are displayed, just double click on the icon for the program required. Follow the on-screen instructions, clicking on the green 'OK' button to move on to the next screen. It should be noted that these programs are still under development. It is hoped that they are fairly robust; but it is possible that there are undiscovered 'bugs' in them. If the program appears to get stuck (or 'hang'), press the 'Esc' key, close the window then reload the program.

The six programs cover:

Representing tens and units (*Numbers 1–99 demo*)
Methods of mental addition and subtraction (*Mental methods demo*)
Representing multiplication (*Multiplication demo*)
Representing fractions (*Fractions demo*)
Multiplying and dividing by powers of ten (*Powers of ten demo*)
Proving the angles in a triangle add up to 180° (*Angles in triangle*)

Glossary

Any definition must reflect the context for which it has been written. In this glossary, we have tried to give robust and informed descriptions, which will be useful in the primary school context. Inevitably there are compromises between mathematical rigour and easy intelligibility. After each entry there are references to chapters in which more detail can be found.

Addend	One of the numbers in an addition sum, e.g. in 5 + 3, both 5 and 3 are addends. (4)
Algorithm	A procedure (or set of rules) for carrying out a calculation. (4)
Alternate angles	If a line cuts two parallel lines, then the angles shown are equal. (14)
Angle	A measure of rotation or turn, usually given in degrees. There are 360° in one full turn. (14)
Area	A measure of the amount of surface in square units such as square centimetres or square inches. (11)
Associative law	Addition and multiplication are associative, that is if there are three numbers added or multiplied together, it does not matter which pair of numbers is treated first, e.g. 2 + (3 + 4) = (2 + 3) + 4 and 2 × (3 × 4) = (2 × 3) × 4. (3)
Attribute	A characteristic of an object, e.g. its length, mass. (Part 3)
Bar chart	A chart with bars whose lengths are proportional to the value of the data or number of cases in a given class, e.g. rainfall chart. (19)
Basic operations	The four basic arithmetic operations are addition, subtraction, multiplication and division. (3)
Binary system	Numbers written to the base-2 using only 0 and 1, e.g. $1011 = 1 \times 8 + 1 \times 2 + 1 \times 1 = 11$ (denary). (4)
Block graph	A simple chart in which each unit is represented by a block. (19)
Box and whisker diagram	A diagram showing median, quartiles and range of data. (19)
Capacity	A measure of the amount of liquid a container can hold. The most common units are litres or pints. (12)
Carroll diagram	A simple 2 × 2 contingency table, e.g. a table with four cells in which 2-D shapes are classified as triangles or not triangles on one side and as red or not red on the other. (19)

Cartesian coordinates	A system, in which the position of a point is determined by its distance from two lines of references, usually two lines at right angles called the *X*-axis and the *Y*-axis, the *x* coordinate given first, e.g. the point A is (3,4). (9)
Categorical data	Data classified by categories, e.g. by eye colour such as brown, blue, green. (19)
Circle	A closed 2-D shape traced out by a point which moves at a fixed distance from another fixed point (the centre of the circle). This is sometimes described as the locus of a point moving at a fixed distance from another fixed point. (10, 11, 16)
Circumference	The length around a circle; the perimeter of a circle. (11)
Commutative law	Addition and multiplication are commutative, that is the result does not depend on the order of the number, e.g. $2 + 3 = 3 + 2$ and $3 \times 4 = 4 \times 3$. Note: subtraction and division are *not* commutative.
Conditional probability	The probability of multiple events in which one event affects the probability of subsequent events, e.g. in the National Lottery the probability of the first ball being number 17 is ¹⁄₄₉, but if the first ball is 17, then the probability of the second ball being 17 is 0. (20)
Cone	3-D object possessing a circular face, and a curved surface tapering to a point not in the same plane as the circular face. It may be thought of as a circular pyramid. (12, 18)
Conjecture	A statement, often derived from a limited set of cases, which can either be proved or disproved. (2)
Conservation	The principle that the amount (number or measurement) is not altered by its position or arrangement. So, for example, if 8 blocks are rearranged, the number is not changed; the length of a rod is the same whether it is horizontal or vertical; the total weight of plasticine is not altered if it is divided into several parts. (4, Part Three, 10)
Continuous data	Data measured on a continuous scale (between limits any number is possible), e.g. height of children. (19)
Correlation	A measure of the relationship between two variables or attributes. (19)
Corresponding angles	If a line cuts two parallel lines, then the angles shown are equal. (14)
Cube	A solid figure (3-D shape) which has six equal square faces. Each face meets adjacent faces at right angles. One of the regular polyhedra. (12, 18)
Cube number	A number that is the third power of an integer, e.g. $8 = 2^3$. (3)
Cuboid	A solid figure (3-D shape) which has six rectangular faces (3 pairs of congruent rectangles). Each face meets adjacent faces at right angles. (18)
Cumulative frequency curve	Curve obtained by joining the points of cumulative frequencies of data. (19)
Cylinder	A 3-D object with two congruent circular ends which are joined by a straight curved surface; a circular prism. (18)
Decimal point	A dot used to separate the whole part of a number from the fractional parts; it is placed immediately to the right of the units digit, e.g. in 2·34 the dot between the 2 and 3 shows that the 2 means 2 units and the 3 means 3 tenths. (7)

Deductive reasoning	Drawing general conclusions from initial statements or assumptions using logical steps. Mathematicians often have to work backwards. They may have a conjecture which seems to fit all the cases tested so far. They then go back and clarify their initial assumptions and definitions. Then they try to prove what they think they know already! (2)
Denominator	The divisor in a fraction, e.g. in $5/7$ 7 is the denominator. (7)
Density	The mass per unit volume of a material. The standard units are kilograms per cubic metre or grams per cubic centimetre. (13)
Directed number	A number with a positive or negative sign, showing whether it is more or less than 0. (6)
Discrete data	Data measured on a discrete scale (only certain numbers are possible). (19)
Distributive law	Multiplication is distributive over addition (but addition is not distributive over multiplication) e.g. $2 \times (3 + 4) = (2 \times 3) + (2 \times 4)$. (3)
Dividend	In a division calculation, the number which is divided by another number, e.g. in $12 \div 3$, 12 is the dividend. (5)
Divisor	In a division calculation, the number which divides another number, e.g. in $12 \div 3$, 3 is the divisor. (5)
Dot graph	A simple graph in which each value is shown by a dot beside a number line. (19)
Equation	A statement that two mathematical expressions are equal, e.g. $3x + 2 = 5$; $2 + 5 = 7$; $(x - 1)^2 = x^2 - 2x + 1$. Note: the first equation only holds for one value of x, the last for all values of x. (8)
Even number	A number (integer) that can be divided by 2; this means it can be represented by two rows (of equal cubes) of the same length. (2, 3)
Factor	A number which divides another number exactly, e.g. 3 is a factor of 6. (5)
Fraction	A number with parts less than 1. It can be written as one number divided by another e.g. $3/4$ (when it is called a common fraction), or as a decimal, e.g. 0.75. If the numerator is less than the denominator, e.g. $3/8$, it is a proper fraction. If the numerator is more than the denominator, e.g. $5/3$, it is an improper fraction. Improper fractions can also be written as mixed fractions, which are made up of an integer and a proper fraction, e.g. $5/3 = 1\frac{2}{3}$. (7)
Frequency table	A table summarising the frequencies of the values in a set of data. (19)
Function	A mathematical relation between two sets (usually of numbers) in which each element of the first set corresponds to one and only one element of the second set. It can be expressed as a rule, e.g. 'add 2' or an equation $y = x + 2$. (9)
Graph	A diagram, usually using Cartesian coordinates with X- and Y-axes showing a relationship between two variables (a function). (9)
Histogram	A bar graph which represents a frequency distribution. The areas of the bars are proportional to the frequencies. If the class intervals are equal it is a bar chart. (19)
Horizontal	Parallel to the Earth's surface or sea level. (14)
Imperial units	A system of units of measurement developed in the UK based on the foot, pound and second. (Part 3)
Independent events	Two or more events which do not affect each other, e.g. throwing a coin twice. Obtaining a head the first time does not affect the probability of getting one the second time. (20)
Index (indices)	A method of writing powers of numbers, indicating how many times a number should be multiplied by itself, e.g. $3^2 = 3 \times 3$; $2^3 = 2 \times 2 \times 2$; $2^0 = 1$; $3^{-1} = \frac{1}{3}$. (3)
Inductive reasoning	A method of drawing general conclusions from a limited set of observations. (2)

Integer	The positive and negative whole numbers including 0, e.g. $^+4$, $^-8$, 0, $^+56$, $^-12$. (3, 6)
Interval scale	A measurement scale where 0 is arbitrary, e.g. time of day, temperature in °C. (19)
Irrational numbers	A number which cannot be written as one integer divided by another integer; they are infinite non-repeating decimals, e.g. $\pi, \sqrt{2}$. (3)
Kite	A quadrilateral with two pairs of adjacent equal sides. (16)
Lowest common multiple	The smallest number that is a multiple of two or more other numbers, e.g. 33 is the lowest common multiple of 3 and 11; it is the smallest number which can be divided by 3 and 11. (2, 5)
Mass	The amount of matter in a body. It is measured in kilograms or pounds. (13)
Mean	The arithmetic average of a set of data, obtained by adding all the data values and dividing by the number of observations. (19)
Median	The 'middle' value of a set of observations. The observations are arranged in order of magnitude, then if there are an odd number of observations it is the value of the middle one; if there are an even number of observations it is the average of the two middle observations. (19)
Minuend	In subtraction calculations, the quantity from which something is taken away, e.g. in $5 - 3$, 5 is the minuend. (4)
Mode	The most frequently occurring value in a set of data. (19)
Multiple	A number which is the product of a given number and an integer, e.g. 6 is a multiple of 2. (5)
Natural number	The counting numbers, e.g. 1, 2, 3, . . . (3)
Numerator	The dividend in a fraction, e.g. in $\frac{5}{7}$ 5 is the numerator. (7)
'Oblong'	This has no very precise mathematical meaning, but in common speech it refers to rectangles which are not squares. (16)
Odd number	A number (integer) that cannot be divided by 2 to give a whole number; this means that if it is represented by two rows (of equal cubes) one row will be one longer than the other. (2, 3)
Ordered list	A list of values arranged in order of magnitude (usually from smallest to largest). (19)
Ordinal scale	A method of ordering objects, e.g. the star system for hotels. (19)
Parallelogram	A quadrilateral where each side is equal in length to the side opposite to it and each side is parallel to the side opposite to it. (11, 16)
Percentage	A fraction expressed as a number of hundredths, e.g. $25\% = \frac{25}{100} (= \frac{1}{4})$. Percentages may be greater than 100, e.g. $120\% = 1\cdot2$.(7)
Perimeter	The length around the edge of a polygon or closed curve. (10)
Perpendicular	At right angles to each other. Two lines are perpendicular if they meet at right angles. (14)
Pictogram	A pictorial representation of data in which each picture or symbol represents one or more units. (19)
Pie chart	A circle with sectors proportional to the frequency of the data in classes. (19)
Place value (denary)	The convention by which the position of the digit within the number determines its value. In the common denary (base-10) system 123 means 1 hundred, 2 tens and 3 units (one hundred and twenty-three) whereas 321 means 3 hundreds 2 tens and 1 unit (three hundred and twenty-one). (4)
Polygon	A closed 2-D figure (shape) formed by three or more points joined by straight lines which do not intersect. (10, 16)

Precedence	The order in which arithmetic operations must be applied, i.e. BIDMAS. (3)
Prime number	A whole number greater than 1 which is only divisible by 1 and itself, e.g. 2, 3, 5, 7, 11. Every natural number greater than 1 is either prime or can be written as the product of primes, e.g. $12 = 2 \times 2 \times 3 = 2^2 \times 3$. (5)
Prism	A solid figure (3-D shape) with two congruent parallel ends and the other faces parallelograms. (In the examples of prisms met in primary school the 'other faces' are normally in fact rectangles.) If the ends are triangles, the prism is a triangular prism, if the ends are squares, the prism is a square prism, and so on. (18)
Probability scale	A measure of probability ranging from 0 (impossible) to 1 (certain). (20)
Pyramid	A solid (3-D) shape formed by a polygonal base and a number of triangular faces meeting in an external common point. If the base is a square, then it is called a square pyramid. (12, 18)
Pythagoras' theorem	A theorem, which states that in a right-angled triangle, the square on the hypotenuse is equal to the sum of the squares on the other two sides; number triples in which $a^2 = b^2 + c^2$. (10)
Quadrilateral	A closed 2-D figure (shape) with four straight sides. (16)
Quartile	In an ordered set of data, the lower quartile is the value which is greater than ¼ and less than ¾ of the observations, and the upper quartile is that value which is greater than ¾ and less than ¼ of the observations. (19)
Quotient	The result of dividing one number by another, e.g. in $12 \div 3 = 4$, 4 is the quotient. (5)
Range	The difference between the smallest and largest value in a set of data. (19)
Ratio scale	A measurement scale in which 0 means 'nothing', e.g. length, weight, time interval, angle. (Part Three)
Rational number	A number that can be written as one integer divided by another integer, e.g. ½, ³⁄₇, ⁸⁄₅, ⁻³⁄₄. (3, 7)
Real numbers	All the rational and irrational numbers together. (3)
Rectangle	A quadrilateral in which all four angles are right angles. (11, 16)
Regular dodecahedron	One of the five regular polyhedra. Each of the 12 faces is a regular congruent pentagon. (18)
Regular icosahedron	One of the five regular polyhedra. Each of its 20 faces is a congruent equilateral triangle. (18)
Regular octahedron	One of the five regular polyhedra. Each of its 8 faces is a congruent equilateral triangle. (18)
Regular polygon	A polygon with equal sides and angles, e.g. a regular pentagon is a five sided polygon where all the sides and angles are equal. (16)
Regular polyhedron (or regular solid)	3-D shape all of whose faces are congruent regular polygons, e.g. all the faces of a cube are congruent squares. In addition, whatever face the solid is resting on, it looks the same. (18)
Regular tetrahedron	One of the five regular polyhedra. Each of its four faces is an equilateral triangle. (18)
Remainder	The amount remaining after one number has been divided into another an exact number of times, e.g. in $14 \div 3 = 4$ remainder 2. (5)

Rhombus	An equal-sided quadrilateral with opposite sides parallel. (16)
Scatter diagram	A 2-D plot of a set of paired observations. (19)
Sector	Part of a circle lying between two radii and the arc they define; 'a slice of pie'. (2,11)
Sequence	A succession of terms formed according to some rule. It can be a sequence of numbers, e.g. 3, 5, 7, . . . or of patterns, e.g. □ □□ □□□. (8)
SI units	Système Internationale d'Unités. A coherent system of units of measurement, based on the metre, kilogram and second, and using the denary (base-10) place value system. (Part Three)
Sphere	A closed 3-D object whose surface is the locus of all points that are a given distance from a fixed point; a ball. (18)
Square number	A number that is an integer squared (multiplied by itself), e.g. $4 = 2^2$. (3)
Subtrahend	In subtraction calculations, the quantity subtracted, e.g. in $5 - 3$, 3 is the subtrahend. (4)
Supplementary angles	Angles which add up to 180° usually 'on a straight line'. (14)
Transitivity principle	If three numbers or measurements have the relations $x > y$ and $y > z$ then x must be greater than z ($x > z$); ancestors. (Part Three)
Trapezium	A quadrilateral with one pair of opposite sides parallel, and the other pair not parallel. (This 'exclusive' definition is disputed by some. See Chapter 16.)
Tree diagram	A diagram used to work out probabilities of multiple events. (19)
Triangle	A closed shape formed by three straight lines; a 3-sided polygon. Scalene triangle – a triangle with no equal sides. Equilateral triangle – a triangle with equal sides. Equiangular triangle – a triangle with equal angles. Isosceles triangle – a triangle with two equal sides (see Chapter 16 for brief discussion of this 'exclusive' definition.)
Triangular number	A number that can be represented by a triangular array of counters or dots. (3)
Variable	Usually a letter, or other symbol, which takes the value of any member of a set (usually a number), e.g. in $y = 2x + 3$, x and y are variables. x can take any value and is called the independent variable. Once x is selected then the value for y can be calculated, so y is the dependent variable. (9)
Venn diagram	A diagram showing relationships between sets. (19)
Vertex	Used of 3-D shapes and not of 2-D shapes. A vertex may be thought of as the place where the edges of a 3-D shape meet at a 'point'. So a cube, for example, has 8 vertices. (16, 18)
Vertical	Perpendicular to the horizontal. (14)
Vertically opposite angles	If two lines cross each other the pairs of opposite angles are equal. (14)
Volume	A measure of 3-D space in cubic units such as cubic centimetres or cubic inches. (12)
Weight	The force exerted between two bodies, e.g. the force attracting a body to the centre of the Earth measured in newtons. It is equal to the mass × acceleration of free fall. (14)

Formulae

Perimeter

Rectangle

Perimeter = 2 (length + breadth)
= 2 × length + 2 × breadth

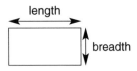

Circle

Circumference
= 2π radius
= π diameter

Area

Rectangle

Area = length × breadth

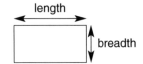

Triangle

Area = $\frac{1}{2}$ × base × height

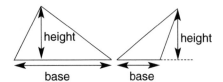

Parallelogram

Area = base × perpendicular height

Trapezium

Area = $\left(\frac{a+b}{2}\right) \times h$

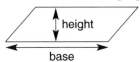

Circle

Area = πr^2

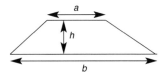

Volume

Cuboid

Volume = length × breadth × height

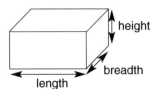

Prism

$$\text{Volume} = \text{area} \times \text{length}$$

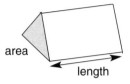

Cylinder

$$\text{Volume} = \pi r^2 h$$

Pyramid

$$\text{Volume} = \tfrac{1}{3} \times \text{area} \times \text{height}$$

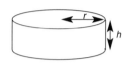

Cone

$$\text{Volume} = \tfrac{1}{3} \pi r^2 h$$

Sphere

$$\text{Volume} = \tfrac{4}{3} \pi r^3$$

Bibliography

Association of Teachers of Mathematics (1986) *10², an ATM Activity Book*. Derby: ATM.

Association of Teachers of Mathematics (1991) *Exploring Mathematics with Younger Children, an ATM Activity Book*. Derby: ATM.

Bolt, B. (1995) *A Mathematical Jamboree*. Cambridge: Cambridge University Press.

Bryant, P. and Nunes, T. (1996) *Children Doing Mathematics*. Cambridge, Mass.: Blackwell.

Burton, L. (1984) *Thinking Things Through*. Oxford: Basil Blackwell.

Carpenter, T. P., Fennema, E., Franke, M. L., Levi, L. and Empson, S. B. (1999) *Children's Mathematics*. Portsmouth, NH: Heinemann.

Daintith, J. and Nelson, R. D. (1989) *The Penguin Dictionary of Mathematics*. Harmondsworth: Penguin.

Davies, G. (1993) *Practical Data Handling*. London: Hodder and Stoughton.

Davis, A. and Pettitt, D. (eds) (1994) *Developing Understanding in Primary Mathematics*. London: Falmer Press.

Dickson, L., Brown, M. and Gibson, O. (1984) *Children Learning Mathematics*. Eastbourne: Holt, Rinehart and Winston.

Donaldson, M. (1978) *Children's Minds*. Glasgow: Fontana (Collins).

Frobisher, L., Monaghan, J., Orton, A., Roper, T. and Threfall, J. (1999) *Learning to Teach Number*. Cheltenham: Stanley Thornes.

Grouws, D. A. (ed.) (1992) *Handbook of Research on Mathematics Teaching and Learning*. New York: Macmillan Publishing Company.

Harries, A. V. and Spooner, M. (2000) *Mental Maths for the Numeracy Hour*. London: David Fulton Publishers.

Haylock, D. and Cockburn, A. (1997) *Understanding Mathematics in the Lower Primary Years*. London: Paul Chapman.

Hopkins, C., Gifford, S. and Pepperell, S. (1996) *Mathematics in the Primary School*. London: David Fulton Publishers.

Hughes, M. (1986) *Children and Number*. Oxford: Basil Blackwell.

Jacobs, H. R. (1994) *Mathematics, A Human Endeavor*, 3rd edn. New York: A. H. Freeman and Company.

Joseph, G. G. (1991) *The Crest of the Peacock*. Harmondsworth: Penguin Books.

Land, F. (1960) *The Language of Mathematics*. London: John Murray.

Langdon, N. and Snape, C. (1984) *A Way with Maths*. Cambridge: Cambridge University Press.

Mason, J., Graham, A., Pimm, D. and Gowar, N. (1985) *Routes to/Roots of Algebra*. Milton Keynes: Open University Press.

Merttens, R. (ed.) (1996) *Teaching Numeracy*. Leamington Spa: Scholastic.

Murray, J. for Association of Teachers of Mathematics (1998) *Primary Points of Departure*. Derby: ATM.

Papert, S. (1980) *Mindstorms: Children, Computers and Powerful Ideas*. Brighton: Harvester Press.

Pimm, D. (1995) *Symbols and Meanings in School Mathematics*. London: Routledge.

Skemp, R. R. (1989) *Mathematics in the Primary School*. London: Routledge.

Snape, C. and Scott, H. (1991) *How Puzzling*. Cambridge: Cambridge University Press.

Straker, A. (1993) *Talking Points in Mathematics*. Cambridge: Cambridge University Press.

The Mathematical Association (1987) *Maths Talk*. Leicester: The Mathematical Association with Stanley Thornes.

The Mathematical Association (1992) *Mental Methods in Mathematics: a first resort*. Leicester: The Mathematical Association.

Thompson, I. (ed.) (1997) *Teaching and Learning Early Number*. Buckingham: Open University Press.

Thompson, I. (ed.) (1999) *Issues in Teaching Numeracy in Primary Schools*. Milton Keynes: Open University Press.

Wells, D. (1986) *The Penguin Dictionary of Curious and Interesting Numbers*. Harmondsworth: Penguin Books.

Wells, D. (1997) *The Penguin Book of Curious and Interesting Mathematics*. Harmondsworth: Penguin Books.

Index

Many topics can be found in the contents page at the beginning of the book as the subject matter is divided into chapters and sections. Such topics are not included in this index. The glossary provides the meaning of mathematical terms and the chapters in which to read more about them.